THE PERIOD SHIP HANDBOOK

THE PERIOD SHIP
HANDBOOK

Keith Julier

NAVAL INSTITUTE PRESS
Annapolis, Maryland.

Published and distributed in the United States of America and Canada by:

Naval Institute Press
118, Maryland Avenue
United States Naval Academy
Annapolis
Maryland
21402-5035

ISBN 1 55750 678-7

Library of Congress Card Number 92-63338

Front cover illustration: *The Royal William*
Back cover illustration: *La Toulonnaise*

Phototypesetting and design by The Studio, Exeter
Printed in Singapore

Contents

List of Colour Plates

(between pages 112 to 113)

Introduction

Building model boats is all about enjoyment and the construction of a period ship model is, in particular, a source of great pleasure and relaxation. It affords the modelmaker the opportunity to be creative, to demonstrate his craftsmanship and, perhaps, to acquire new skills.

Many would-be modellers are hesitant, I am sure, because they feel that they either do not have the ability or possess an adequate workshop. For these people the kit is often the solution to the problem and it is to them that this book is largely addressed.

One of my aims has been to encourage the hesitant and enthuse the beginner to take on more ambitious projects. There is always a new challenge to be met and always something new to learn; in fact you can spend a lifetime in the hobby and still come up against a new experience and new techniques to master.

The book is not intended to be a contribution to the age-old, kit-built versus scratch-built discussion but an attempt to show the newcomer to the hobby that a high class model *can* be built from a kit. My efforts have come together by looking at a series of kits for models of varying degrees of difficulty and type. They have been selected to provide the widest possible range of features the modelmaker may come across; they are not in order of degree of difficulty — the *Royal William* has been chosen to head the list because it encompasses the majority of techniques likely to be encountered by the modelmaker. This book will be of use to any person building a model of a period ship, whether from a kit or from scratch.

Many of the techniques described are fairly standard procedures used by many modelmakers while others are perhaps more unique to my own way of working.

Nothing is mandatory, and the best way is usually the way that suits *you*, and the way that gives you the required result in the easiest possible manner. Always be prepared to listen to, and try, new ideas and methods but, at the same time, develop your own skills and ingenuity. I trust that you, the reader, will find things of interest, encouragement and pleasure in this book in which case I will be well satisfied.

As you will gather from going through this book, it was not the work of just a few weeks. However, it was a project that gave considerable pleasure. Nonetheless it would not have come to fruition had it not been for the help, advice and support of a number of people and it would be remiss of me not to acknowledge their services.

Nothing could have been made, or written, without the kits of Amati, Artesania Latina, Billings, Corel, Euromodel Como and Panart. I am particularly indebted to Dennis Horne at Euro Models of Twickenham for his assistance with *The Royal William*.

The help of John Cundell at *Model Boats* magazine was absolutely invaluable; I learnt a lot from him that made the preparation of this book so much easier.

The photographs of the models taken during the course of construction are from my own camera, but the far superior colour photographs of the finished models were taken by Manny Cefai.

My wife, Edna, has not only tolerated my many hours of modelmaking and the horrendous mess I make, but has actively contributed to the building work. Technical adviser and seamstress on sailmaking, manuscript typing, preparation of rigging blocks, and organiser of the most essential workroom catering, are all disciplines in which she has totally excelled. Her support and enthusiasm have been overwhelming.

CHAPTER 1

The Tool Box

Obviously, the more you have in the way of tools and equipment, the easier everything becomes, but it certainly is not the case that the potential builder has to acquire an all singing and dancing workshop before he can start.

Thus, it is really a matter of deciding *needs* rather than *wants* and, for kit building, the needs are relatively small. However, please be warned that this is an extremely personal choice you have to make and one that depends largely on your own skills, innovative talent and, of course, the depth of your pocket. Your own feelings on this subject will undoubtedly change as you progress further down the path of modelmaking. What was at the beginning a luxury item, rapidly becomes a tool without which you wonder how you coped. I have tried to make my suggested list of tools as realistic as possible and can only call on my own experience and memories as to how I started.

Basic Tools

A modelling knife, preferably with a selection of differently shaped insertable blades, a razor saw, fine-nosed pliers and side cutters together with a light hammer are, in my opinion, absolute essentials. A range of twist drills up to about 2 mm diameter and a pin chuck with which to turn them will cover most needs. A small David plane will also be a useful tool to have.

Clothes' pegs make very useful holding devices, particularly the wooden ones which lend themselves to a bit of customising at the business end. However, I have to say that a few electricians' crocodile clips are vastly superior in terms of size/grip ratio.

As I recall, the next major addition to my kit was a 12 volt electric drill and transformer. I was fortunate enough to receive some good advice at this time and, as a result, spent perhaps a little more than I had originally intended and bought a high output transformer with several outlets. This was a purchase really appreciated later on when I added further electric tools to my collection.

There aren't many kits that couldn't be built with the basic kit of tools so far listed until you get towards some of the 'Biggies' and, even then, it will often be more a matter of ease and convenience rather than absolute necessity to have something more sophisticated. Not that I'm against sophistication, and I certainly do not subscribe to the argument that a model has an extra quality for having been built on the dining room table with only the use of a razor blade and a piece of sandpaper. You *can* usually tell!

Extending the tool box

So, just what are we talking about when we consider more sophisticated tools? I suppose the first things that come to mind are further pieces of 12 volt equipment, a sander, jig-saw, pedestal drill, the list goes on and on. Now you get to appreciate the better quality transformer.

Over the years I have tried all sorts of dodges for bending planks and there are some very pricey bits of gear around; but I have to say that the tool that gets most use during my planking sessions is the Amati plank nipper.

There are gadgets for clamping long strips for tapering and universally adjustable cradles for holding the model under construction. Most of the specialist shops will provide a list of these items and you can add to your tools in the way that best suits *your* way of working. Of course there are many more tools that I haven't mentioned — the list is endless and I have no doubt that my critics will express their absolute amazement that I didn't list a balzover pad with a built-in gotcha pin! Never mind.

Having dealt with the 'capital' equipment, now let us have a look at what is required in the way of consumables. These fall mainly into two categories, fixing and finishing; we are therefore talking about adhesives, abrasive papers and varnishes.

Adhesives

Adhesives have advanced in their technology so much

over the last few years that it is now just about possible to stick anything to everything. However, for optimum convenience when building model boats, I usually manage to find a use for four different types and while they may not be needed on all kits, I always make sure that I have an adequate supply in hand before starting a project.

White PVA (Evostick Resin W) is an absolute must — it has a reasonably fast grab capacity permitting work to continue after about 20 to 30 minutes — always remembering though that total curing can take up to 24 hours. Its other main attribute is that it has an almost complete absence of smell, which is very handy if you work indoors rather than in a shed or garage.

There is a wide range of contact adhesives from which to choose, my own particular favourite being Dunlop's Thixofix. I choose this mainly because of its viscosity; being what is best described as a gel, it makes for easier application and cleaner working.

An equally wide choice is available in the field of superglues, those liquid and gel adhesives that give you instant stick capacity. A little goes a long way and thus, with practice in their application, they don't turn out to be as expensive as you might at first think. They come in very handy when rigging and constructing small deck fittings; just make sure you get the bits together correctly first time!

Finally, for those times when metal has to be stuck either to wood or other pieces of metal, Araldite epoxy is a life-saver. However, its success is largely dependent on adequate joint preparation, cleanliness and correct mixing of this two-part adhesive.

Adhesives are not the only means of fixing that are used. Brass or steel pins are frequently used to supplement a glued joint. More often than not, these are provided in a kit so you do not have to make a choice of length or material. If you do have to buy, you will find that 10 mm and 14 mm brass panel pins or 'lost head' style will suit most purposes.

Abrasive Papers

We are all familiar with what we commonly call sandpaper. In fact, this is a misnomer and what we really refer to is glasspaper. Yet again in this field, research has brought about advances in abrasive materials to the point where there are a number of new papers available that can take a lot of the tedium out of the rubbing down process. Just take a look along the shelves of your local DIY store and you will see that there are several grades of glasspaper, garnetpaper and papers coated with silicon-carbide, the latter better known as wet-and-dry.

For general use, glasspaper is quite adequate although you should find that garnetpaper provides a much cleaner cut and retains its 'bite' for a longer period of time. Provided that the model can withstand a degree of

dampness, wet-and-dry papers can be used with wood for early stages of 'sanding', but do remember that damp wood will not take a final finish with any type or grade of abrasive paper.

Don't go mad with the coarse grades — you may get rid of a lot of material fairly quickly, but the scratches they leave can be horrendous. Work down through to the finer grades until the required finish is attained. Worn coarse paper does *not* equate to a finer grade.

A cork sanding block, preferably shaped to have a concave face, is most beneficial to getting a nice even finish on a planked hull. Large areas of hardwood may sometimes be better dealt with by the use of a cabinet scraper or even a single-edged razor blade.

Do spend a little time to make the right selection.

Finishes

Stains and varnishes form the basis of most finishing operations, there being only a minimal requirement for large painted areas. Colron stains are ideal for colour and Cuprinol acrylic clear matt varnish serves as both finish and rigging sealer, *and brushes can be cleaned with water.*

If paint is called for, then the vast range of Humbrol enamels can usually fit the bill. Should you get involved in larger areas, such as the below waterline surfaces, I can recommend a look amongst the Dulux Colour Testers. They come in 50 ml pots and are ideal for the job, very cost effective too. Testers from the Dulux Woodtones range can also solve some of the smaller wood colouring requirements.

I would like to stress that where I have referred to specific products and trade names, it is because I have particular experience of them. There are undoubtedly many equally good alternatives and, like many things in the building of model boats, it comes down to personal choice; what suits you and what helps you to produce the best result.

Tool Condition

Tools need to be maintained in tip-top condition if they, and you, are going to produce the best results. Blunt tools are not only useless for working with, but are downright dangerous. An oilstone to keep them keen at all times is, therefore, a worthwhile investment.

Safety

Some of the operations involved in the building of model boats are potentially hazardous and a couple of common sense precautions are advisable. The rubbing down of hull surfaces produces a lot of dust, so do wear a mask to prevent breathing it in. I'm not sure whether we have serious fire hazard conditions here, but I have always kept a small domestic fire extinguisher in my workroom, just in case.

If you are fortunate enough to have your work area inside the house, as I have, then personal experience tells me to recommend that you have a vacuum cleaner handy *and use it fairly frequently*. Dust is a hazard and is best kept down; consideration for other members of the household is also not only commendable but can be positively advantageous.

I have not mentioned lighting at the workplace and I suppose that, indirectly, it could be classified as a safety item. Good lighting can certainly reduce any strain on the eyes and, of course, contribute to better and more accurate work. Two sources of fluorescent light as a minimum are usually required to provide any degree of shadowless illumination. Of course, if you can run to an adjustable lamp for optimum working, so much the better. This should, I hasten to add, be an additional not an alternative source.

CHAPTER 2

Choosing The Kit

Kits come in varying degrees of building difficulty and some are definitely not for the beginner. I should also add that the cheapest ones are not always the easiest to construct. Many kits will provide the means of producing a fine museum standard model, albeit that a little bit of extra work and research may be necessary to attain such standard.

The kit usually provides all the necessary materials and drawings, the research has already been done and, due to the pre-cut and pre-shaped parts often featured in today's product, the model builder's tool kit needs only to be fairly basic. In spite of this preparatory work, do not run away with the idea that the construction is merely an assembly job — it isn't! In fact, the innovative skills sometimes required when building from a kit surpass those of the more fortunate amongst us who possess a sophisticated workshop, where switching on and turning a couple of handles does the job in a fraction of the time.

Making all the right decisions when choosing a kit is absolutely vital to get the most out of this fascinating hobby. If you are a complete beginner, don't be over-ambitious in your selection of subject. A good guide to the degree of difficulty can often be obtained by looking at the general shape of the hull. Tightly rounded bows are always going to be a problem, particularly if you don't have some sort of plank bending aid. The old Coast Guard cutters and Baltimore clippers offer a reasonably trouble-free shape, where the planking lines at bow and stern are not too severe. It pays to look at the box carefully too, sometimes the manufacturer will indicate the standard of expertise required.

Don't be put off by what appears to be an absolute mass of unintelligible rigging. It has more to do with quantity than with difficulty and it just takes a little more time to rig three masts than two. Comprehensive rigging details are normally provided in the kit.

Consider too, where you are going to build the model. It has to be said that they are not normally dining room table projects and, ideally, you need a place where partially completed work can be left undisturbed until your next modelling session. When considering the space required, remember that it is not only the size of the finished model that has to be catered for; you also need space to work on sub-assemblies that have to be built away from the main structure.

With regard to kit quality, I can only recommend that you select from a range of models kitted by a reputable manufacturer. Take a look through the pages of *Model Boats* magazine, for instance, where major dealers and distributors list what is on offer. They won't knowingly handle rubbish and poor quality will not stay in the market place very long. Many retailers are enthusiasts themselves and will willingly give advice and answer any specific questions you may have. It may be possible to look inside the box in the shop, but please do ask first. Many boxes are packed in a particular sequence and, if things don't go back in the right order, you just can't get the lid back on!

So, having got the lid off, what do you look for? Make sure you aren't holding a big box that is only half full. It's an old dodge sometimes used to make you think you are buying more than you actually are. That is not often the case of course, but it should make you wary and look a little more closely at the contents, just in case. The instruction manual can often tell you a lot about the kit and a well-illustrated one bodes well, particularly for the beginner. Don't be put off by any foreign kits, the manuals are often multi-lingual or, at least, have the main part of the instructions translated into English. If it doesn't, then you have to decide on the basis of the drawings and whether any illustrations and sketches are adequate without the written word. These comments assume that there is, in fact, a manual or set of instructions to look at in the first place. If nothing comes to light, or what there is amounts to only a couple of typewritten sheets, then either the kit is directed towards the more experienced or is of fairly poor quality. Either way, it is one that should be purchased only after very careful consideration.

It won't usually be possible to examine all the fittings because of the way that they are normally packed, but these are not generally too much of a problem. The main difficulty encountered with them is that sometimes kits are made up using standard packs that form the basis of a manufacturer's fittings catalogue. Thus there are occasions when items like capstans, pumps, winches, etc. are not quite the right size or style for the ship in question. This is not usually disastrous of course, but don't look upon standard fittings as items that can just be taken straight from the pack and assembled onto the model.

Sheet material often provides laser-cut or press-cut parts and these should be flat pieces without distortion. Similarly, strip material should be straight and twist-free. Should you encounter any large blocks of hardwood, even though roughly pre-shaped, think about whether you have the facilities to carve or finish shape such material. In fact, you come to realise after a while that some pre-shaping is not always as advantageous as first thought, particularly with regard to block-work.

Kits of any consequence usually include several sizes of cordage for the rigging. Normally, you would expect to find two colours, black or dark brown and tan, for the standing and running rigging respectively. White is really not suitable and, unless you are willing to substitute it with something else, you can be faced with a messy dyeing job. I always get the feeling when I see white rigging thread that the kit manufacturer has bought up a cheap job lot somewhere that just happens to be the required diameter. That's probably not true, but it is this lack of thought that makes the difference between a poor kit and a good one.

The same can be said for sail material. White, for most period ship models, is going to look too artificial and can spoil the effect of an otherwise excellent construction. Strangely, most modellers will accept the dyeing process for sails whereas it is felt that the cordage

is more the responsibility of the kit manufacturers to get right. Apart from the colour, the texture is also important. However, at the stage when you are buying the kit, it is most difficult to make the assessment as to whether it is going to hang right when converted into a sail. Some kits do not provide any material at all on the basis that sails cover up all that beautiful work you have put into the building and rigging. This is a valid point and many modellers refrain from rigging sails because of it. Also you might listen to the argument that a material has not yet been found to properly simulate a wind-filled course. But more of that later in the book.

All that I have written so far about kit selection has presupposed that the prospective purchaser has the opportunity to visit a model shop with an adequate stock from which to make a considered choice. So, what do you do if you have no option than the use of mail order? As I said earlier, the people who distribute and retail kits and fittings are often both specialists and enthusiasts and are most willing to offer advice and assistance. However, if you want their help, might I suggest that you confine your telephone call to a midweek afternoon and not expect their best response at times when they are likely to have a shop full of people.

The Mailboat page in *Model Boats* magazine will often yield comment and advice from readers and, in some cases, your letter may be passed on to someone known to have specific knowledge concerning your problem.

One of the purposes of this book, of course, is to offer as much valid information as possible on the kits used for building the various models, as well as the construction techniques involved.

CHAPTER 3

Making A Start

Do not be too anxious to start cutting and sticking pieces together. A thorough, and I *mean* thorough, study of the plans and instructions will pay dividends as you proceed through the building of the model. Many kits will provide a list of materials and fittings; check these out and familiarise yourself with all the bits and pieces and where they all go.

One particular manufacturer goes as far as to provide a cutting list that defines from which pieces of stock material each item is cut. This, of course, helps to ensure that there is enough material in the kit, but not too much! It also means that you deviate from the list at your peril, since you could finish up needing a 200 mm length of dowel with only a 180 mm length left in the box. So beware.

It is often worth identifying particular features of a model and treating them as separate projects within the overall construction. Winches, capstans, anchors, ovens, etc., all lend themselves to this and there is a psychological aspect to this way of working that frequently makes for better results.

If you have decided that the kit is to be the basis of a more enhanced model, you should, in conjunction with the necessary investigation and research, identify the areas which will benefit from extra detailing or modification. It is important to make these observations at this stage since your decisions could well influence the sequence and procedures laid down in the kit instructions. It might be sensible to make a note of these points just to jog the memory when the particular stage of working is reached. Note should be made as to any additional materials needed and bought well before they come up for use.

Some of the kits specifically for the more experienced modelmaker may be found to have instructions so sparse as to make the formulating of your own procedures the first task. The usual problem here is one of sequence of working, and careful in-depth study of the construction is needed to ensure that the required access to areas of later development are not shut off.

As to the actual construction techniques involved, the following pages look at a range of models of different shapes and sizes which, hopefully, provide the opportunity to examine most of the major procedures that you have to contend with when constructing a model boat. While much of what I have written describes ways and means around those problems arising when building from a kit, there is also much that, hopefully, may be helpful if starting from scratch. There is absolutely nothing mandatory about these procedures and they are not purported to be the only, or the best, way to tackle particular facets of construction. They are ways that I have found successful over a period of some fifty years of modelmaking.

Make sure that your tools are in good shape and that you have everything you need to hand. There is nothing worse than finding you have run out of adhesive, for instance, just five minutes after the shops have closed!

CHAPTER 4

The First Rate
Royal William 1719

The *Royal William* was launched at Portsmouth in 1719. It was the third vessel to be so named and was built using much of the usable material from its earlier namesake.

The treatment afforded its planking by charring prior to fixing proved to be highly successful. The ship survived a very active career at sea, being part of Vice Admiral Sir Charles Saunders' squadron at Quebec in 1759 and taking part in the Gibraltar operation of 1782. After the successful storming of the Heights of Abraham, General Wolfe's embalmed body was put aboard the *Royal William* to be brought to England for what Saunders believed would be a state funeral. The ship was finally broken up in 1813 after being assigned

anchor watch at Portsmouth. Ninety-four years of fairly active service was quite an achievement.

With an overall length of around 310 ft and an armament of 104 guns, it went to sea with a complement of 730 men. *(See front cover illustration for picture of the finished model.)*

The Kit

This is one of the larger kits currently available and comes from the Euro Model Como stable. It produces a model of nearly 45 in (1140 mm) long, of considerable weight and, if you have back trouble, requires

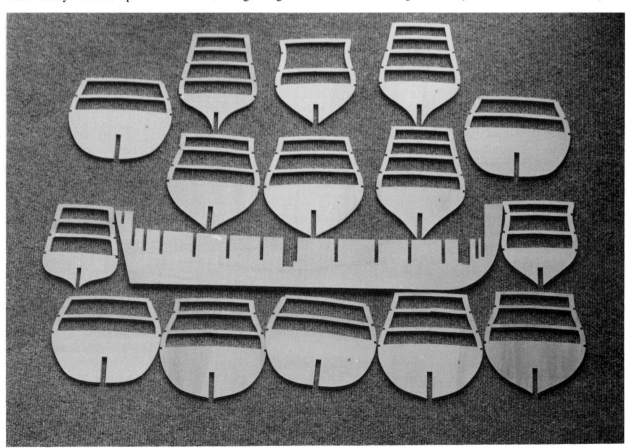

Fig. 4.1. The main 'bulkheads' and false keel as supplied in the kit.

Fig. 4.2. Some of the fittings, gun barrels, anchors etc.

help when lifting the box. The weight is primarily due to the large number of diecast parts provided for the figurehead and other considerable ornamentation, all of which come as basic castings needing fettling and gilding. Fettling is a minor job as flash on the castings is minimal.

The quality of all materials is excellent, the main 'bulkheads' and false keel, plus much of the basic block-work being pre-shaped (Fig. 4.1). Masts and spars are ready tapered and the strip material is straight and true. There is the usual supply of fittings one has come to expect in quality kits; brass gun barrels, pre-formed carriages etc., all of which make the fingers itch to get started (see Figs 4.2 and 4.3). Strangely, no fixing pins are provided and these will most certainly be needed, at least for the first planking.

The drawings, all seventeen sheets, are superb; the detail, dimensions, scrap and exploded views are among the best I have seen in a kit. The builder will do well to study these at great length before starting, because all his skill and experience will have to be brought to bear in order to determine methods and sequences of assembly. Apart from a sheet giving a few historical notes, there are only two A4 pages of suggested procedural instructions — from then on, the modeller is on his own.

Everything that needs protection is either bagged or boxed and, generally, the kit is very well presented.

Building the Hull

It was not long before I realised just how true it was that foresight and planning were the order of the day. All the notes on the drawings are in Italian and while most are fairly obvious in meaning, it soon became apparent that there are two distinct types of drawing contained within the kit. Some sheets are concerned with the details of the original vessel and some were constructional drawings for modelmaking. However, some of the former have been marked up with material sizes for certain features and constant reference to several sheets is going to be necessary right throughout the build.

How much detail is incorporated into the model is left to the whims of the modelmaker, although all the detail is recorded on the drawings. Some of the pre-cut parts, for the decks for instance, are shaped specifically to afford the builder the opportunity to keep his options open. The main framework comprises a series of bulkhead/frames cross-halved into a false keel (Fig. 4.4). All the pieces are pre-shaped and no adjustments to slot widths were found necessary. On the contrary, some fits were a little on the sloppy side and needed some packing. I did a dry run of the assembly first just to get the feel of things and it turned out to be a most worthwhile exercise.

It is only when you get these early pieces assembled

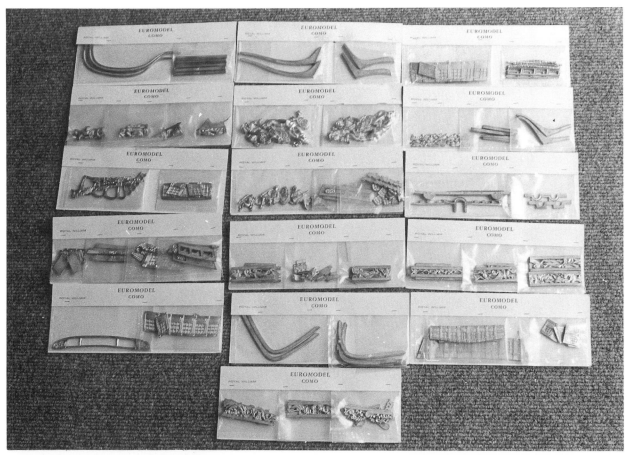

Fig. 4.3. Some of the diecast ornamentation.

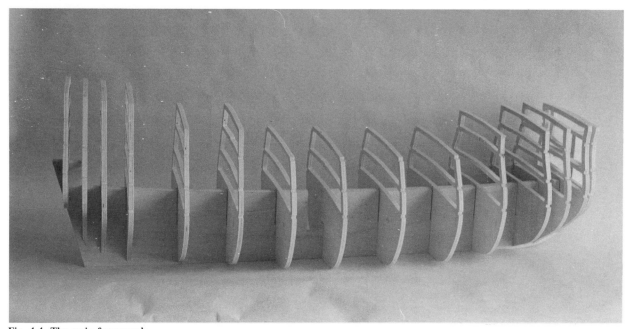

Fig. 4.4. The main framework.

that you realise just how big the finished model is going to be. The dimensions on the box certainly didn't prepare me for the enormity of the model and full realisation only came when I had the three dimensional carcass in my hands. It was obvious that I was going to have to reorganise my work area. Like most model-makers, I tend to work in one spot, moving the partially assembled model to one side while I make or cut the next bits and pieces. Just 'moving the model to one side' in this case was not going to be so easy, particularly in the later stages of construction. I therefore devised a sliding false top to my workbench for assembly purposes

19

which, running on old drawer runners, slid out of the way to leave my bench top proper clear for construction work.

One thing led to another and it became apparent that there was also some mileage to be gained in making the stand at this stage (Fig. 4.5). The pre-cut parts needed some attention to afford nice tight joints that would be adequate without being glued, since the pieces would need to be taken apart later for finishing. How gratifying to find, at last, a kit with a stand supplied.

Fig. 4.5. The assembled stand.

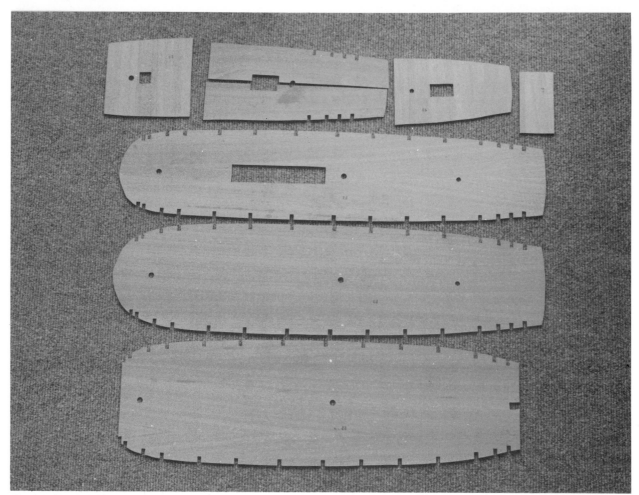

Fig. 4.6. The deck blanks as supplied. Note one is cut down centre line, some others will need the same treatment to aid assembly.

Getting back to my dry run assembly, I needed to be sure which way to pack the sloppy joints. The edges of the decks come shaped and ready notched to fit into the frames (Fig. 4.6), so it seemed sensible to use these as an alignment jig. The lower decks need to be slit down the centre line, stem to stern, and slid into position from the aft end. In fact, because of the restriction of the high contours at the ends of the false keel, the lowest deck also had to be cut across the beam at a convenient frame to enable it to be correctly positioned.

Having seen that everything lined up and having decided whether the packing required needed to be positioned in the keel slots fore or aft of the frames, the assembly was dismantled ready for gluing. PVA adhesive was used and all the cross halving joints reassembled, the packing being slipped into place where necessary and the deck pieces positioned dry to maintain correct frame separation and squareness while the glue dried.

This assembly needs to be left for the glue to thoroughly cure, since the next stage of construction involves the application of three longitudinal stringers each side (Fig. 4.7). These are of substantial section and have to take a certain degree of bend; thus the framework has to be as strong as possible to sustain the forces subtended by these pieces.

Leaving the deck pieces in place helps too, in that they prevent any flexing of the frames while applying the stringers. In order to help with the bending it is advisable not to cut the material to length before fixing and leave a minimal amount of overhang at the stern. The residue overhanging at the front end helps with bending and provides length to tie and clamp while the glue sets. Again, the adhesive must be left for at least 24 hours to properly cure before trimming the ends flush with the first and last frames.

Block-work

The blocks at the main and foremast positions can now be identified and fitted. At the stern there are two shaped pieces which do little more than increase the thickness of the last frame. However, their position in the vertical plane is important as their top edges delineate the end of the upward sweep of planking under the stern. This line also controls the position of the lower of the two stern gallery blocks to be fitted later, and need to be placed according to dimensions extracted from the drawings.

A little more dry assembly of the deck pieces reveals that the front end of one of them has to be cut off square to the front face of the most forward frame. This permits the fitting of the bow blocks right up to the underside of the main deck. The bow blocks themselves need to be carefully marked out on the piece of timber provided or you will find that it is of insufficient length. The right-

Fig. 4.7. The three longitudinal 'stringers' each side in place.

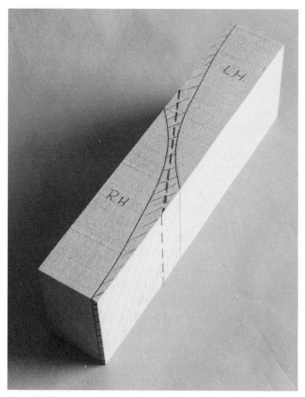

Fig. 4.8. The bow blocks need careful marking out as shown.

hand and left-hand pieces have to be overlapped within the length and then separated by a diagonal cut (Fig. 4.8). It is advisable to do as much shaping as possible before gluing them to the hull, leaving only the minimum amount of material to attain the continuous flow of line from the hull frames to the blocks. When thoroughly set in position they can be finally shaped together with the frame edges.

Holding the hull

Holding the hull for the shaping of the blocks and the frame edges caused a bit of a problem. It was not a manageable option to hold it by hand, either on the bench, or in the lap.

Therefore I made up a device comprising three pieces of 75 mm × 50 mm timber in the form of a shallow 'U', the two uprights being planed on width to suit the space between frames B and C and 4 and 5. They were then slotted along their top face 10 mm wide × 50 mm deep before screwing them to the third piece separated by the same distance as measured between frames B and 4. The secret is to make the fit between the selected frames as snug as possible, thus, the loads applied when working the hull will be taken either on the frames where they are jointed into the false keel or, in the other plane, at the bottom of the slots on the edge of the false keel. Apart from the fit of the uprights between the frames, this piece of gear does not have to be anything special and 'chicken-run' carpentry is adequate. The centre part of the rig is held in the vice with the shorter pieces upright and the hull framework lowered down onto it, either way up as required. The hull is now sufficiently supported and stabilised to withstand the sharp tool work and sanding loads required (see Fig. 4.9).

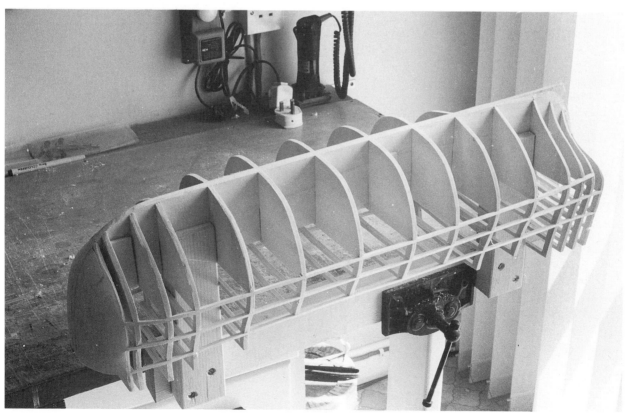

Fig. 4.9. The carcass inverted on the holding frame until the bottom planking is done. It can also be held 'the right way up'.

Final framework shaping

Excess material can be planed from the stringers and the entire outer surfaces, ie. frame edges and blocks, sanded to suit the lines of the hull. Use a strip of planking to continually monitor progress, remembering that when planking is carried out, the plank should make contact over the entire thickness of each frame.

The false keel in the area of the stern post needs special attention in that its thickness has to be considerably reduced from 10 mm and tapered in to match the run of the planks over the last four or five frames. This is to ensure that the combined thickness of the false keel and planking matches the thickness of the stern post that is to be applied later.

The first planking

The drawings depicting the build-up of the hull framework show all decks fitted in position. This is not a very practicable proposition on two counts. First, it shuts off all access to the 'tween decks areas for gun fixings and any other internal detail desired and secondly, it limits the use of the holding device described previously. Therefore it is imperative at this time to decide what features you want to construct between decks before you start planking. Remember too, that no transom work can be done before fitting the decks since this is the access point for all three main gun decks.

I decided to dry fit all the decks again in case the loads imposed by the stringers, or any work latterly done on the hull framework, had tightened anything up. Having satisfied myself that they could all be easily slipped in and located in position, they were all removed in preparation for the planking to begin. The first planking is done in 6 mm × 1.5 mm lime and, although the area to be covered is considerable, the lines are quite friendly and a minimum of tapering is required (Fig. 4.10). The curves at the bow are severe however, and some sort of bending aid is necessary. I used the Amati plank nipper, a tool which permits fairly sharp bends to be attained without marking the outer surface.

The line of the main deck was used as a guide and I applied an untapered strip in the first instance to gauge the natural run of the plank. Having fixed a similar plank on the opposite side of the hull, the number of planks required to cover the hull at the midships frame can be measured. Taking further measurements along the edges of the fore and aft frames will allow the width of the plank at these points to be calculated and hence the degree of taper required (see Fig. 4.11).

The notes provided with the kit suggest that the aim should be to avoid gaps between the planks at prow and stern. Quite frankly, with regard to the first planking, the natural run of the strips is likely to give a more even surface and thus a stronger hull for later working. The use of stealers (those fill-in triangular bits), particularly at the stern, is quite acceptable in my opinion (Figs 4.12

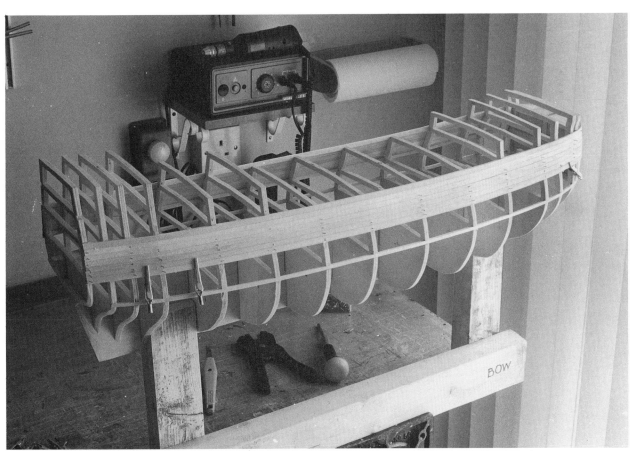

Fig. 4.10. **The right way up on the holding frame for first planking. Note amati plank nipper and pin pusher on bench.**

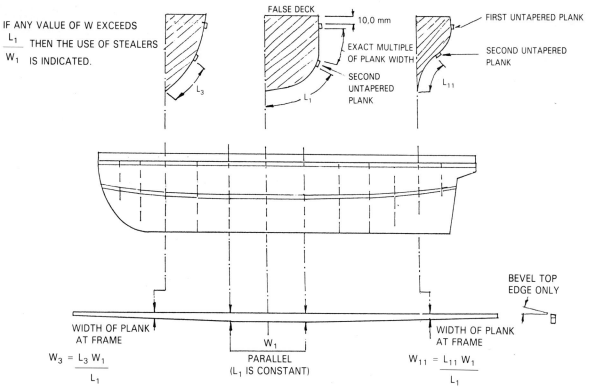

Fig. 4.11. Tapering planks.

and 4.13). Again, white PVA adhesive is ideal with planks pinned in place at each frame position. I used 10 mm brass pins partially pushed home with a pin-pusher. If the frames have been edge-tapered correctly and the end block-work properly shaped, the pins perform only a light holding task and need not, except in one or two places under the stern, be pushed right in up to the head. This makes them so much easier to extract before sanding.

Glue should be applied to both the frame edges and the edge of the preceding plank. When completely planked, the entire surface should be carefully examined for any seam not adequately glued and the condition corrected before any sanding is done. Failure to do this makes the final sanding very difficult since a sprung plank just 'gives' under the pressure of the abrasive paper; reducing its thickness to match that of the adjacent planks is almost impossible.

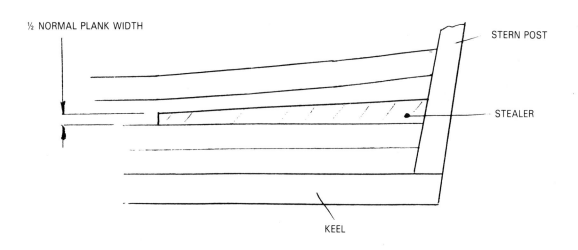

Fig. 4.12. Stealers.

Fig. 4.13. The unsanded first planking under the stern. Note the 'stealers'.

Gunports

With the section of the hull below the main deck smoothed off to satisfaction, it appeared to be a convenient time to mark out and cut the gunports in the area so far planked. I chose this particular time because the tumblehome on the vessel is considerable and, to continue the planking above the level so far achieved, would reduce the working access through the top of the model.

The lowest deck was now fitted in position and its level accurately marked on the outside of the hull. The top and bottom edges of the gunports relative to this deck can now be established and their lateral positions measured from the drawings. No difficulty was experienced cutting the apertures out using a sharp scalpel (Fig. 4.14). However, several positions are coincident with bulkheads and these too should be cut away as required. A constant check on alignment is recommended and the best, and simplest, way to do this is to eye down the length of the hull along the line of the ports. Consideration should now be given to the fixing of the dummy gun barrels.

Dummy gun barrels

The blocks for fixing these barrels should be cut from stock provided and, ideally, each barrel needs its own block. This allows the protrusion of each barrel outside the hull to be controlled. The correct dimension can be taken from the drawings and, having drilled the block to take the barrel spigot at the correct height, it can be glued to the deck in the right position. A small tee-shaped gauge can be made up from scrap material to ensure that every block is the same distance in from the outer surface of the hull (Fig. 4.15).

The block into which the mizen mast is stepped should also be glued in place before installing the second gun deck and its barrel blocks in the manner described above.

The main deck

Before fitting the deck remember to cut away the top of the first fo'c'sle frame as indicated on the drawings. Assuming that you aren't going to 'chicken out' of making the staircase that leads down from the main deck to the gun deck, a 20 mm wide aperture needs to be cut into the deck halves before fixing. Once these pieces are permanently in place, a little forward planning is necessary.

The fascia to the cabin area under the quarterdeck can hardly be seen once the model is completed unless you really get down to close examination. On the basis that someone will, now is the time to trim and decorate the relevant diecasting because it will need to be fitted before assembling the next deck level (Fig. 4.16). It seems early days to be thinking about painting and

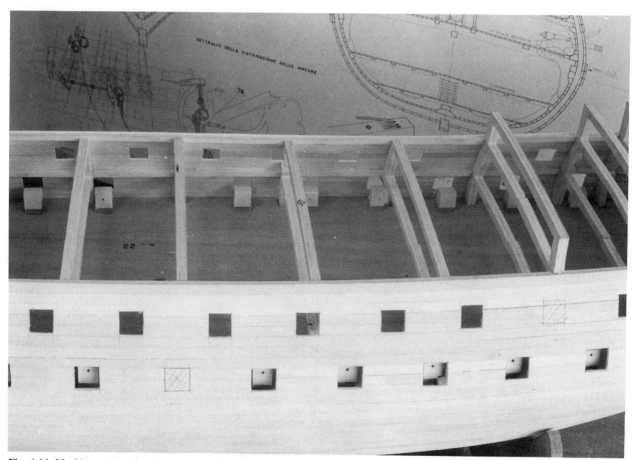

Fig. 4.14. Marking and cutting the gunports. Note blocks on the lower gun deck for the dummy barrels.

Fig. 4.15. Positioning the blocks for dummy barrels using the 'tee' gauge.

Fig. 4.16. The fascia to the cabin area below the quarterdeck.

decorating, but this area is totally inaccessible once the quarterdeck is in place.

After trimming any flash from the diecasting, I painted the whole front face, with the exception of the glazed areas, with matt black and, later, dry-brushed the colour and the gold ornamentation on top. The black emphasised all the edges and the impressed detail and, generally speaking, it looked pretty good. If I learnt anything at this stage, it was not to use too stiff a brush that tended to push paint into places where it wasn't wanted!

The main deck can now be planked from the cabin fascia below the quarterdeck right through to the bows. Cut the planks to the lengths shown on the drawings and ensure that butt joints are correctly positioned with three full planks between joints on any one frame.

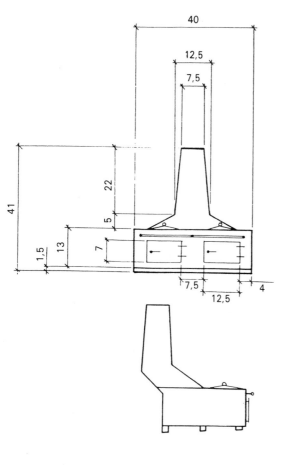

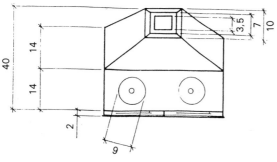

Fig. 4.17. The ship's stove.

The ship's stove

Another feature, of which not too much is seen on the finished model, is the ship's stove. The upper part of the chimney stack protrudes above the surface of the fo'c'sle deck but it isn't going to look quite right just to make this part and stick it to the deck. The drawings give full dimensional details of the whole unit (Fig. 4.17), which can easily be fabricated from a few small blocks of scrap, then mounted onto the main deck prior to fitting the fo'c'sle deck. Painted dark grey with a couple of pin heads to simulate the oven door knobs and you have a very presentable stove (Fig. 4.18).

Fig. 4.18. The ships stove ready for final rub down.

The main deck staircase

I was most surprised that the kit did not provide turned wooden spindles for this feature. Even with a small lathe, without the use of a form tool, it is almost impossible to produce identically shaped parts. Thus you are left with two options; purchase proprietary parts or, use the plain 2 mm diameter dowelling supplied.

I chose the latter path and made the assembly up from several sections, the last being the actual staircase and bannisters, all coming together with the aid of super-glue. Each section comprised a top and bottom rail, drilled as a pair to ensure correct spindle alignment, and a series of 2 mm diameter spindles. The rails were made from scrap 5 mm × 1 mm strip and reduced to 3.5 mm × 0.75 mm after assembly (Fig 4.19).

The drawings are again fully detailed and, if carefully made, the staircase and bannisters slip down into the aperture in the deck and the side balustrading sits flat on the surrounding area. However, I considered it wise not to permanently fix the unit until after the side planking had been finished.

Finishing the first planking

Before proceeding further, it is as well to check the alignment of holes for the masts and make any corrections necessary, noting particularly any rake that has to be applied. The hull planking can now be extended to those surfaces above the level of the main deck and the remaining gunports marked and cut out (Fig. 4.20).

In the midships area, some of the planking is unsup-

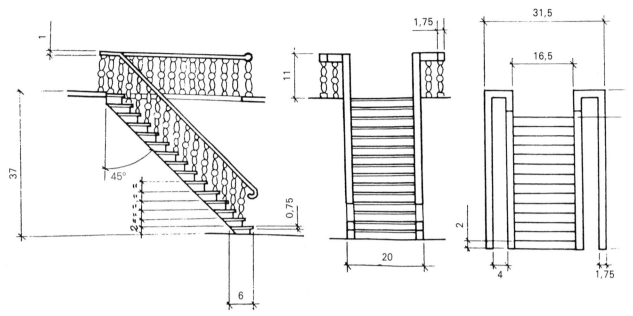

Fig. 4.19. The main deck staircase.

Fig. 4.20. The first planking finished.

ported and thus, some edge-to-edge work is involved. This is an occasion when the crocodile clips come in handy to keep the planks in line with each other. Plank higher than is finally required and do not worry at this stage about the line of the ship's rails; any excess planking can always be trimmed off later. I also found it a good move to line the inner exposed surfaces with strips of *second* hull planking before fitting the decks. This provided greatly increased strength to the unsupported timbers but also fulfilled the cosmetic requirements.

Fitting the remaining decks

Check where *complete* gun carriages will be mounted on the main deck and where further blocks for dummy barrels are needed. Fit such blocks along with the staircase before fitting the quarterdeck and fo'c'sle decks in place. The remaining decks are all fitted following the same procedure described previously, constantly checking that you are not making any areas of later detailing inaccessible.

The upper decks all come in one piece and therefore can be planked, trimmed and sanded prior to assembly if desired.

The second planking

You need to spend some time sorting through the mass of diecast ornamentation and identifying which piece goes where on the sides of the hull. Having sorted out the left-hand from the right and laid them out in their relative positions, they were then clipped to the sides of the hull with clothes' pegs. This needs to be done fairly precisely in order to determine the line of the planking, the bottom edge of the lower row of castings denoting the top edge of the first plank.

Now it is decision time again. What method do you use to apply the planking? Frankly, there are really only two options available using the kit materials and each presents a different set of problems.

Due to the curvature of the hull, long strips of the 5 mm × 1 mm provided will not lay flat against the surface of the first planking. Thus, the first option is to cut the strips into scale length planks, cutting the ends to make neat butt joints. However, using this method it is very difficult to get tightly fitting edge-to-edge joints between successive rows of planking.

The second option is to use long strips, but use a pair of fine side cutters to nip across about a third of the width of the strip, on the outside of the bend at intervals along the length. This permits a nice snug fit between the edges of the planks but, of course, the small cuts tend to open up as the plank is applied and will need some sort of filling. I tried both methods on a piece of ply board and decided that the second option gave the more acceptable results.

A choice of adhesive now becomes available — PVA

Fig. 4.21. The start of the second planking. Do not size gunports at this stage.

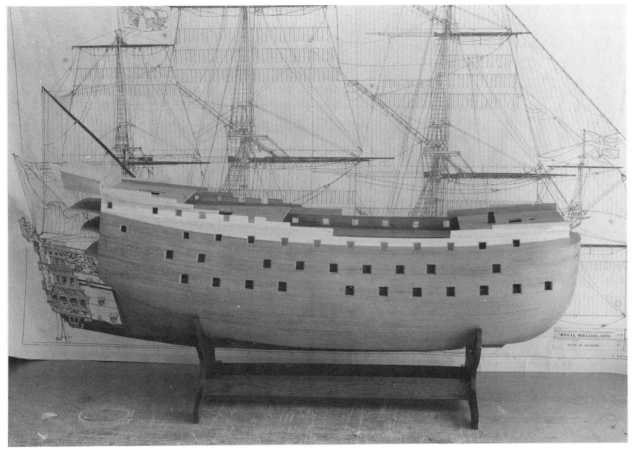

Fig. 4.22. The second planking complete.

or a contact type. The PVA is probably best for establishing the position of the first plank but after that, it is really a matter of personal choice.

As planking proceeded over the lines of gunports, I found that it was wise to cut, or leave, an opening at the position of each port (Fig. 4.21). However, I considered it *unwise* to try and attain final shape and size at this stage but merely left a space into which a tool could be inserted later on. There really isn't too much to say about the planking; a fairly regular check on the required tapering keeps things in good order and the compounding of the curves is reasonably kind (Fig. 4.22). The nasty bit is the rubbing down afterwards, particularly under the stern. A short length of broom handle wrapped with fairly coarse wet-and-dry cloth is as good a solution as I've found. Used dry, it doesn't seem to clog like glasspaper and the marks it leaves on the wood surface do not appear to be too deep or difficult to later remove with a finer grade.

The gunports

Having finished off the hull surface to satisfaction, attention should now be given to trimming out the gunports to size. If the positions and sizes cut into the first planking were accurate, they act as an excellent guide to this final sizing and a sharp scalpel is more than adequate for the job.

All ports need to be framed and this was achieved using spare hull planking (Fig. 4.23). Some are open ports and should be framed flush with the hull surface; others that have lids or side-hung doors should be recessed. The latter need quite a bit of care since the thickness of the planking to which the framing is glued has been considerably reduced.

The prow, stern post and keel

The back edge of the false keel and the planking should be trued up and the stern post fixed in place. Ideally, the post should be a little thicker than the combined thickness of false keel and planking, thus leaving just a small amount to remove to blend in with the planks.

The prow comes pre-shaped and the amount of adjustment required to attain a nice fit around the forward curves of the hull is minimal. However, getting it lined up centrally from deck to keel is not so easy unless you find a way to hold the hull steady while you true it up. (An extra pair of hands to stabilise the hull on its stand is a winning move.) I drilled the prow with three small holes into which I push-fitted panel pins and, having lightly marked its position on the front of the hull, the prow was then glued and the pins pushed home. Do remember to wipe off any excess adhesive with a damp cloth before it dries. If you don't, resultant stains are difficult to get rid of and are accentuated with the later

31

application of varnish.

The keel is made from three strips laminated together and, with the stern post trimmed on its lower end and the prow firmly glued in place, the fitting of the keel is easy.

The stern galleries

You need to study the drawings at considerable length before embarking on the construction of the back end. For a start, the drawings show a scratch-building procedure and not one using the diecast ornamentation provided in the kit. Just a straightforward transference from wood to metal you might think, but it is not quite as simple as that, since the castings are not absolutely identical in size as the details on the main drawing. That really is the crux of the problem, and once this has been fathomed out, it is really down to making careful and sensible adjustments.

Without doubt, the simplest way to proceed is to start at the bottom and work upwards, building one level on top of the previous one. I use the term 'simplest' in the very broadest sense because the next stage is the most difficult one so far encountered. The lowest part of the structure comprises two main pieces which, in plan, have to conform to the shape of the hull planking but, at the same time, in end elevation, have to be curved to match the deck camber. This is woodcarving pure and simple; no short cuts, just a lot of hard work with

constant checking for size and shape. The blocks concerned are in walnut and fairly easy to work with sharp tools. However, in retrospect, I think that I would have preferred a pair of plain blocks rather than the pre-shaped pieces supplied. I don't want to sound ungrateful but, carving the convex and concave surfaces top and bottom of each piece so that they fit snugly together would have been much easier if the blocks could have been held firmly in the vice. As it was, the pre-shaping prevented this and I finished up with a rather precarious system of G-clamps and wedges. This rather limited the amount of 'push' that could be exerted with the chisels, but it worked, albeit over quite a number of hours of precision carpentry.

Once I had attained a satisfactory fit between the blocks and the hull, it was then a matter of deciding whether to fit the ornamentation before assembly, or later, when the whole structure was built. I chose the former procedure and gently trimmed and bent the pertinent diecast parts and fixed them in place with a two-part epoxy adhesive.

This sub-assembly should be offered up to the hull to check for the final fit. Using the rudder blank, the helm port position should be marked onto the assembly and carefully gouged out before gluing this first stage into place. When set, this provides a sound base for making up the inner parts of the lower open gallery (Figs 4.24 and 4.25).

Fig. 4.23. The framed and recessed ports, ready for final clean-up.

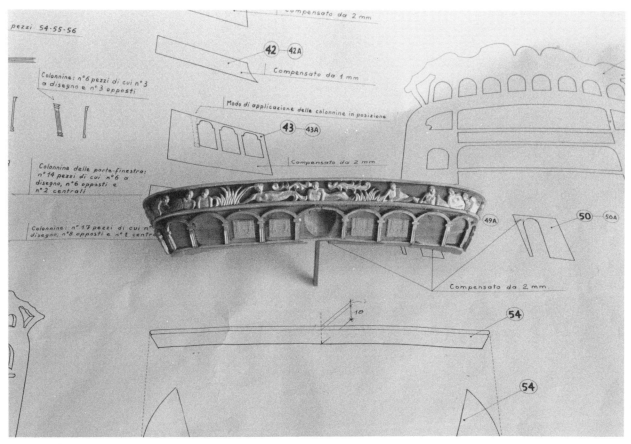

Fig. 4.24. The lower gallery assembly (the vertical prop is not part of the unit!).

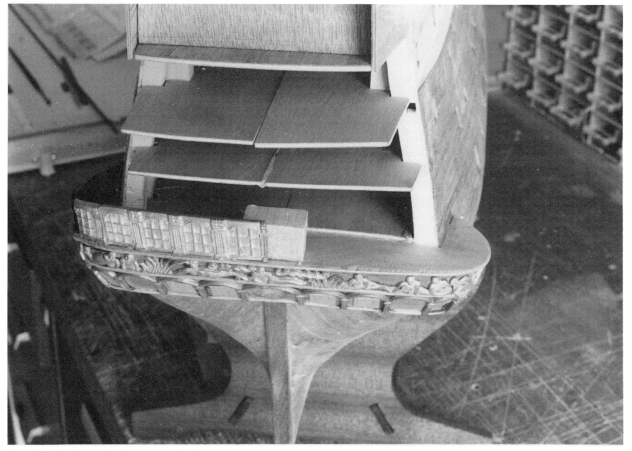

Fig. 4.25. Starting to build up the galleries.

Fig. 4.26. Paint and gild diecast parts before permanently fixing in place.

Identify and gather together all those diecast parts that are concerned with the stern and quarter galleries. File off all flash and die lines and generally clean up ready for putting together. This is not an arduous task as the castings are very clean and crisp. What is a fairly lengthy chore is the accurate measurement of what you have so far built and its comparison with the sizes of the castings supplied. I found that there were differences between them and the drawings, nothing drastic I hasten to add, but an accumulation of several odd half millimetres will add up gradually as the construction of the galleries climbs up towards the poop deck. In my particular case I found that I had a little bit more space than I had casting! This amounted to 2 mm in total and this I easily took up by increasing the two gallery deck thicknesses by 1 mm each. Don't forget that both faces of these decks need to be planked, the underside being the planked ceiling of the gallery below.

The inner facings of each gallery and the access partitions to the quarter galleries must be painted and gilded before assembly (Fig. 4.26). Build the stern galleries first, then varnish the decks and ceilings before fitting the transom. The reason for making this suggestion is again associated with minor differences between the drawings and the quarter gallery diecastings, all of which have to be carefully bent to shape to fit between hull and transom (Fig. 4.27).

Fig. 4.27. Building up the quarter galleries.

Similarly, the two apertures in the upper port and starboard corners of the transom should not be cut until after fitting all the diecast ornamentation to the stern. Again, I found it easier to start from the bottom and work up, leaving most of the adjustment necessary to be made to the lower edges of the large casting that spreads itself right across the top of the transom. This only needs to be done so as to enable it to fit over and between the eight small windows that should sit in a neat curve across the top of the upper gallery. Fit the four figures on the sides of the transom, without spears at this stage, then proceed to work on the bending and fitting of the upper quarter gallery parts. Before fitting the rails to the upper gallery, the two transom apertures can now be cut from the stern, missing the ornamentation already assembled.

I did not like the cast strips of spindling for the balustrade around the lower gallery, and it was purely a personal choice to substitute some boxwood columns I had in my spares box (Figs 4.28 and 4.29).

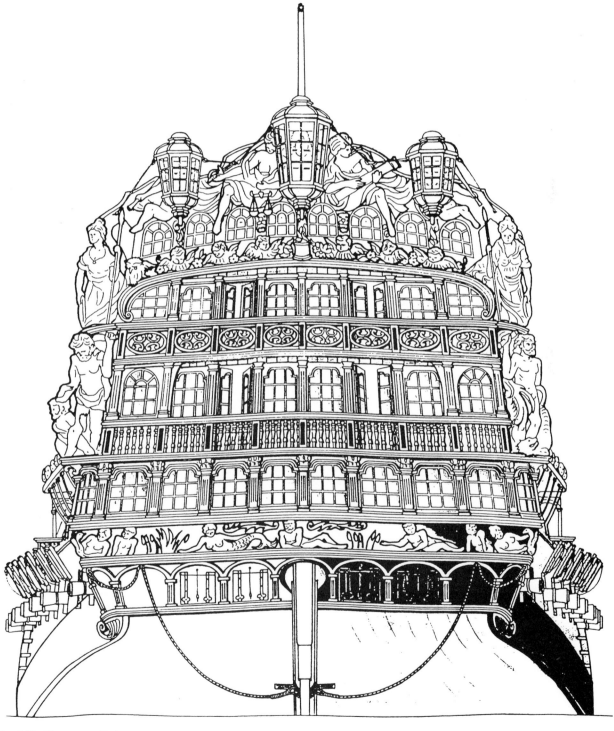

Fig. 4.28. The stern galleries.

Fig. 4.29. The transom and ornamentation in place.

Fig. 4.30. The wales and fenders.

The wales

The main wales, between the waterline and lower gun deck comprise three planks, edge-to-edge; the middle wales are two planks wide and the channel wales two separated strips of 3 mm × 2 mm, the lower of which lines up with the edge of the exposed deck at the bows. The alignment and spacing of these is important and you should be guided by the position of the gunports, the quarter galleries and, as just mentioned, the bow deck. They are fixed following exactly the same procedure as the second planking, but using PVA adhesive is essential. Do not attempt to cut those gunports that intrude into the wales until after the glue has thoroughly set (Fig. 4.30).

The fenders

There are four per side and should be shaped to snugly fit the tumblehome. To achieve the desired fit, a cardboard template was made, the shape then being transferred to the wooden strips selected for the purpose. The fenders were made over-length at the top end for later trimming and shaping after making up the bulwark rails. Once these are in place, the side ornamentation can be fitted (Fig. 4.30).

The side ornamentation

Unlike the planking procedure, where alternate side to side working was the order of the day, you should decorate one side at a time. The fenders, when correctly positioned relative to the gunports, offer an ideal starting place to fit the numerous diecast pieces involved. As with previous castings, the amount of cleaning up re-

quired is minimal, but be careful not to overlook those very small apertures within the design that may have that thin residual flash. A set of good needle files are obviously the tools for this job. File the ends of the first section square, scrape the rear surface clean and fix in place with cyanoacrylate. The second section should be treated in the same way, but first dry-fitted to ensure the best possible joint with the first section. The only problem I encountered was a marginal difference in thickness between some of the sections. However, a little bit of technical adjustment, better known as 'tweaking the ends', allowed adequate matching.

Before fixing each piece, make sure that the lower or upper rail has been cut away if necessary to match a gunport position (Fig. 4.30). This is not easy to do after the event and it is certainly not wise to try and remove the section, once fixed. OK, so when you have got them all glued in place, you can still see the joins. Not to worry, help is at hand in the form of the fine grade of Polyfilla. A speck on the finger gently rubbed across the joint does the trick. Any residue is soon titivated away with the appropriate needle file and the joint completely invisible when gilded. Plan ahead a little before fixing the most forward section on each side of the fo'c'sle deck by carefully marking the position of the two relevant head rails and catheads. The length of the forward side section can then be cut accordingly.

The top edges of the wooden bulwarks left over-high can now be trimmed to match the top edge of the diecastings. The combined metal and wooden edges can now be capped overall with a 4 mm × 0.5 mm strip, ready bent to follow the several places where diecast scrollwork forms the ends of different levels of bulwarks (Fig. 4.31).

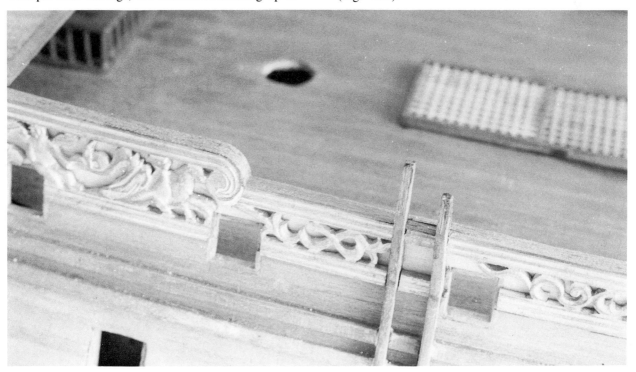

Fig. 4.31. The bulwark capping. Note over-length fenders.

The head rails

It is fortunate that the head rails come as diecast parts (Fig. 4.32) and do not have to be bent up or otherwise fabricated from wood — the shapes and curves are quite horrendous. Even so, the work content in carrying out this part of the construction is somewhat formidable and not to be recommended if you have had a bad day at work!

All rails, even though cast basically to shape, require matching to the curve of the hull. Such shaping is a long and tedious business, best started at the thick end, working along the rail gradually adjusting the curve, either by filing or bending, until the overall length can be assessed and the thin end cut and shaped as required. The top and bottom rails were fixed with two-part epoxy adhesive, each rail having been drilled to permit it to be pinned in place (Fig. 4.33). Cyanoacrylate was used for the remaining parts due to the awkwardness of applying any form of mechanical clamping necessary with a longer curing adhesive.

The gammoning hole and bracket should be correctly positioned before painting the inside faces of the timbers and the fitting of the beakhead grating. Any gaps between the forward ends of the rails and the rear shape of the figurehead should be filled and trimmed ready for external painting.

The bulwark rails

Over one hundred rail supports each 5 mm high need to be cut and shaped from 5 mm × 1 mm strip and fixed in place along the capping strips that trim the top edge of the bulwarks. I made a simple sawing jig to ensure that each piece was cut to exactly the same length. A scalpel was used to taper the sides and superglue employed as the adhesive.

The rails proper, in the majority of cases, have curved ends to match the scrollwork on the side ornamentation. In order to achieve these curves in a relatively simple manner and to ensure that with the passing of time they didn't open out, I decided that each rail would be laminated using two pieces of 4 mm × 0.5 mm strip. The ends of each were curved using the Amati bending nipper, then stuck together with white PVA. Crocodile clips held the bent ends firmly together and when set, the rail took on a rigidity that aided correct trimming and assembly to the supports fixed earlier.

The rails across the ends of the fo'c'sle and quarter decks by contrast, were of simpler construction and really warrant little comment.

Channels

The channels should be made up in pairs, port and starboard, to ensure identical lengths and deadeye positions. The inner edges must be shaped to match the curved side of the hull. This is an essential factor in attaining a strong assembly which ultimately has to take a fair load when setting up the shrouds. To further assist in the strengthening of the channels, a series of knees or brackets fit between the top of the channel boards and the side of the hull. It is worth spending a bit of time on these, again to get good fitting joints. PVA adhesive is entirely suitable for assembling these parts, but it is recommended that it be left at least 24 hours to properly cure before adding the deadeyes and chainplates.

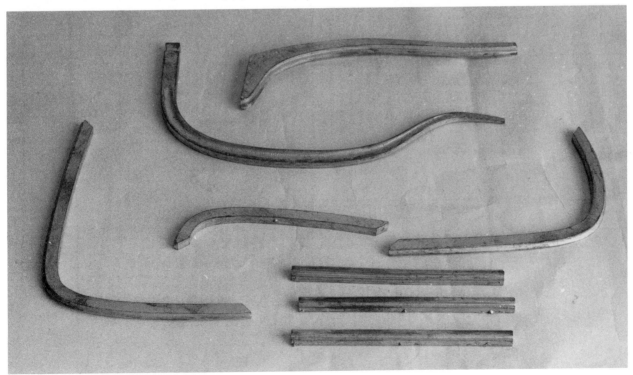

Fig. 4.32. The headrail diecastings.

Fig. 4.33. The head rails assembly.

Fig. 4.34. Channels and lower shroud deadeyes.

The lower deadeyes

Pre-formed 'chainplates' are provided in the kit but could really do with being a little bit longer in order to make a strongly fitting unit. The deadeyes snap into the hooped end of the chainplate whose lower end is then passed down through the channel board (Fig. 4.34). I bent the end of the chainplate tail inwards towards the hull, passed it through the top eye of the preventer link and then on into a hole in the hull. It is important to get the hole in its correct position, not only relative to the underside of the channel board, but also such that the line of the chainplate assumes the correct angle relative to its associated shroud. The tail of the chainplate was glued into the hole using an epoxy adhesive. Before this set, the lower eye of the preventer link was aligned to the same angle as the chainplate and fixed to the hull with a dome-headed pin.

The smaller deadeyes on the mizen channel were a sloppy fit in the chainplates supplied and, to get over the possible loss due to them falling out, they need to be held in place with just a touch of epoxy, making sure that the three holes in the deadeye are in their correct attitude. The larger deadeyes for the fore and main masts are a much tighter fit in the chainplates and are better left without adhesive for final alignment when actually setting up the shrouds.

The forecastle ornamentation

I concluded after two unsatisfactory attempts to ornament the forecastle facing 'on the boat' to try a completely different tack. I had found that the height at which I had to work and the fact that the surface in question was set back from the stem made everything just too awkward. I therefore decided to make a false facing on the bench complete with the two roundhouses.

The basis for this was two layers of veneer, cross-laminated together, onto which the various pieces of ornamental stripping could be added. This was then cut to shape to snugly fit on the head of the ship, then returned to the bench for further work.

I first made the two roundhouses, checking their size and position with the diecasting provided for capping the front of the forecastle deck. The two closed gunport lids were then located in position together with the central doorways and a coat of matt black paint brushed on. A length of 2 mm wide strip was sanded and gilded with gold paint and when dry, cut into suitable lengths to make up the ornamentation. The whole assembly was then glued to the forecastle deck facing.

It may be, of course, that it was my particular size of hand, or length of arm from elbow to wrist, that caused the awkwardness in the first place. Whatever the reason, the method that I ultimately adopted worked well and I commend it as a worthwhile alternative to working directly on the model itself. The aforementioned diecasting can now be properly cleaned up and painted before fitting in place across the front of the forecastle deck (Fig. 4.35). If you have done the initial marking out for the ornamentation correctly, the roundhouses

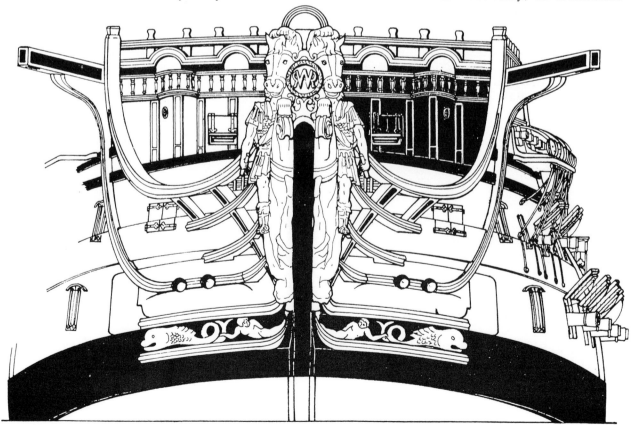

Fig. 4.35. Elevation showing forecastle ornamentation, roundhouses and capping across front of deck.

should now be nicely capped and the diecast archway sat centrally above the doors. The diecasting needed a little bit of gentle tweaking in order that its lower edge properly matched the camber of the deck, but nothing more radical than that was needed. I found that super-glue gel was a most convenient adhesive for this fitting.

Fitting Out

The curved staircases

The drawings show the proportions of these left- and right-hand assemblies quite well, but alas, the builder is left entirely to his or her own devices when it comes to modelling methods. The first thing to recognize is that whatever procedure you choose to adopt, it has to be repeatable in order to produce an identical, albeit, opposite hand. This then was not the time to be thinking about fixing lots of tiny bits together in the hope that I could duplicate the same sizes on both units.

I therefore opted to cut two rectangular blocks of balsa equal in size to the height, width and depth of the finished staircase (Fig. 4.36). These I shaped in plan view according to the curve of the steps, remembering to cut one right- and one left-hand. Having divided the height into the required number of risers, I then care-fully cut in all the steps in both pieces, cutting each alternatively in the right- and left-hand parts. This kept a tighter control on making each the same size.

When I was happy with the result, each riser was faced with 0.5 mm strip and, when completely set, each tread was added using the same material. The ends of both treads and risers were trimmed to follow the inner and outer curve of the staircase and the side strings added to follow the 'going' of the risers. Careful use of superglue helped a lot in getting all these parts together but, even so, I still left the assemblies overnight before

attempting to carve away the balsa still visible. Fitting newel posts completed the project and, what at first sight had appeared to be quite a daunting task had not in fact proved too difficult at all.

Anchor and riding bitts

Since these sustained considerable loads in use, they were extended down and fixed to the beams of the orlop deck below. However, should the modeller not wish to go to this degree of accuracy, they can be made up 'as seen' and fixed to the relevant deck surface. A word of warning though — the cross section of the material to be used is not very great, thus it is advisable not to rely on a plain glued joint, but reinforce it with a dowel. The joints between the cross pieces and uprights are of simple cross slot form and really should not require any further strengthening.

The rudder

The rudder is provided already cut to basic shape. Accurate measurement is needed to mark out and cut the apertures for the hinges, remembering to make them large enough to be able to slide the pintle and pin (on the rudder) over the gudgeon (on the hull), then drop the assembly down to engage the pins. It may be that you wish to simulate more authentically the way the rudder was built up. For this I refer you to Fig. 4.37.

The hinges supplied in the kit are cast and very sub-stantial. They look very good, but you must take care when trying to bend the gudgeons to match the curve of the hull planking. Don't overdo the force or they will snap. File or scrape the inside faces and you will find that epoxy adhesive is just the job for fixing the parts in place. Avoid superglue in this instance, it will not give you enough time to adjust the position.

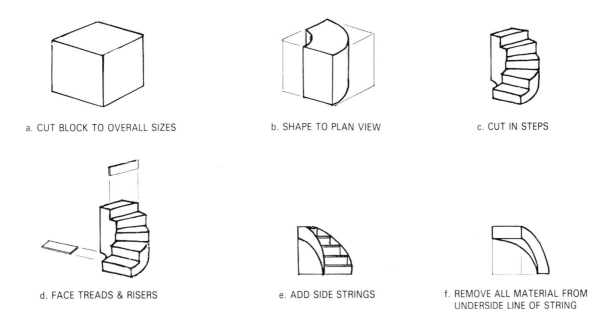

a. CUT BLOCK TO OVERALL SIZES

b. SHAPE TO PLAN VIEW

c. CUT IN STEPS

d. FACE TREADS & RISERS

e. ADD SIDE STRINGS

f. REMOVE ALL MATERIAL FROM UNDERSIDE LINE OF STRING

Fig. 4.36. Construction of curved staircase port side shown – make starboard concurrently.

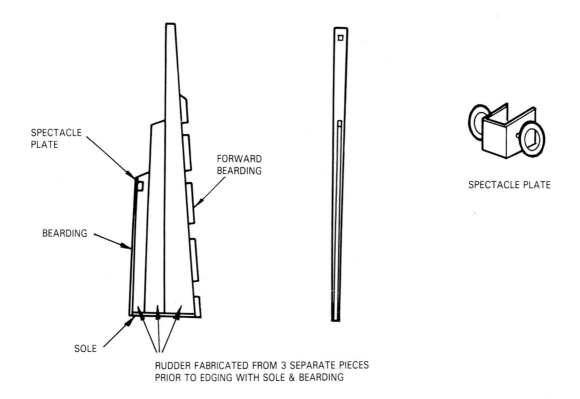

SPECTACLE
PLATE

FORWARD
BEARING

BEARDING

SOLE

RUDDER FABRICATED FROM 3 SEPARATE PIECES
PRIOR TO EDGING WITH SOLE & BEARDING

SPECTACLE PLATE

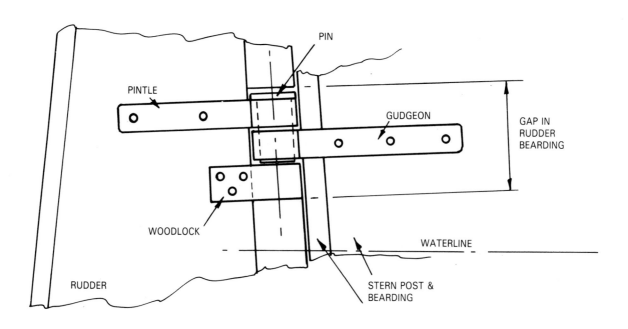

PIN

PINTLE

GUDGEON

GAP IN
RUDDER
BEARDING

WOODLOCK

WATERLINE

RUDDER

STERN POST &
BEARDING

NOTE: WOODLOCK FITTED ONE POSITION ONLY IE ON
STARBOARD SIDE OF GAP IMMEDIATELY ABOVE WATERLINE

Fig. 4.37. Rudder assembly.

The ship's boat

This is not quite the straightforward job that the pre-shaped hull supplied leads you to expect. Considerable work is necessary to reshape the shell to look anything like the real thing. The first area for attention is the line of the gunwales which have quite a curve from stem to stern (Fig. 4.38). In producing this shape, the routered step provided around the inside of the hull shell becomes redundant and should be carefully pared away. Add the slatted floor and build up the inside features at prow and stern before fixing the thwarts. The pre-machined slot for the keel is definitely an asset and, after a bit of work quite a presentable little boat can be produced (Fig. 4.39).

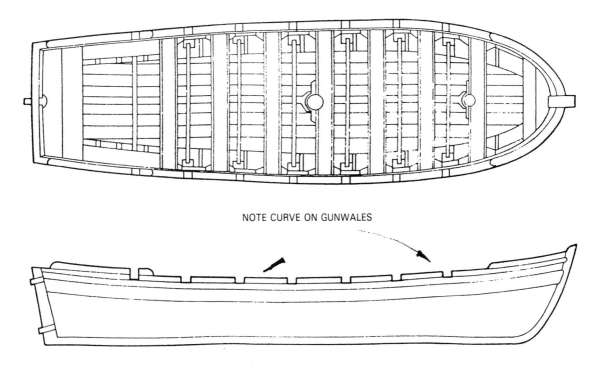

NOTE CURVE ON GUNWALES

Fig. 4.38. The shape of the ship's boat.

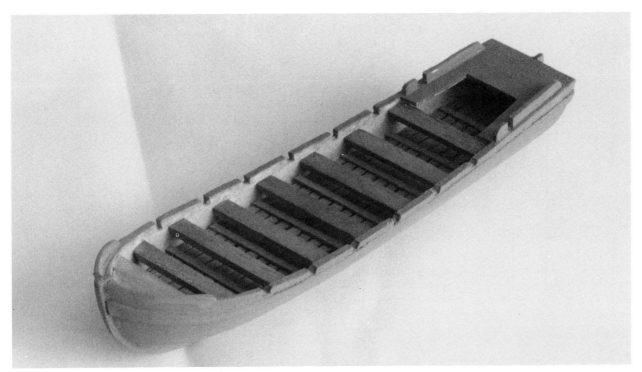

Fig. 4.39. The ship's boat.

The gun carriage assemblies

The basic assemblies are made from pre-formed parts supplied with the kit and comprise the carriage, wheels, axles, barrel and pivots. However, depending upon how much detail you wish to include in your particular model, there are further additions that can be made (Fig. 4.40).

The drawings are well detailed and show the rigging of the guns to deck and inside of bulwarks. This entails the fitting of some 144 small double blocks for the guns that can be seen in their entirety on deck. Watch out for the wheel sizes — each carriage has a pair of larger diameter wheels at the front than at the back. There are two different sizes of carriage and the smaller wheels on the large carriage are the same diameter as the large wheels on the small carriage.

Axle diameters need to be reduced for the two smallest size wheels. Tapering is not good enough, and can result in broken wheels; opening out the holes in the wheels can be equally hazardous. Make sure that the axles protrude well through the wheel. Remember that tapered cotters were used to hold the wheels on the axles and, although it might not be possible to faithfully produce such cotters, it would be incorrect to have over-short axles.

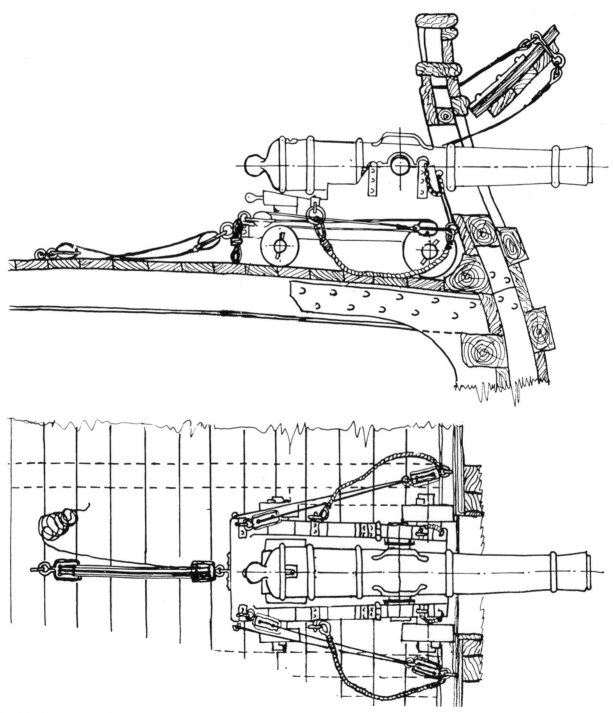

Fig. 4.40. The gun assembly.

Brass wire is provided for making the pivots. However you choose to cut the wire, do not forget to file the ends flat to remove the pinch marks of side cutters or the burrs from sawing. Wedge blocks should be cut from scrap material and glued to the carriages under the rear end of the barrel. With care, these can be positioned to present all barrels at the same level and, in a more practical sense, provide a third fixing point for the barrel on the carriage.

Whatever you wish to add to this basic assembly, do it now. There are far too many obstructions and a lack of space to work in once the assembly is fixed to the deck.

Gunport lids

The construction of the gunport lids is a self-contained project in itself. The total number involved, each made from the assembly of five pieces, gives the modelmaker scope to express ingenuity as to how best to make them identical to each other without a lot of repetitive measuring and marking out.

The main piece comprises two parts, glued together edge to edge and backed up by a third, but smaller, square piece. The first job is to glue two full length strips together to make up the correct depth of the lids then, when dry, cut off identical lengths to suit the lid width. Having fitted the third piece, the two hinges can be fixed in place which you may find are better painted

before assembly using a touch of superglue. The entire underside and edges of the completed lid should be painted matt red before fixing to the hull. Two holes drilled in the hull accept extensions of the hinge diecasting and while these holes should be drilled at this time, it is a matter of personal choice as to when the lids are put in place. I found that later, rather than sooner, was the better bet.

Making the Masts and Yards

The timber for the masts comes already tapered, but you should not run away with the idea that this makes the fabrication merely an assembly job. Diameters, especially in the area of the tops, need adjusting as do the shapes at the butt end of the upper masts, which should also feature a rectangular hole to take the fid. I have to say that in spite of the high quality of the drawings provided with this kit, I found that a copy of *The Masting and Rigging of English Ships of War 1625–1860* by James Lees (see References at the end of this chapter) was absolutely invaluable.

The woldings should be added to the lower masts before assembling the tops in place. The number and position together with the correct number of turns is clearly shown on the drawings. I used the hidden end method (Boy Scouts to the fore) for producing a neat and tidy job. Making each top is a project in itself and care-

Fig. 4.41. The underside of the main top. Note woldings.

ful measurement is required to permit a snug fit of the assembly around the mast. Cross-halving joints are favourite for putting the crosstrees and trestletrees together, taking care that the upper surfaces are properly true and flat to take the subsequent planking. Full dimensional details are given, but just check the actual mast diameters that you have finished up with, in order to get the spacing of the various elements correct (Fig. 4.41).

Each top has to be edged, but before doing this, add the battens to the upper surface of the planking. The ends can then be trimmed to match the outer shape of the platform and provide a bit more support for the edging strip. The aft edge of the platform should be done with one piece then, with care, one continuous strip can be used to edge the remaining sides (Figs 4.42 and 4.43).

The holes for the fixing of the deadeyes and futtock shrouds should be drilled, as should the holes around the front rim of the top to take the crowsfeet. Bolsters should be fitted adjacent to the lower mast aperture. These are of quadrant section over which the shrouds are ultimately pulled down.

The topmast trestletrees and crosstrees are made up in a similar fashion to those described for the lower mast tops. However, the crosstrees curve back over about a third of their length each side so that the end of the forward crosstree is in line with the centre of the topmast. These parts obviously have to be cut from fairly wide strip of the correct thickness and it is best to make three together in order to finish up with three identical pieces (Fig. 4.44). After assembly, drill all necessary holes for the upper futtock shrouds then fit bolsters as mentioned earlier for the tops.

Fig. 4.43. Main topmast and cap.

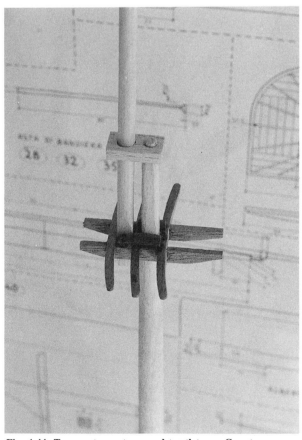

Fig. 4.44. Top mast crosstrees and trestletrees. Crosstrees curve back.

Fig. 4.42. Upper surface of main top edges trimmed and holes for futtock shrouds drilled.

The hounds should be fretted out to shape and cleaned and tidied before assembling to the lower masthead. It is important to recognise the rake of the mast and the related angle of the tops before finally fixing them in place. The top, upper masts and crosstrees can now be brought together as a complete mast unit, constantly checking for straightness and alignment.

The bowsprit construction follows along the same procedures as the masts. However, you have several additional features to watch. First, and not least, is the angle which the bowsprit makes with the hull and the clearance of its underside with the figurehead and top of the prow. Temporarily fix the main stem of the bowsprit in position to ensure that the angle is correct, making any corrections necessary. The position of the cleats for the gammoning should be marked relative to the hole and bracket made earlier. Accurate alignment of the sprit top and topmast should now be made and these parts permanently fixed in place.

The bowsprit can now be removed from the hull for making up and fitting the gammoning cleats in the positions previously marked. The jibboom saddles should also be fashioned and fixed in place, then the jibboom itself, noting that it passes through the sprit top and is lashed at its heel to the bowsprit. The mast and bowsprit assemblies can now be varnished and painted. Those areas around the tops, crosstrees and trestletrees should be painted matt black as should the mast caps and the tip of the jibboom. All should be set aside to thoroughly dry before a total coat of matt varnish can be applied.

Study the rigging details to identify the positions of the many and various size blocks involved. Many of these are far more easily rigged before the mast is stepped, particularly those that hang below the tops and through which are roved the leech and buntlines. Even the blocks for the braces might well be rigged at this time. Remember, it is not only getting the fingers in amongst rigging to tie knots that can be difficult at a later stage, but one slip with a trimming blade can be absolutely disastrous. Don't forget the bowsprit — there are a number of deadeyes and blocks that are better fixed while you have the assembly on the bench and can move it around.

I find that on a model having a lot of complex rigging, certainly one where sails are to be hoisted, it is well to concentrate on one mast at a time and highlight on the drawings all the blocks concerned. On this particular project, because so many sheets need to be referred to for a total picture, I drew a very basic diagram of each mast assembly and used coloured pencils to mark in the different sizes and styles of blocks to be used. It takes quite a bit of time, but you can be assured that it is well worth the effort. Having more or less completed the hull, it is quite amazing how strong the temptation is to step the masts. Be satisfied with a dry run!

The yards

I describe the making of the yards at this point as it seems a natural follow-on to the completion of the masts. However, it may be that in reality, like myself, you may like to consider leaving this part of the project until after the completion of the standing rigging. It is purely a matter of personal choice and there are considerations for and against either decision. On the one hand, making the yards and miscellaneous spars (not forgetting the flag staff at the stern) at this juncture brings an end to the carpentry part of the project with its attendant sawdust and drillings. On the other hand, if you make them now, you have to find somewhere safe to keep a dozen assemblies comprising yard, stuns'l booms, blocks, footropes and pendants. Whichever way you choose, the procedures are the same, but the latter option has a lot going for it.

The lower yards are provided already tapered but you have to do some very careful work to recognise that the centre portion of the lower yards are octagonal in section. Thus, having filed the given circular section to the required eight-sided shape, this section is now too long and the ends have to be retapered in circular section accordingly. This all needs to be done with the utmost care because the diameter of the yards as supplied is only just about large enough to take in the diameter of the octagon size across corners. However, it can be done . . . just!

Having sorted out the lower yards, the upper yards have to be made from plain parallel dowel rod. Most modelmakers building this kit will almost certainly have their favourite way of tapering masts and yards developed during the building of earlier models. It does, however, largely depend on what equipment you have available. Those modelmakers with a lathe will no doubt use it to good effect, but what is to be done if you do not have this facility? A method that I have found to be very effective is to file the basic dowel rod to an octagonal section at the same time including the taper toward the end of the mast or spar. The size across the flats of the octagon should be slightly larger than the finished diameter required. An electric drill, preferably with variable speed and held in a horizontal drill stand, is then used to spin the roughly tapered spar whilst various grades of abrasive paper are applied to convert the rough octagon section back to the round. This does tend to be a bit on the slow side because of the constant checking that needs to be done on the length and diameters of the tapers involved. But it does work if your workshop kit has nothing more sophisticated.

The next stage is to make and fix the sling cleats (Fig. 4.45) and yard arm cleats (Fig. 4.46). I find that it is usually better to make each of the sling cleats from two pieces of strip material cyanoed together and then shaped up to suit. This is far less difficult than trying to make them from one piece and certainly easier to attain matching pairs.

47

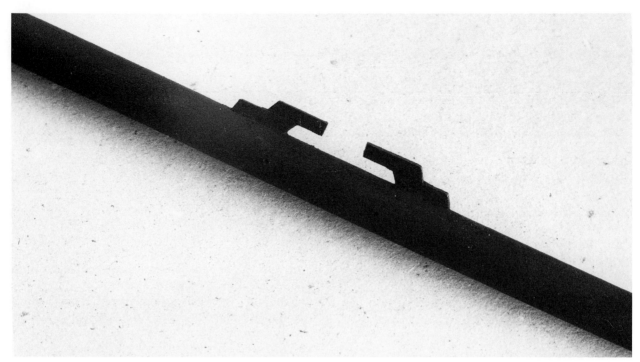

Fig. 4.45. Sling cleats.

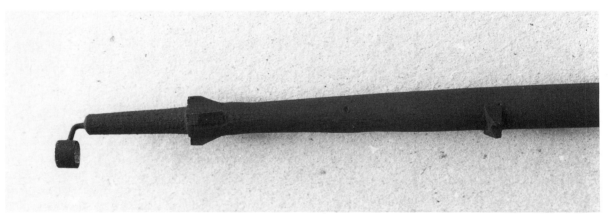

Fig. 4.46. Yard arm cleats and stunsail boom irons.

Now that we have a set of yards all shaped and sized, the next step is to add the stirrups and footropes. In days gone by, rope stirrups were an absolute pain because you could never get them to hang right and footropes took on a curve that was anything but natural. Times have changed and the advent of superglue has brought the solution to many former modelmaking problems. I will say right now that my method is a simulation of how stirrups were applied, but at this scale the result is most effective.

First the yard has to be marked at the position of each stirrup and 1.00 mm diameter holes drilled through the yard at 90° to the sling cleats. In the same way drill holes at the position of the end of each footrope. Now take a length of 0.75 mm diameter thread at least three times the length of the finished stirrup, thread through one of the holes until the end protrudes about 8 mm then apply a spot of cyano and pull the end of the thread back into the hole. We now have the free length of thread

hanging down from the underside of the yard.

The next stage needs to be done with a certain amount of speed and may require a couple of practice runs, but it isn't difficult to get the hang of it. Hold the yard in the left hand (the right if you are a southpaw), and liberally coat the hanging thread with cyano to within about 20 mm of the free end. Quickly take the uncoated portion between index finger and thumb of the right hand and, keeping it taut, pull the thread UP the FORE side of the yard, over the top and DOWN the AFT side (Fig. 4.47). Maintain the tension until the cyano has gone off and, voilà, you have a nice stiff stirrup.

Having done the two or three stirrups concerned with one footrope, put the yard to one side while you prepare the 'jig' for the footrope. This entails knocking a couple of pins about 150 mm apart into a piece of board or the top of the bench, between which, at about 2 mm from the surface of the board, you stretch a length of 0.75 mm diameter thread about twice the total length of the foot-

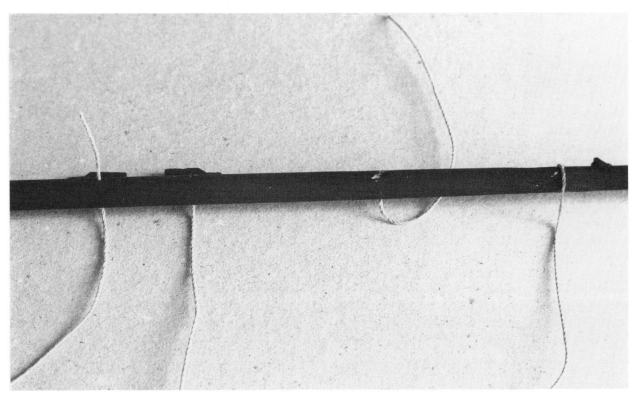

Fig. 4.47. The four stages of making footrope stirrups.

rope. A slip knot at one end and simple winding at the other is more than adequate to maintain the tension. Taking the yard, lay it parallel to the footrope so that the stirrups lay on top of it at the correct distance from the yard. A steel rule, augmented by a bit of added weight (a pair of pliers in my case), laid across the end of the stirrups keeps everything in place while a careful appli-

cation of cyano is made at the junction of the footrope and each stirrup (Fig. 4.48).

When set, the ends of the footrope are fed up through the remaining holes in the yard and superglued in place. The ends are then trimmed off flush with the top surface of the yard. The ends of the stirrups are then also trimmed to the underside of the footropes to complete

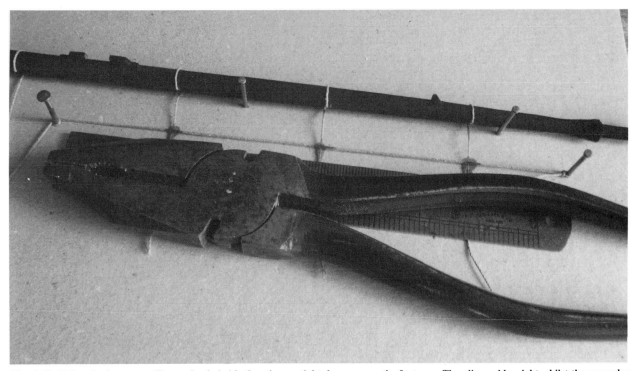

Fig. 4.48. Fixing the footropes. The steel rule holds the stirrups tight down across the footrope. The pliers add weight whilst the superglue is applied.

the job. The stuns'l boom irons should next be fabricated. There is nothing supplied in the kit to make these so it was a case of delving into the scrap box to find something suitable. I finally came up with a short length of brass tube 4.0 mm diameter from which I cut eight collars each 3 mm long. I then drilled a hole to suit the diameter of some brass pins I had to hand centrally into one side of each collar. Eight pins were then bent to an 'L' shape with legs 4 mm and 10 mm long. The 4 mm legs were then tapped into the holes and soft soldered in place with the 10 mm legs parallel to the centre line of the collar diameter. The end of the pin inside the collar, which should only just be protruding, should now be filed off flush with the inside diameter. Finally, a 4.0 mm diameter cup washer should be soldered in place on the 10 mm leg about halfway along its length. A hole drilled into the end of the yard accepts the end of the 10 mm leg and the assembly should then be adjusted radially to position the boom centre at 45° to the sling cleats before finally fixing with cyano. It then only remains to make the small boom supports and glue them in position (Fig. 4.46).

The yards at this time should be painted matt black, remembering that the stunsail booms are left natural and varnished, with only the ends that protrude beyond the end of the yards painted matt black. As in the case of the masts, it is well worth studying the drawings closely to identify the size and position of the various blocks that need to be tied to the yards. Again, it is much easier to fix these in place before rigging the yards to their respective masts. When tying these in place, note that some accept rigging from the fore side of the sail and some from the aft side, thus they should have their radial position on the yard biased accordingly. The pendants should also be rigged at this time, remembering that those on the mizen yards are rigged forward rather than aft.

The flagstaff at the stern must not be forgotten, or the blocks that fix it to the inside of the transom. The pole itself is made from 3.0 mm diameter dowel × 160 mm long and tapered to drawing. The two fixing blocks were each made by drilling a 3.0 mm diameter hole centrally through a 10 mm length of 8 mm × 2 mm strip which is then slit down with a scalpel tangential to the hole. The edges are then cleaned square and the corners chamfered to make a piece which holds the butt end of the pole against the inner face of the transom. A small single block, 2 mm for preference, should be tied at the top of the pole to take the line that hoists the flag. Again, it is a matter of choice, but I chose to leave the fixing of the flagstaff until later, since it had every chance of being knocked off during the following rigging process.

We have now basically finished the construction and carpentry involved and now is a good time to go back over everything that has been made to ensure that no final touches are required. Look particularly at the gunport lids; these are potential features for getting damaged or knocked off. Make sure that eyebolts have

not come loose and study the ornamentation to ensure that there are no unsightly gaps between adjacent diecast parts. Having satisfied yourself that everything is in order, a good tidy up around the bench area clears the deck for the rigging process where different tools and materials come into play. A clean up of the ship itself is not a bad idea — it is surprising just how much muck hides itself between decks and around the prow between the head rails.

Before the model gets any bigger and therefore more unwieldy, the stand could well be finished off and the nameplate fixed in position. Up until now, my stand had relied on tight joints to hold it together, but obviously now is the time to decide on the manner of finish to be adopted. The timber provided in the kit is of excellent quality and will undoubtedly take polish well — even several coats of varnish, whichever takes your fancy. It is well worth considering edging the supporting surfaces of the stand with strips of substantially thick felt material. This makes for a very snug seating for the hull, and certainly will protect the surface of the ship's bottom.

The stand should be reassembled and the joints thoroughly glued up. You will have realised, when taking the model off of the temporary stand construction, just how much weight there is going to be in the finished job. Remember how heavy the box was when you first bought the kit? The stand has certainly got to have those well fitted and glued joints.

So now we come to the rigging and another set of problems and different materials to handle. Also there is that unavoidable decision to make. To fit, or not to fit, sails? That is the question. Whether it is better to suffer the leechlines and buntlines of extended rigging etc. etc. My apologies to Shakespeare, but he never built a model of the *Royal William*!

The Standing Rigging

Before starting to rig the model, it is well worth doing a bit of reading on the subject in general and, if possible, on the rigging of ships of the particular period in question. I have already mentioned *The Masting and Rigging of English Ships of War* by James Lees and I make no apology for repeating my opinion that it is the best work on the subject currently available. It is especially useful in that it contains a section on seamanship and advises on the order of dressing the masts and yards, ropework, blocks and belaying. The modelmaker will find this invaluable when building the *Royal William* because whilst the belaying points are given in the plans, sequence of rigging is not.

A few general notes on rigging procedures and technique before we get to work. First of all let us consider the materials. Cordage usually comes in hanks of the various sizes required, but if you are looking for the correct cable laid and rope laid material, then you are likely to look in vain. Kits do not usually recognise the difference and if you wish to be absolutely correct on your model, then you have no other choice than to lay your own. To make a winding head and ropewalk is not overly difficult and descriptions of more than adequate gear have appeared in *Model Boats* magazine. Harold Hahn, in his *Ships of the American Revolution and Their Models*, devotes considerable space to the subject and there is no doubt that the results of doing it yourself are far more satisfactory from both the accuracy and cosmetic aspects. However, if you do not have such facilities and are therefore having to proceed with what you have been given, there are still several things that need to be done before rigging actually starts.

Let us consider colour. There are many fine models in museums and exhibitions rigged throughout in one colour, usually tan. There are equally fine examples where the standing rigging is in dark brown or black, using tan for the running rigging. So, I am going to sit on the fence and say do what you feel looks best on your model. If you do go for colour, and what you have been supplied with is all natural or tan, then you are in for a dyeing job. In any case, the rigging thread should be uncoiled and rewound into hanks about 250 mm long and washed, dyed if required, then hung up to dry with some weight suspended on the bottom. This takes most of the natural stretch out of the material and helps to avoid that annoying twist that can occur when tension is applied.

Another means of introducing some stability to the threads is to work in some white PVA adhesive. Do this when you have actually cut off a length for rigging by coating the thumb and forefinger with adhesive and pulling the cut length through. This has two further advantages — first it lays down all those minute surface fibres that would otherwise stick up and act as hooks for dust to cling to later on and, secondly, it helps to induce and maintain a more natural sag to those lines that do not have to be tensioned up.

It is worth paying a little bit of attention to the rigging blocks and spend some time clearing out the holes. It is usually fairly evident which way the drill went through; there is a nice clean hole one side, while on the other, several whiskers hang around the edge of the hole. Redrill in the opposite direction to clear the hole. It may seem pointless to redrill holes already provided, but there are few things more frustrating than having successfully got the end of the thread into the hole, only to find it won't come out the other end! You can also lay odds that such a block will have been rigged in the one place you can't get a drill into. One very useful ploy that helps the threading of blocks is to smear the end of the rigging thread with superglue over about a 10 mm length. This stiffens up the thread to provide a built-in bodkin and is particularly handy for rigging lanyards through deadeyes when setting up the shrouds.

As far as tools are concerned, I have found that a selection of different ended tweezers are almost mandatory. A slim-handled scalpel (kept specifically for rigging) is quite a handy tool but, for trimming ends really close, I find that the most efficient tool is a pair of good nail clippers. Choose either the square-ended gentleman's pocket style or the smaller variety of side cutters used by pedicurists. Generally speaking, the clippers are safer than the scalpel; one slip with the sharp edge whilst in amongst the rigging can cause havoc. Supplement these items with a few different sizes of crochet hooks for general 'fishing' and you should be well set to start rigging.

At this stage, it may well be worth saying a few words about knots and ropework. Having studied more model ships than the normal modelmaker gets to see, it is apparent to me that the majority of fixings are simulated rather than tied in the authentic manner. There are good reasons for this — scale, accessibility, not to mention less efficient eyesight that may come with advancing years. If you wish to really go to town, then reference to *The Ashley Book of Knots* is recommended. However, there are other ways which look pretty good. Seizings around blocks and deadeyes are a prime example. Trying to seize the thread around a 2 mm or 3 mm block can be quite a task and will often look bulky if not a bit of a bodged job. Try taking the short end around the block, applying a touch of cyano and quickly twisting the threads together. Pull and untwist the short end back to leave the twisted portion about 4 mm long and trim off. The result can look a good sight better than many a 'proper' seizing I have seen.

However, for the larger features, the job must be done properly and I suspect that every modeller will have his, or her, own favourite way of tackling the task. One of my pet procedures involves the use of small crocodile clips as shown in the accompanying sketches (Fig. 4.49).

A far more difficult aspect to cover is that of tension; how tight to apply each part of the rigging. I would be less than honest if I said that there were rules to follow that would guarantee correct results. How do you explain a sense of 'feel' or gut feeling that a particular tension is about right. I guess only experience will tell, but there are one or two things to remember to try. The first essential is not to over-tension. This can not only pull masts or spars out of alignment, but is a totally irreversible situation. There are always ways and means of tightening things up — albeit cheating — but it is almost impossible to slacken a line once set up.

One simple technique for gauging tension involves the use, yet again, of the small crocodile clip. Attach one clip to the line midway between its fixing points and tension up until the line is pulled straight. Alright, I know that the length of the line and the weight of the clip are academically significant, but at least it provides a consistent basis for working and one that can be varied with experience. Maybe two clips for a longer run of thicker rope? Remember too, that if you are going to rig sails, the tension on the fore and aft stays needs to be

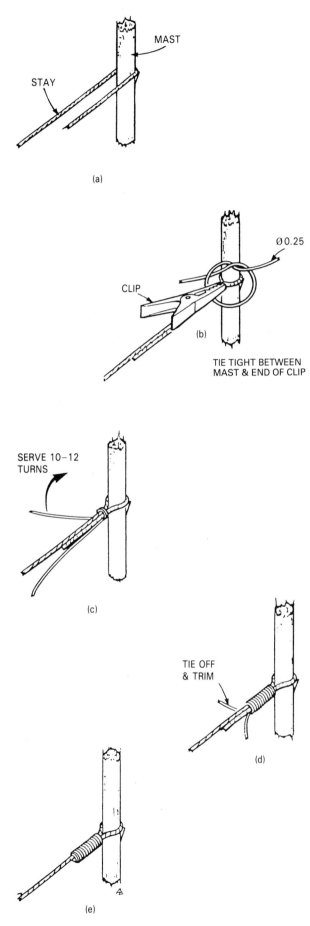

MAST

STAY

(a)

Ø 0.25

CLIP

TIE TIGHT BETWEEN
MAST & END OF CLIP

(b)

SERVE 10–12
TURNS

(c)

TIE OFF
& TRIM

(d)

(e)

Fig. 4.49. Seizings.

greater if they are not to sag under the weight of the sail.

Having discussed lines under tension, let us now consider those that hang slack. To get these to look right is yet another problem not too easy to solve. The thread always seems to have a mind of its own and it can be the devil's own job to get that natural curve that doesn't get noticed on a model when it is right, but stands out like a sore thumb when it's not. The aforementioned washing and adequate pre-stretching makes a large contribution towards success, but even so, a little extra encouragement is usually required. I have found that the PVA treatment is a good start, but let the adhesive go off a bit before setting up the line. If this is seen to be insufficient, try brushing a further light coating onto the thread and gently stroking the inside of the sagging line with a piece of dowel or a pencil. Depending on the nature of the material, it may be found that instead of PVA an application of acrylic varnish will do the trick. For thicker threads a very light moistening prior to brushing on the varnish may be advantageous.

Finally, before we start to go into action on the *Royal William*, a further note about adhesives. A touch of cyanoacrylate is good for sealing off knots, seizings and lashings. However, although it takes a little longer before ends can be trimmed, acrylic varnish is better, cleaner and less hazardous. It is also easier to apply in all those difficult and less accessible places. With both media, be careful not to overdo the application and perhaps foul holes in blocks or deadeyes.

Rigging the bowsprit

The bowsprit can now be permanently fixed in place. Having previously checked the relative angles of bowsprit and sprit topmast, the only care needed at this juncture is to make sure that when making this permanent assembly, the topmast is in the vertical position. The hole in the hull should take the butt end of the bowsprit in a fairly snug fashion prior to applying glue and having made the assembly, it should be left to thoroughly set before attempting to start any rigging.

The first stage is the gammoning and the *Royal William* has two (Fig. 4.50). Although much is hidden by the head rails, it should be noted that the gammoning was not just a series of turns around the bowsprit and through the stem or gammon bracket, but rather rove in such a way as to give the appearance of a twist. This was done by keeping the turns to the fore on the bowsprit but then to the aft end of the hole and bracket. The gammoning was then tightened up by the application of frapping turns in the middle, these usually numbering the same as the turns of gammoning. One of the main problems to overcome is the inaccessibility due to the close proximity of the head rails. The various shapes of tweezers come into their own on this operation as do the crochet hooks.

A six-sheave rack block should be lashed to both the port and starboard side of the forward gammoning as

Fig. 4.50. Bowsprit gammoning.

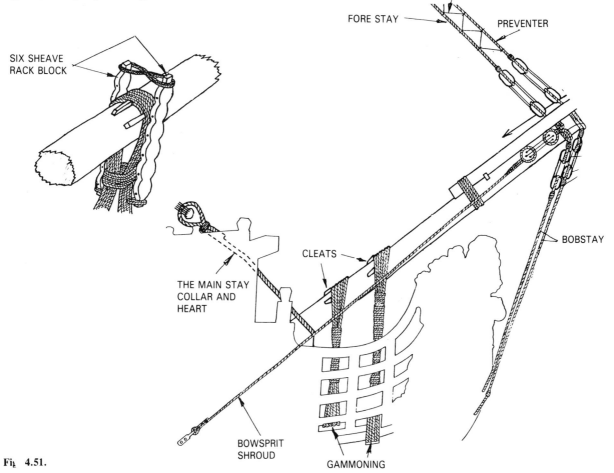

SIX SHEAVE
RACK BLOCK

FORE STAY

PREVENTER

BOBSTAY

THE MAIN STAY
COLLAR AND
HEART

CLEATS

BOWSPRIT
SHROUD

GAMMONING

Fig 4.51.

Bowsprit shrouds and bobstays.

The foremast area bitts and grating.

shown in Fig. 4.51. The two bobstays are the next to be rigged. These should pass through holes in the stem then up to the underside of the bowsprit where they are pulled up with lanyards through a pair of deadeyes. The two shrouds are rigged in a similar manner from a point just above the main wale and to the fore of the first gunport, again to a pair of deadeyes each side of the bowsprit.

The sprit topmast also has shrouds and ratlines and these should be added now to complete the initial bow-sprit rigging (Fig. 4.52). The formal sequence of putting on the shrouds should be observed; forward starboard, forward port then starboard and port alternately. The deadeyes for the shrouds are set up on the sprit top in futtock fashion to the bowsprit below, remembering to keep the three holes in the deadeyes in their correct alignment. Similarly, the shrouds are tailed with dead-eyes and then pulled down with lanyards. Fig. 4.53 shows the sequence for seizing deadeyes to the shrouds. The lanyard is started through the right-hand hole of the upper deadeye from the inboard side and knotted to prevent it pulling through. It is then sequentially reeved through the holes of the deadeyes until it finally emerges from the inboard side of the left-hand hole in the lower deadeye. The end of the lanyard is then taken up through the throat above the upper deadeye with a half-hitch, then seized to the shroud after several turns (Fig. 4.54). Incidentally, this system of setting up was for use where shrouds were made from shroud laid rope. If cable laid

shrouds were employed, the start of the lanyard would be from the left-hand hole in the upper deadeye.

We now come to the first of the many ratlines that have to be tied. It is a most tedious job and one which no modeller I have ever met has any liking for. There have been one or two gadgets put on the market for 'simplifying' the process, but I have yet to find one that works *properly*. I have tried all sorts of so-called short cuts, but I am constantly reminded of the old saying that the laziest man always takes the greatest pains. I therefore feel that the best way is to tie them on in the fashion described on the following pages.

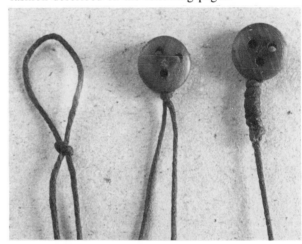

Fig. 4.53. Seizing deadeyes to shrouds.

Fig. 4.52. The sprit topmast with its shrouds and ratlines.

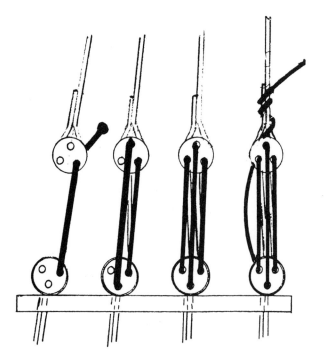

Fig. 4.54. Sequence for rigging lanyards. Note relative position of deadeyes.

First, let me say that I cheat and use single hitches rather than clove-hitches throughout. Having cut a suitable length of thread for one ratline, I take one end and pass it behind the most left-hand shroud, pull it forward and tie a hitch. This leaves one end tied to the shroud with the free end of the thread to the right. This is taken behind the next shroud and hitched to it in the same way, and so on, working from left to right. A pair of fine tweezers in the right hand greatly assist in the feeding and tying. I usually tie about five or six ratlines then touch all the knots with the slightest amount of acrylic varnish to be left overnight before trimming. Refer to Figs 4.55 to 4.60 to see the sequence adopted. These illustrate those on the foremast shrouds but the same procedure applies. Points to watch. Do not put so much tension on as to distort the line of the shrouds and, when cutting off the required length of thread, make sure you cut a sufficient amount. It is surprising how much length goes into a knot (there are ten on each ratline on the fore and main mast shrouds), extra length also being required for handling. The process always seems quite wasteful in terms of material, but it is better to err by cutting overlong pieces. Trimmed ends are often long enough for tying blocks etc., later on. Should you be left-handed, you will probably find that it will be easier working from right to left rather than in the manner I have described previously.

I think that at this stage it will be seen that it would be unwise to set up the spritsail and sprit topsail yards as they will be extremely vulnerable to damage during the ongoing rigging process.

Fig. 4.55. Tying ratlines — if right-handed, work left to right. Feed end of ratline inboard between shrouds 5 and 6.

Fig. 4.56. Take end behind shroud 5.

Fig. 4.57. Pull end outboard between shrouds 4 and 5 and through loop.

Fig. 4.58. Control the run of the tightening knot with the tweezers.

Fig. 4.59. The knot pulled up.

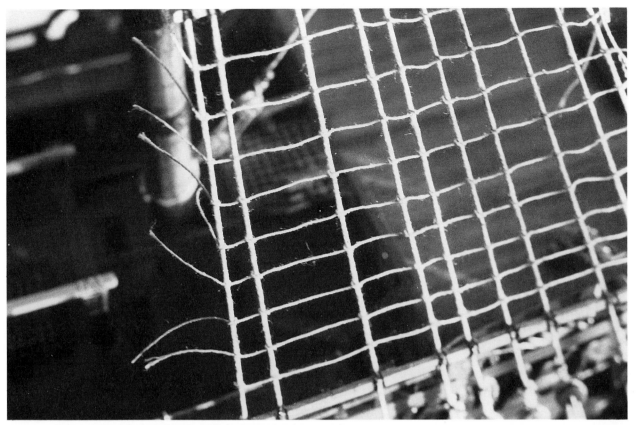

Fig. 4.60. When complete touch all knots with acrylic varnish before trimming.

Stepping and rigging the foremast

First make sure that all of the rigging blocks, eyes, etc., have been identified and fitted where possible. If previous work has been done correctly, stepping the mast is simply a matter of dropping it in place, checking again that it stands upright when looking down the centre line of the model, and that it adopts the correct rake angle when viewed from the side.

Should some small adjustment be required, do not rely on doing it by tension on the rigging. The easiest way is to remove the mast, open up the hole in the uppermost deck by about 0.5 mm on diameter and tap in wedge blocks to make the corrections necessary. Obviously, the wedges are inserted deeper on the side required to correct the perpendicularity or the rake, whichever is in need of adjustment. The wedges should be glued in place and when set they can be trimmed off flush with the level of the deck. Do not forget to slip the heel rings onto the bottom of the mast before assembly; these will slide down and thus cover the ends of the wedges.

Setting up the shrouds

When the mast has set in position the shrouds can be set up following the same procedure as described earlier for the sprit topmast. The ten lower shrouds, together with their respective sheer poles, should be rigged first followed by the five futtock shrouds to the upper mast.

The sheer poles will stabilise the shrouds for the rigging of the ratlines. Any tendency for the futtock shrouds to pull the lower shrouds outwards should now be corrected by rigging the upper caparthins. These are formed by running a single line back and forth between the port and starboard shrouds at the level of the upper sheer poles. Only the aft six shrouds are so treated and the line is frapped centrally in groups of three or four lines to pull up the tension. Do not rig the lower caparthins at this stage.

The ratlines

We now come to the continuance of that task which is the nightmare of most period ship modelmakers — the ratlines. It is suggested that they be done as each mast is set up, rather than leaving them until later when the total becomes a somewhat daunting exercise. Incidentally, it is as well not to rig the two standing backstays until after the ratlines have been done, since they tend to get in the way. Refer again to Figs 4.55 to 4.60.

Due to the extent of ratlines on the fore and main masts, a further problem comes to light that was not too evident when tying the ratlines on the sprit topmast. It is one of spacing and keeping control thereof. A pair of dividers or callipers set to the required dimension is all that is needed for the occasional check that the right spacing is being maintained. The eye is normally very accurate for gauging repetitive dimensions, but beware,

The main mast area bitts staircase and rails.

Main top.

there is an illusory factor to contend with — as you work upwards the line of the shrouds converge, whereas the ratlines remain horizontal. Thus the space enclosed by the shrouds and the ratlines at deadeye level is basically a horizontal rectangle. Midway between deck and top, the shape tends towards a square, finally becoming a vertical rectangle at the top. The eye can find it difficult to adjust to this gradual change of shape and, without fairly frequent checking, the natural tendency will be to tie the ratlines closer together at the top, so that the original horizontal rectangular shape is maintained.

The main and mizen masts

These are each stepped and shrouded in the same way as the foremast, again omitting the standing backstays and each being rattled down in turn. With these two mast assemblies, it is even more important to ensure that all possible blocks and eyes are fitted before stepping since, as each successive mast is put up and more and more rigging added, the less space there is available to drill holes or get fingers in to thread and tie knots.

The stays

Basically, the sequence of setting up the stays on this model is on the principle of bottom first, hence the first rigged is the main stay. The main stay is taken from a collar around the bowsprit to the main top. A heart is

seized in the collar such that it is positioned just behind the head of the forecastle. The collar fixing comprised an eye on the end of one tail, the other and longer end, passed through it and was seized to itself. This fixing was usually on the port side, albeit that the position of the heart should be such as to permit the main stay to pass to the starboard side of the foremast. The stay itself was secured around the main mast at the top using an eye and mouse. The lower end was fitted with a heart and the whole tightened up with a lanyard running between this and the heart in the collar (Fig. 4.61).

The preventer stay was rigged in the same way except that it was fixed to the lower part of the foremast instead of the bowsprit and was pulled down with a lanyard in deadeyes rather than hearts. The main stay and preventer stay were snaked. Like the tying of ratlines, this is an awkward and tedious task and one for which modellers have favourite methods. These vary from hitching the snake ratline fashion alternately between stay and preventer, to actually sewing the snake through the stays. See Figs 4.62 and 4.63 which show snaking on the forestay.

My own method is to use 0.25 mm thread well stiffened with PVA, which is then lashed at each juncture with a separate piece of thread. Because of its stiffness, the snake can be bent to a fairly sharp angle, thus keeping each 'leg' reasonably straight. Using this method, you need to start at the top and work down so that the hang of the snake's free end is more conducive

Fig. 4.61. The lower end of the main stay.

Fig. 4.62. Forestay and preventer stay snaked. See also fiddle block at lower end of fore topmast stay.

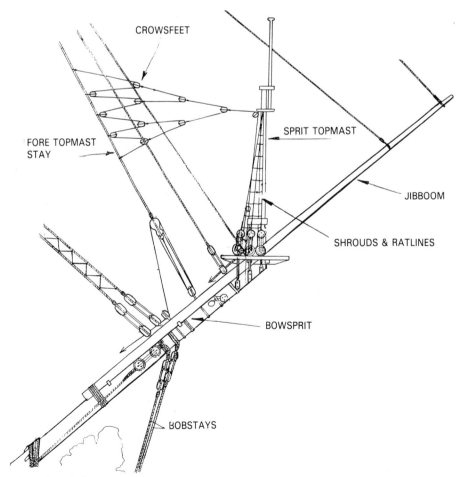

CROWSFEET

FORE TOPMAST
STAY

SPRIT TOPMAST

JIBBOOM

SHROUDS & RATLINES

BOWSPRIT

BOBSTAYS

Fig. 4.63. Features of standing rigging.

towards getting the pitching right. The fore stay and its preventer are set up in the same way as the main stay and run from bowsprit to fore top, the lower ends being pulled down with lanyards in deadeyes rather than hearts and the two are snaked together.

The fore topmast stay is set up via a fiddle block to the bowsprit (Figs. 4.62 and 4.63). Once this has been tensioned, the backstay pendant from the sprit topmast and its associated crowsfeet can be rigged (Fig. 4.64).

The mizen stay is rigged next, again in a similar fashion to the others. It has no preventer and runs from deadeyes and lanyard at the base of the main mast up to the mizen top.

Euphroe blocks and crowsfeet

The euphroe blocks, one for each mast, have to be made from scratch. For clean, sharp and precise work, these should ideally be made from hardwood scrap strip of suitable size. Having looked a little further ahead, I noted that a fourth was needed to rig the lifts to the lateen yard on the mizen mast, so I decided to make all four together.

The holes were drilled first before attempting to shape the blocks, the number of holes being half the number around the front edge of the related top less one or, half the number of lashings to the upper end of the lateen yard. Having drilled and shaped each block, a groove was filed all round longitudinally. When finished, the

euphroe block has a single block stropped to its tail end and a further block is seized in the appropriate position to the stay in question. The line rigging the two together starts from the single/euphroe block, passes around through both blocks and is then tied off to a cleat seized to the stay below the lower block. I am not too sure about the validity of this cleat and it could be that the line was tied off directly on to the stay. This tackle should be left slack at this time until the crowsfeet have been rigged (Fig. 4.65).

The crowsfeet start with a line around the euphroe block taken up to the top, down through the centre hole then threaded up through the next hole to port. The line then passes down to, and through, the upper hole in the euphroe block and back to the top and down through the next hole to starboard of centre. This procedure continues until all holes in the top and euphroe block have been threaded, finishing at the outer hole to starboard where the line is tied off. A little bit of tweaking and adjustment of the tackle is now required to tighten everything up, being careful not to over-tighten and so distort the line of the stay (Fig. 4.66).

Once the crowsfeet have been rigged to all three tops, the stays to the upper masts can be added, plus the standing backstays to the fore and main masts. Note that the lower deadeyes for these stays sit on stools to the rear and above the channels (Fig. 4.67). You should not attempt to pull the lanyards up too tight since the area of adhesion of stool to hull is not very large and thus will

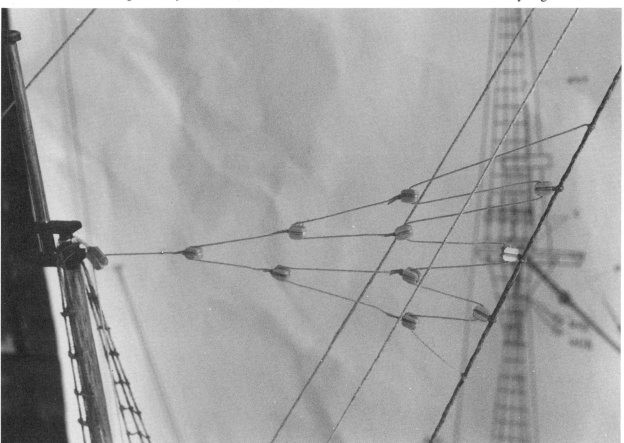

Fig. 4.64. Crowsfeet from sprit topmast to fore topmast stay.

Fig. 4.65. Euphroe block and tackle.

Fig. 4.66. The crowsfeet to the foremast top.

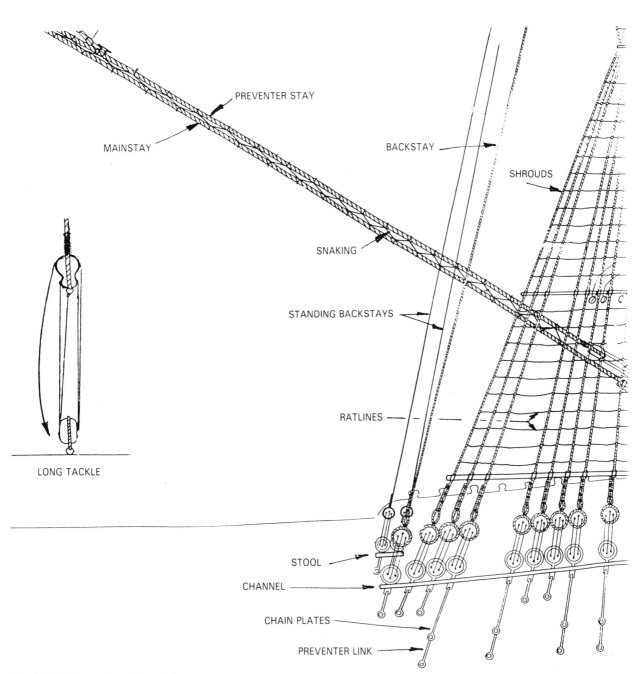

Fig. 4.67. Features of standing rigging.

not sustain too much load. As before, you should start with rigging the upper stays from the bowsprit to the foremast and finish with those between the main and mizen mast.

Consulting the drawings, you will see that there are a number of blocks that are tied to the stays for the later rigging of the braces. Following the principle that you should tie all blocks in place at the earliest available opportunity, now is the time to put these in place.

Mounting the yards

We have now reached that stage of the construction where a final decision has to be made about the fitting of sails. With sails, the yards will be rigged high on the masts whereas they will be down on the caps if they are

to be left bare. It would be a most impractical job, if not totally impossible, to alter things one way or the other later on.

The assembly of each yard to its respective mast involves rigging the parrals, slings or jeers and the lifts. Parrals comprise two or three rows of wooden balls, or trucks, each separated from its neighbour by wooden ribs. These permit easy rotation of the yard about the mast. For modelmaking, a number of small beads are required, the ribs being made from scratch using scrap material from the kit. One end of the parral assembly should be tied to the yard then, offering up the yard to the mast, the free end of the parral is taken round behind the mast, brought forward and secured to the yard (Fig. 4.68).

The jeers can now be set up. These consist of blocks

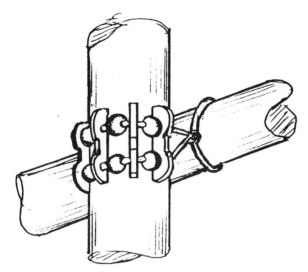

Fig. 4.68. Typical two row parrals.

and tackle for raising and lowering the yards on the mast in conjunction with the lifts. The lower yard jeers comprise two pairs of triple blocks closely spaced about the centre of the yard with the standing part of the tackle taken from the upper block (Fig. 4.69). For this period, the lower block was often a double rather than a triple, with the standing part of the tackle seized to the yard just outboard of the block. The line is taken down towards deck level where it terminates around a double block and rigged with long tackle to the jeer bitts. Ties to the upper yards (Fig. 4.70) comprise one pair of blocks and come below through a block stropped to a ring fixed in the deck, then up to the rail between the bitts. The yard to the sprit topmast is set up in a similar fashion, but the spritsail yard on the bowsprit is slung in a fixed position.

The mizen yard is suspended by a sling from the lower masthead through a single block stropped to the centre of the yard. Parrals are fitted as before. Lifts are next rigged from masthead to yardarms (Fig. 4.71) then back to masthead and down to long tackle at the deck. A simpler arrangement is used for the uppermost yards where lifts run direct from yardarm to masthead before going down to deck level. The lifts on the mizen yard take the form of crowsfeet from the upper end of the yard, through a euphroe block, on to the mizen

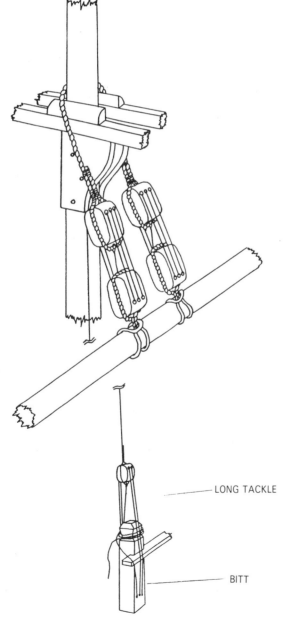

LONG TACKLE

BITT

Fig. 4.69. Jeers to the lower yards.

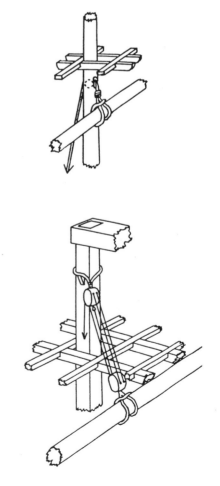

Fig. 4.70. Ties to the upper yards.

Midships showing capstan and boat interior. Note stove chimney stack and belfry on forecastle deck.

Head rails. Note 6 sheave rack blocks seized to forward gammoning.

masthead, then down to the port mizen chains (see Fig. 4.72). Bowlines should be rigged to the lower end of the mizen yard, taken through blocks tied to the aft main shroud and tied off to the timber heads each side. These will balance out the tension on the crowsfeet lifts and keep the yard nice and stable. The standing lifts on the spritsail yard are taken from deadeyes collared to the bowsprit then out to the yardarm, the tension being taken up with lanyards.

If it has been decided to fit sails, it will be found better not to rig the braces at this time since these will restrict the space available to manipulate further rigging. Just leave the pendants hanging from the yardarms until later.

Apart from the aforesaid braces, the standing rigging is now complete and we come to the running rigging, some of which can be affixed to the sails on the bench before hanging them on the model. However, before you hang them you have to make them and it is to that subject we now come.

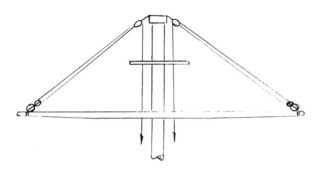

Fig. 4.71. Lower yard lifts.

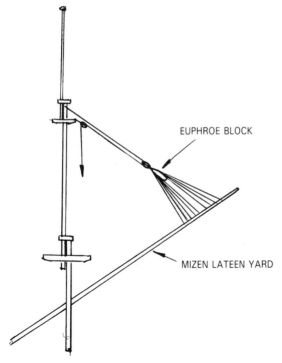

EUPHROE BLOCK

MIZEN LATEEN YARD

Fig. 4.72. Lifts on the mizen yard.

Sails and Sailmaking

Take a look around any exhibition of model ships and you won't find very many static models with a full suit of sails. Ask modelmakers why they don't fit them and you usually get one of three answers. They never look right, they hide all the craftsmanship in the woodwork or, I haven't got the facilities. All very valid reasons. On the other hand, one could respond that they *can* look right and they can *add* to the craftsmanship to be seen. I sometimes wonder if the reason sails are seldom fitted is because needlework is not seen in the same light as woodwork and metalwork! However, it has to be said that poorly made sails, or the selection of the wrong material, can spoil what is otherwise a fine piece of modelmaking.

While it is true that the basis of this text concerns the construction of the kit for the *Royal William*, I feel that a more in-depth discussion on the subject of sailmaking is in order. The material in the kit was pretty good and was used to make the sails that can be seen in the photographs herein. Alas, that is not always the case and all too often the material supplied is totally inadequate and has to be discarded and replaced. Thus my following words are, hopefully, of value to kitbuilder and scratchbuilder alike, both often having need to visit the haberdashers for a rummage through the remnants box.

Let us first, therefore, consider the material question and those aspects that are important to the modelmaker.

Sail material

There are several basic qualities to think about; the size or coarseness of the weave, the 'hang' factor, the thickness and what it looks like in overall terms and finally, the colour.

The coarseness affects stiffness or pliability, also the material's overall look. Remember that a cloth woven from threads 0.25 mm diameter will have a thickness of at least 0.50 mm, which at 1/50th scale represents a sail 25 mm or one inch thick. A tight or close weave usually means a stiffer material whereas, a loose open weave could scale up to a sail having all the properties of a thick string vest! For the smaller scales we may, therefore, not be looking for a woven cloth at all but rather a rag tissue or parchment suitably lacquered. Thus, it becomes obvious that we are in a compromise situation. We really need a fairly fine thread, woven close enough to avoid the string vest situation, but loose enough to provide adequate semblance of natural 'hang'. One material that does have this quality is fine silk. Unfortunately, it also has a sheen which is just about impossible to get rid of without treating the material in such a way as to destroy the very qualities it was initially selected for. A material which freely frays and comes apart at the edges when cut should not be selected.

The 'hang' factor has a direct influence on the way the assembled sails will finally look on the model. What we don't want are sails that finish up flat and stiff like pieces of cardboard. On the other hand, the fully wind-filled sail on a static model looks equally artificial. There are one or two things that can be done to create shape in the finished sail of course, and these will be discussed later.

Colour is less of a problem, the requirement normally being from a fairly narrow spectrum. But do think carefully before using white unless there is a need to dye it to a colour that is unobtainable off the shelf. Obviously, you should avoid a material that has a sheen like the aforementioned silk, and look for a cloth that has the same basic flat finish on both sides. The material I tend to favour, and one that fills most requirements, is unbleached calico. The weave varies slightly from bolt to bolt, but nothing to worry about. It normally comes in a shade of very light oatmeal or natural colour and will take to colouring with dyes if required. There are no problems with fraying edges and it works well in the sewing machine or when hand sewing with needle and thimble. When thoroughly washed, its pliability is just right for model sailmaking.

Making the sails

Assuming that the material has been selected and is to hand, we come to decision time again. How are the sails to be made or, more to the point, who is going to make them? My hand sewing is fairly atrocious but I reckon I could handle a sewing machine with a bit of practice. A word of warning if you are going to ask someone to

make them for you. Make sure that it is perfectly understood that making a set of fifteen sails for the *Royal William* for instance, is not just a Saturday afternoon job and that the commitment is for something in the order of thirty-five to forty hours work. I would also add that if you can get them made as well as my wife makes them, it has got to be worth a night out on the town — and you would still be getting the best part of the deal. But let us assume that, for one reason or another, you are lumbered with making them for yourself.

The first essential is to thoroughly wash the material to get any dressing out of it then, whilst still damp, press with a hot iron. On a scrap piece, practice turning and machining as small a hem as possible. When you are satisfied with your efforts, unpick the hem and measure exactly how much extra material you need to leave outside the line of the finished sail size. Patterns for all sails are required and these should be made from a fairly strong tissue paper. Using a fibre-tipped pen, trace the finished sail outline and all seams from the drawings adding the measured hemming allowance to each outside line (Fig. 4.73).

Pin the patterns to the material (Fig. 4.74), making sure that the weave of the cloth lies in the same direction for all sails and cut out each item, taking care not to cut inside the outline of the pattern (Fig. 4.75). Unpin the patterns, establish the 'right' side of the cloth, have this upwards and with the pattern now underneath, trace the lines of the seams directly onto the material with a soft pencil (Fig. 4.76).

Fig. 4.73. Sailmaking, trace the outlines.

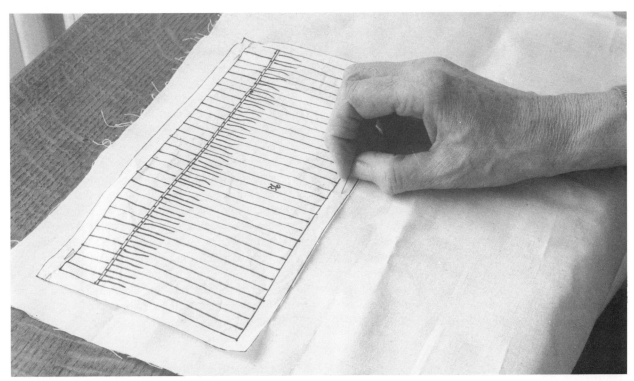

Fig. 4.74. Pin pattern to cloth.

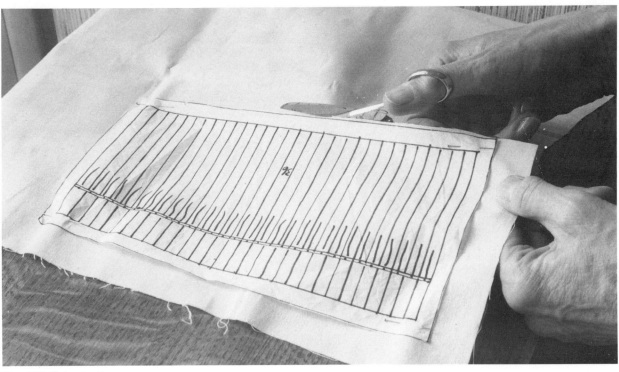

Fig. 4.75. Cut out sail.

Selecting a thread colour slightly darker than the sail cloth, the vertical seams can now be machined, ensuring that the 'right' side of the material is still face up. To save a lot of sewing in of ends later on, all vertical seams from the top edge of the sail to the reef bands can be machined with one length of thread. Starting at the top, the first seam is machined down to the reef band then along the band to the next seam, then back up to the top. Machine along the top edge to the next seam, then repeat the cycle down, across, up, across, until the entire width of the sail has been covered (Fig. 4.77). The same procedure is followed for the vertical seams between the reef band and the bottom edge of the sail, again using only one length of thread. The horizontal reef bands can now be machined in a similar fashion (Fig. 4.78). Obviously, if reef bands do not feature on a particular sail, the vertical seams can run directly from the top to the bottom edge.

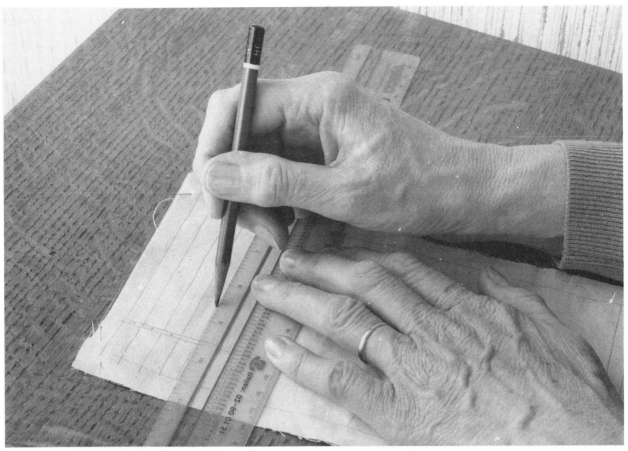

Fig. 4.76. Trace lines on to 'right' side of cloth.

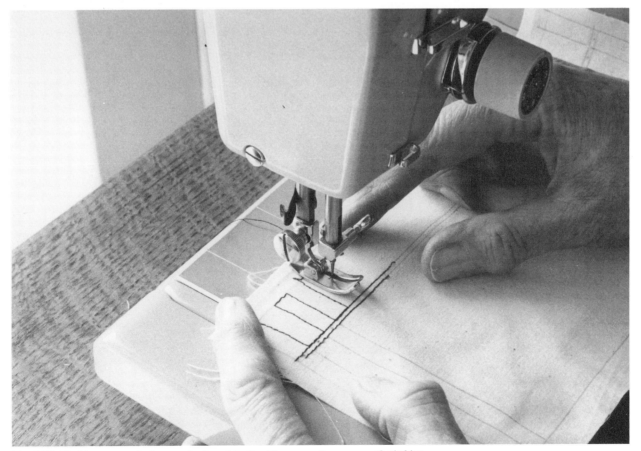

Fig. 4.77. Machine sew vertical seams back and forth with one continuous run of stitching.

Fig. 4.78. Stitch horizontal reef bands.

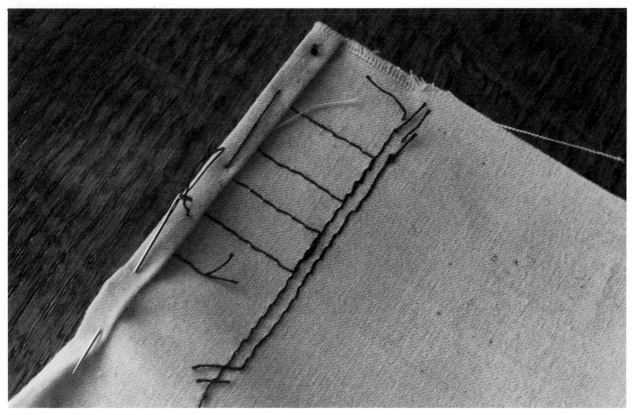

Fig. 4.79. Double fold hems and tack with long-hand stitches.

Now turn the sail over so that the 'wrong' side of the material is on top for hemming. Hems need to be as small as possible and the raw edge of the cloth should be folded in. Thus, the seam is the result of a double fold which, of course, traps the loose ends of the seam stitching. The folded seam should be pinned (Fig. 4.79), then tacked in place with long-hand stitches. When machining the hems, ensure that the corner ends are neatly tucked and that the loose ends of the machining are sewn in (Fig. 4.80).

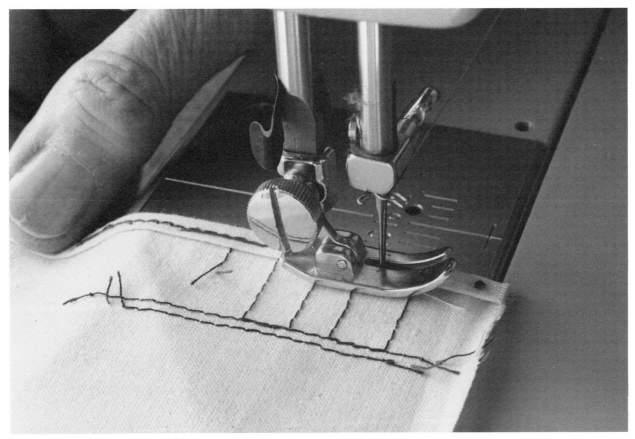

Fig. 4.80. Machine stitch hems.

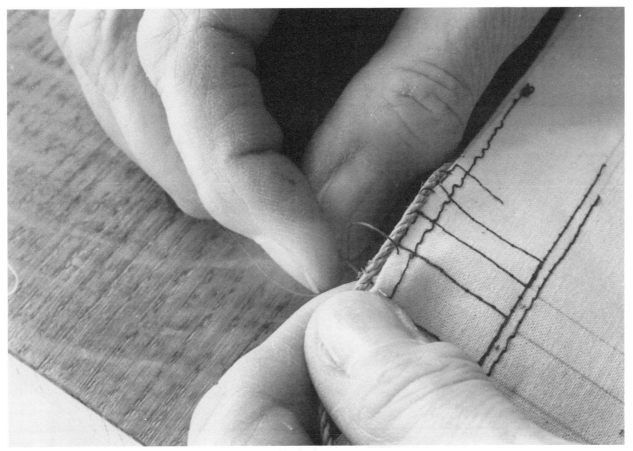

Fig. 4.81. Hand stitch bolt ropes.

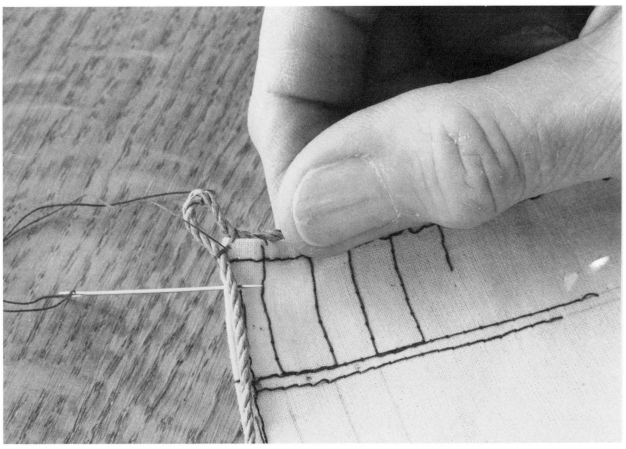

Fig. 4.82. Leave small loops at each corner of sail.

It is a long haul sewing on the bolt ropes — the rope edging all round the outside of the sails. I am not aware of any facility for doing this on the normal domestic sewing machine, so I am afraid it is a case of hand sewing (Fig. 4.81). Select the correct size of thread and start the sewing at one of the corners. As each corner is reached, the thread should be formed into a small loop before continuing to sew along the next edge (Fig. 4.82). As I say, it is a long task to edge all fifteen sails for the *Royal William* but, apart from making the sails look right, it has a practical result in that the bolt ropes provide a means of inducing and retaining a subtle curve to the edges of the sails, more of which later.

The reef points should now be sewn in, noting that the length on the aft side of the sail is about twice that on the fore side. It is probably better to make them over-length and trim them to size when they are all on. That way, they will all be the same length.

Making the anchors and buoys

There are four anchors to make using the shank and fluke castings provided in the kit and fitting them with wooden stocks. The castings need a certain amount of attention to clear away the moulding mismatch lines and the holes through the stocks require squaring out to receive the anchor shanks. The stocks are bound with iron bands and these have to be simulated using thin

timber strips or card. Whatever the material of your choice, note that you cannot use a strip of material simply wrapped around the stock. Due to the tapers involved, a continuous strip would need to be developed for shape. It is therefore worth considering making each band from four pieces, one glued to each face of the stock and the sharp corners rounded off by gentle sanding when the glue has dried. A touch of matt black paint to the bands and to where the castings have been cleaned up, add the rings and you have four anchors ready for rigging (Fig. 4.83).

The anchor buoys are provided as four damson-shaped turned parts which, in themselves, require little or no work. However, to make them look anything like the real thing, they need to be bound in anchor buoy slings and correctly rigged to the anchor flukes and fore shrouds. The slings are quite complex pieces of rope-work and would be very difficult to reproduce at this particular scale. I chose to follow the correct pattern but in a simulated form which, as can be seen in the accompanying photograph, produced a quite acceptable buoy assembly (Fig. 4.84).

Basically, the slings comprise six pieces of thread. One length is draped over one end of the buoy and fixed in place using cyano adhesive. A second length, with a small loop tied midway, is then fixed at ninety degrees to the first. The four ends are then trimmed just below the largest diameter of the buoy. The other end is treated

74

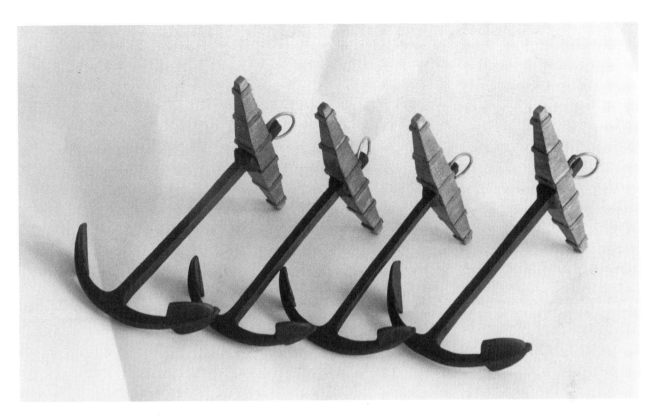

Fig. 4.83. The four anchors.

Fig. 4.84. Anchor buoy with sling.

in the same fashion but the threads disposed 45 degrees further round the buoy. The fifth and sixth lengths of thread are then fixed around the body of the buoy coincident with the ends of the earlier fixed pieces. A coat of acrylic matt varnish stiffens the loops at each end and nicely finishes off the job. Rigging the four anchors previously made can now be done.

First, if they have not already been done, the anchor rings should be bound, or served, all round, making sure that the join in the ring is housed within the thickness of the anchor diecasting. You will probably find that it is more convenient to fit the two smaller anchors first, these being lashed up to the fore channels. The anchor rope takes two turns around the ring, and is hitched twice before the end is seized to itself. Try and get the rope tied in its proper attitude on the ring, since the serving prevents free movement about the ring after it

has been tightened up (Fig. 4.85). Once the anchor has been lashed in position, the rope can be taken to the hawse holes and fixed therein. If your hull construction has been left solid at the bow end and the anchor ropes are not to be fed through to the capstan, they need to be secured well. I don't know what the fascination is, but people's fingers are invariably drawn to rudders, anchors and ships' wheels. They seem to have a need to see if the rudder moves on its hinges, the wheel moves the rudder or if the anchor swings from the cathead and the ropes pass freely through the hawse holes. Therefore, I work on the principle that if it can move, it will be moved and will eventually get broken. So I fix it.

Deepen the hawse holes by about 10 mm with a drill size just marginally larger than the diameter of the anchor rope. Cut the anchor rope to length and moisten the end with superglue to stiffen it up. When hardened off, coat it with PVA and push it right home into the hawse hole. A triple block with a hook is rigged to the cathead and the larger anchor suspended from it by the ring. As before, the anchor rope should be taken to the hawse hole and firmly fixed in place.

Once both anchors have been mounted onto the model, the anchor buoys can be suspended from the shrouds and the excess rope immediately below the buoy coiled up and lashed. The end of the buoy rope should be tied to the anchor at the joint between the flukes and the shank with a clove hitch then have its free end seized to the shank. Both buoy ropes and anchor ropes should have the simulated sag treatment to ensure that they have a realistic hang.

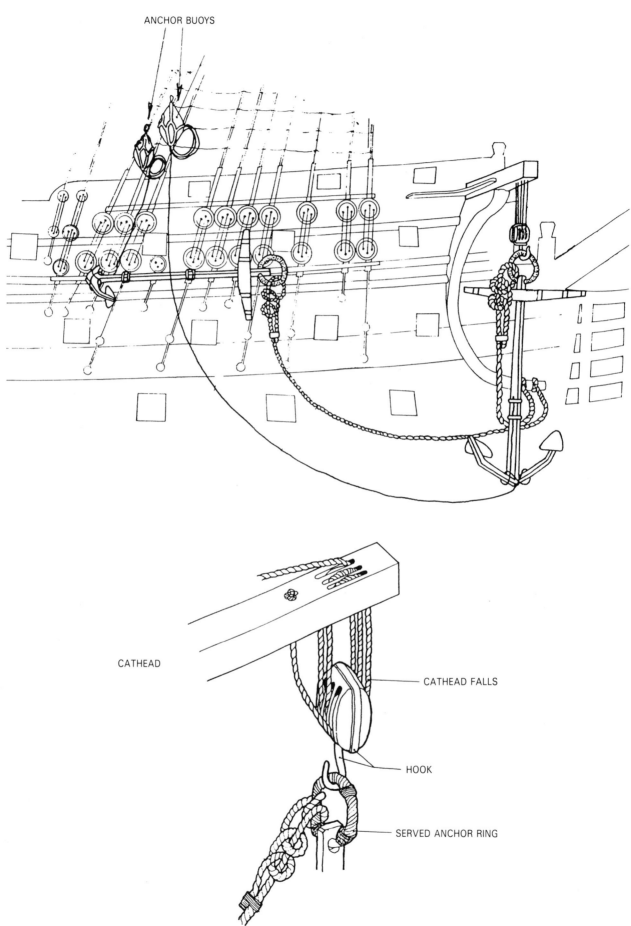

ANCHOR BUOYS

CATHEAD

CATHEAD FALLS

HOOK

SERVED ANCHOR RING

Fig. 4.85. Rigging anchors and buoys.

A view forward showing anchor buoys rigged to shrouds, also curves on ship's boat gunwales.

The Running Rigging

Before putting up sails we have another opportunity to fit some blocks and, indeed, some rigging too while we have the sails on the bench. The fore and aft sails particularly can be fitted with brails, downhauls and sheet pendants (see Fig. 4.86).

The brails, running from the edges of the four-sided sails through blocks at the upper fore corner, normally hang slack. The block is usually a double on the starboard side and a single on the port side. The slackness can be more easily simulated when the sail is lying flat on the bench. Having first applied the PVA treatment to the thread, the line of the sag can be maintained by just the smallest touch of superglue gel to tack the line to the sail. Remember that brails are rigged on both sides of the sail.

The downhaul, from the upper aft corner runs through the same double block as the brail on the starboard side via several loops or hanks along the top edge of the sail. In the same way as the brails, the sag of the downhaul between the loops can be set up. Pendants from the lower aft corner of the sails take the sheets down to the deck. Note that the starboard pendant is longer than that on the port side and drapes over the adjacent stay before being rigged below.

The sail on the mizen lateen yard was a little different in its rig to the other fore and aft sails in that it was

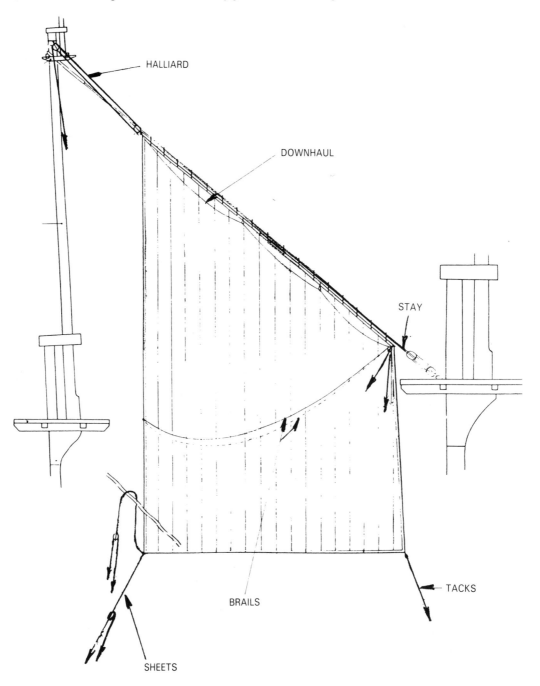

HALLIARD

DOWNHAUL

STAY

BRAILS

TACKS

SHEETS

Fig. 4.86. Four-sided staysail rigging.

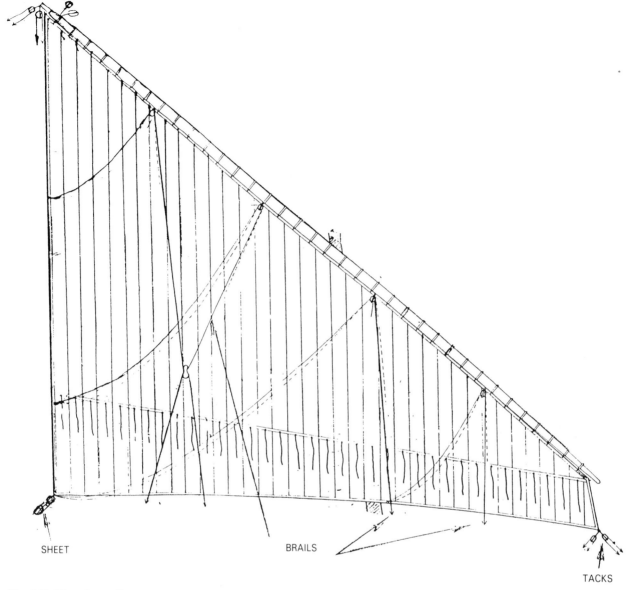

SHEET

BRAILS

TACKS

Fig. 4.87. The mizen sail.

permanently laced to the yard and therefore did not have halliard or downhaul. The brails, however, were more complex involving fiddle blocks each side and single blocks stropped to the yard at several salient points (Fig. 4.87). Square sails do not lend themselves to much work off the model in terms of rigging apart from blocks at the lower corners.

Incidentally, now that we have reached a point in the rigging process where it is increasingly necessary to get in amongst it all, it is a good idea to roll up your shirt sleeves or wear a short-sleeved garment and take off your wristwatch or other bracelets. I say this because anything accidentally caught in the rigging can do untold damage, especially if you don't notice it until the hand is withdrawn. Buttons, buckles, watch winders and cufflinks are all formulae for total disaster.

As has been said several times before, a little bit of forward thinking is always helpful and we have now reached another stage where, if we plough on too far,

things can become unnecessarily awkward. Bearing in mind all the time that each successive step taken reduces the space available for continued rigging, it will become apparent that to fit all the sails, as one specific exercise, is not to be advised. In fact, I have found that to the contrary, it is far better to hang one at a time in a particular sequence and complete its rigging as far as possible before moving on to the next.

It will be further seen that there is a sequence of fitting which adds to the convenience of setting up the remainder of the running rigging. In general terms, this follows the pattern that you work from bottom to top and front to back. In the case of the *Royal William* the sequence is as listed overleaf. Note that fore and aft sails are fitted before the square sails and that braces, also sheets to the lower sails, are not fitted until all the sails have been otherwise rigged. The only exception to this is for the spritsail and sprit topmast sail, where braces are rigged in a somewhat different fashion to the others.

Sail fitting sequence

1. Fore topmast staysail.
2. Jib.
3. Main topmast staysail.
4. Main topgallant staysail.
5. Mizen staysail.
6. Mizen topmast staysail.
7. Lateen mizen.
8. Fore course.
9. Fore topsail.
10. Fore topgallant.
11. Main course.
12. Main topsail.
13. Main topgallant.
14. Mizen topsail.
15. Mizen topgallant.

Setting up sails on the stays is quite straightforward but attaching the square sails to the yards can be a little awkward because, without the braces rigged, the yards do have quite a bit of movement. To get round this, the sail can be held in position with a couple of crocodile clips while the needle and thread is prepared. Thread a needle with about 500 mm of thread then, at each securing point along the edge of the sail, pull the thread through until a tail of about 50 mm is left. Cut the thread on the leading side a similar distance from the sail to leave a total length of 100 mm. This is then tied up and dabbed with a touch of acrylic varnish before moving to the next point. There is nothing magical about the 100 mm length, it is just a matter of leaving enough to get hold of to do the tying.

Remember that some of the blocks already stropped to the yards hang to the fore side of the sail for the buntlines, whereas others hang to the aft side for the sheets from the sail above and for the clew garnets (Fig. 4.88). The procedure for lacing the mizen to the lateen yard starts in exactly the same way as for other sails, by clipping the ends of the top edge in place. The lacing starts at the top end of the yard and winds down to the lower forward end.

The continued rigging of the fore and aft sails is probably best done by setting up the halliards first, then the downhaul, sheets and brails, in that order (Figs. 4.86 to 4.89). Note that the starboard sheets come down to deck from the longer of the two pendants attached to the lower aft corner of the sail. These sheets drape over the adjacent stay and hang slack. It is therefore more of a problem to get both lines to hang parallel to each other and not twist together. To avoid this, the block on the pendant should hang naturally with the hole in the right position before attempting to rig, and should be kept in this attitude when threading the rigging. If it doesn't, a coat of acrylic varnish allowed to dry out under a little tension will usually do the trick. For tackle under tension, the block can be countertwisted so that when pulled up,

the block becomes correctly aligned. Of course, washing the rigging and letting it dry under tension should have done much to have taken out the natural twist of the thread.

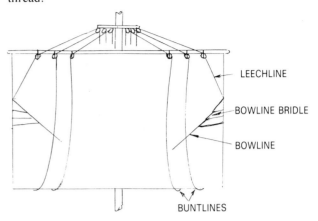

Fig. 4.88. Square sail rigging.

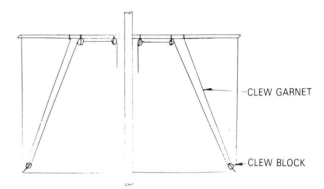

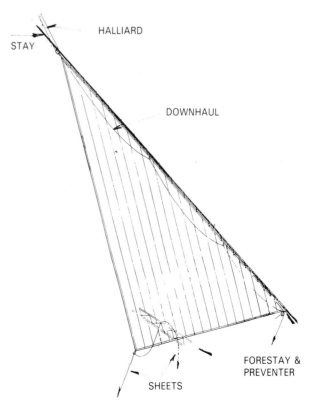

Fig. 4.89. Three-sided staysail rigging.

Slack line can be further coerced into a natural looking sag using the same method of applying acrylic varnish. The aim should always be to confine the curve of the sag to one plane and to remember that the curve is not a true radius unless the two ends are both on the same horizontal level. The curve always tightens up at the lower end and the greater the difference in height between the two ends, the tighter and lower the change in curve becomes. This principle will, of course, apply not only to the sheets, but to any naturally hanging line without tension. Unfortunately, with thread of the size used for rigging model ships, the weight is totally out of proportion to its mass and thus, to look natural, there has to be some artificial aid applied.

Similar circumstances apply to the sails. Again, the 'hang factor' is unnatural because the weight/area ratio is all out of balance. For modelmakers, the practical advantage of the sewn-on bolt ropes now comes to the fore in that, they too, can be brushed with acrylic varnish and then persuaded into shape. Some patience is needed to do this and you must not expect the required result after only one application. The knack lies in knowing when to apply the next coat — 20 to 45 minutes depending on diameter — so that the second coat delays the total drying out of the first coat but takes advantage of, and enhances, its initial stiffening effect. The actual curve can best be induced by stroking the thread on the inside of the curve with a piece of plastic rod, or the side of a ballpoint pen is ideal. I avoid the use of wood, as this can retain some residue of the varnish and, in some circumstances, create a drag condition. The plastic can, and should, be wiped clean after every application.

Rigging the square sails also needs to be carefully sequenced if the work is going to be carried out in the most convenient manner. Discounting the braces, and the sheets and tacks from the bottom corners of the fore and main courses, which should not be rigged until the very last, virtually all the rigging is associated with blocks attached to the yards or tops. Generally speaking, it is better started with those lines that pass through the lowest blocks nearest to the centre of the ship and work outwards. Thus, the buntlines, involving the blocks on the yard to the fore of the sail and those hanging from the underside of the top, will be the last to be rigged in this section.

In the last section of rigging to be set up, I group those features which start at the outside and run inboard, but cross the spaces between masts. These comprise the sheets and tacks to the two courses, the bowlines and bridles and the braces. The sheets and tacks come into that category of slack rigging mentioned previously and should be treated accordingly. Fortunately, the thread size used is somewhat larger than for most other rigging details and so the problem is lessened to some degree.

Because of the more complex system involved in rigging the bowlines and bowline bridles, these should be worked on before the braces, certainly for the sails on the main and mizen masts. The bridle consisted of two or three ropes (depending on the sail) hitched to the leech or side of the sail then taken to deck level by the bowline (Fig. 4.90). For modelmaking, start with the upper, shorter length of rope and secure each end to the edge of the sail. One end of a second and longer piece of rope is hitched around approximately the centre of the first piece and its other end temporarily fixed to the edge of the sail. The end of the bowline is attached to the approximate centre of the second piece then taken down to deck level to its belaying position and again temporarily tied off. The pattern of the bridle can now be adjusted to the required proportions before being permanently hitched up. This is done by gently moving the point at which the second rope and the bowline join the first and second pieces of rope respectively. The lower end of the bowline can now be properly tied off. In the case of the main course, a third piece of rope will be introduced between the second piece and the upper end of the bowline. The points at which the various ropes that go to make up the bridle come together should be touched with a small spot of acrylic varnish to seal off the fixing.

Once all the bowline bridles have been set up, the braces can be rigged, starting with those on the fore yard, main yard and crossjack, before moving up to the topsail and topgallant yards on each mast. The upper braces from the foremast yards start from their respective stay and return to blocks tied just below via the pendants on the end of the yards. The lines are then taken down through guide blocks tied to the stay directly below before passing through blocks, seized to rings in the deck at the forecastle rail, to which they are finally tied off.

To complete the rigging, it remains only to rig the sheets and tacks to the fore and main courses. The sheet to the main course is seized to a ring in the side of the hull adjacent to the quarter gallery, then taken through a block on the lower corner of the sail and taken back to a sheave hole in the hull just above the main wale. The tack is taken forward to a similar sheave hole in the hull between two gunports on the lower gun deck immediately below the end of the forecastle deck. The fore course sheet is rigged in the same way as the main course with the ring and sheave hole being positioned at the line of the aft fender. The tack is run forward to the sheave hole in the head rails below the bowsprit.

Finishing Off

Although the basic construction and rigging have now been completed, there are still several hours of work ahead to tidy up and finish off the model. The first task is to make and fit all the coils of rope at the various belaying points on the rails or laying flat on the deck, whichever is pertinent. In some cases, of course, it is possible to form the coil of rope as a continuation of the same piece used for the rigging. Where that is not

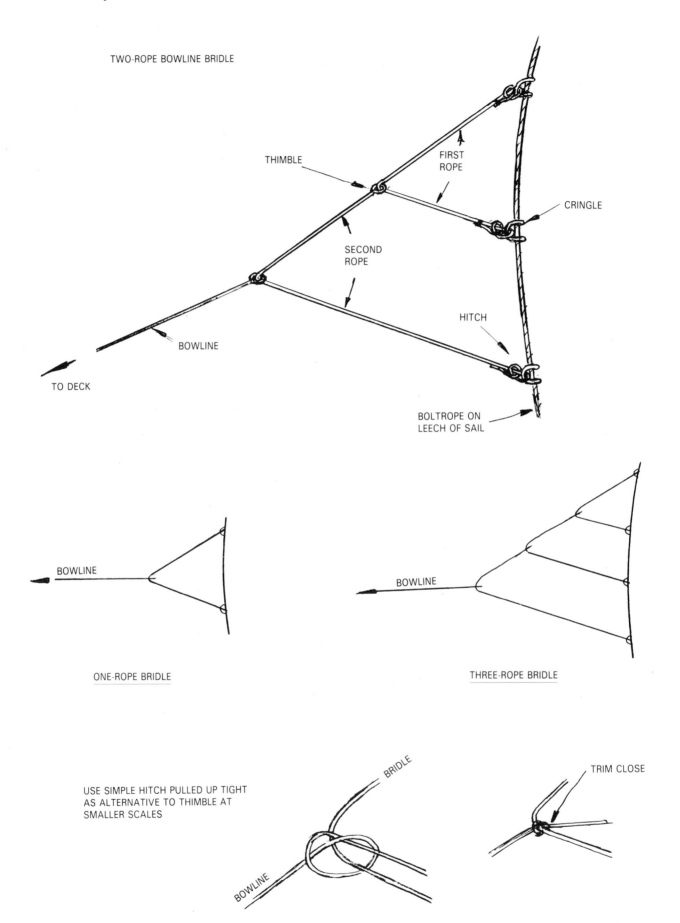

TWO-ROPE BOWLINE BRIDLE

THIMBLE

FIRST
ROPE

CRINGLE

SECOND
ROPE

BOWLINE

HITCH

TO DECK

BOLTROPE ON
LEECH OF SAIL

BOWLINE

ONE-ROPE BRIDLE

BOWLINE

THREE-ROPE BRIDLE

USE SIMPLE HITCH PULLED UP TIGHT
AS ALTERNATIVE TO THIMBLE AT
SMALLER SCALES

BRIDLE

TRIM CLOSE

BOWLINE

Fig. 4.90. Bowlines and bridles.

The stern galleries and lanterns.

possible due to limited access for fingers, it is important to remember to use the correct diameter of thread.

Coils to lay flat on the deck are not too difficult to make up, but those to hang on the rails need a little more thought or they will not look right. It is our old enemy the hang factor again and it will certainly not suffice to make a coil, hang it from the rail and expect it to hang vertically. It really will stick out like the proverbial sore thumb. You need to make up a small jig where the hung shape can be simulated with glue-stiffened thread before applying the coil to the model (Fig. 4.91).

Flags are something of a contentious issue. They suffer from the same hang factor problems as sails, but worse, and many modelmakers choose to leave them off because they invariably spoil the model. However, if you wish to fly flags, make sure that they are the correct ones for the period and are flown from the correct place. Finally, the ship's lanterns should be fixed in place.

The entire model should next be examined to ensure that there are no loose ends left from the rigging process. Any found should obviously be removed with care. There is a law which dictates that any that are left have to be in the most awkward of places so that the greatest risk presents itself when wielding the scalpel. It is then a matter of cleaning decks and ledges of any dust, trimmed ends, or other foreign matter. A useful tool for disturbing muck from inaccessible corners is the photographer's lens brush with puffer attached; the debris can then usually be removed using a soft, damp, paint brush.

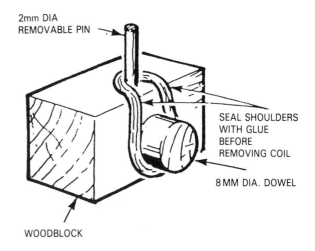

2mm DIA REMOVABLE PIN

SEAL SHOULDERS WITH GLUE BEFORE REMOVING COIL

8 MM DIA. DOWEL

WOODBLOCK

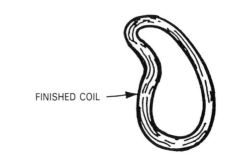

FINISHED COIL

Fig. 4.91. Rope coils.

At the mizen mast, reef points on the sail feature on both sides.

Quarter galleries.

Port side entrance.

View of spritsail and figurehead.

Finally, before installing the model in its permanent resting place, leave it on the bench for a few days and make several more critical examinations. One very good way of discovering the odd loose end or any other problem is to concentrate the eye by viewing through a camera lens, preferably in the close-up mode. Even so, it is usually when showing photographs of the finished model that some *clever clogs* spots a loose or untrimmed end.

So, there we are, one model complete and hopefully your appetite whetted for the next project.

Conclusions

It is always very difficult to be scrupulously fair and correct in one's assessment of a kit and one of this size presents an even greater problem. No kit is ever beyond criticism of course, in the same way that no finished model is ever absolutely perfect. One of the biggest dangers for kit producers and reviewers alike, is to forget the basic reason for having a kit in the first place — to reasonably give the modelmaker all that he needs to build the model of his choice. It is the word *reasonably* that is difficult to interpret in a fair and balanced way.

If the kit manufacturer has produced a kit for a beginner, then it should not be expected to involve advanced construction techniques or the need for specialist tools. On the other hand, the fact that a kit is designated for the expert should not take advantage of the distinct possibility that a fairly extensive *Odds and Bobs* box will be available.

The reviewer, even though he may be an experienced modelmaker, must always put himself in the position of the person who has purchased the kit and offer his criticism on the basis of the standard to which the kit is directed. The first consideration is whether or not the kit permits the builder to make a good scale model of the ship in question. In the case of the *Royal William*, it certainly does. There are excellent drawings supported by good quality timbers and fittings.

The next question that has to be addressed relates to how hard you have to work and plan to achieve the quality results. No modelmaker worth his salt moans about the patient hard work he puts into his hobby. However, I am not so sure about the planning side of things and I suspect that most kits are bought because with the wood, the fittings and the drawings, comes the planning, the sequence of construction and some guidance to the techniques involved. Take those away and one might as well build from scratch.

The kit for the *Royal William* suffers to some extent in this area, but the actual construction is well depicted on the drawings and any modeller embarking on this sort of project would reasonably be expected to have the techniques involved within his grasp. Overall, this kit is a good one, and provides an absorbing project involving something in excess of a thousand hours' work. I made the model basically straight from the box with what was provided and I reckon that if a lot more internal work was done with all guns fully rigged, one could easily find at least another two hundred hours.

With regard to value for money, prices seem to vary depending on source and, of course, it depends on what you are looking for in a kit in the first place. I reckon that it holds its own in the market place and that there won't be too many disappointed buyers.

I am indebted to Dennis Horne of Euro Models of Twickenham, who supplied the kit and to Euromodel Como of Italy for permission to use extracts from their drawings in the preparation of this text.

REFERENCES

The Construction and Fitting of the Sailing Man of War 1650–1850 by Peter Goodwin. ISBN 0 85177 326 5. Conway Maritime Press.
The Masting and Rigging of English Ships of War 1625–1860 by James Lees. ISBN 0 85177 290 0. Conway Maritime Press.
The Galleon by Peter Kirsch. ISBN 0 85177 566 2. Conway Maritime Press.
The Ashley Book of Knots by Clifford W. Ashley.
Ships of The American Revolution and Their Models by Harold M. Hahn. Conway Maritime Press. ISBN 0 85177 467 9.

CHAPTER 5

The Thames Barge
The Will Everard

The finished model.

The Kit

For the most part, Billings have produced a relatively simple kit to build, but I approached the building of this model with mixed feelings. As a kit for the less experienced, I wondered whether there would be sufficient challenge to sustain interest, or that I might be tempted to depart from the confines of the kit and add a few extras to 'improve' it, so to speak. There was no need to worry on either score. Generally it is a relatively

simple model to build, but there are areas where a little thought can do much to improve the results. As far as extras are concerned, forget it, the detail is all there.

The quality of the fittings is excellent and whilst good fittings on a poorly built model provide an obviously poor result, there is no reason why anyone with only basic skills and tools should not build a very acceptable model 585 mm long.

The hull

The hull is built in two halves on a ply 'base board'. It is essential that this board is absolutely flat or the matching of the two finished halves will be difficult. I had no previous experience of building a hull using this process, being more used to bulkheads on a central false keel or true frames, shipyard fashion. Nevertheless, the Billings way does work remarkably well and I produced a straight undistorted hull with no problems. Study of the drawings showed that the inner edges of the hull formers are exposed on the finished model and I decided to fill and sand them really smooth before assembly (see Fig. 5.1).

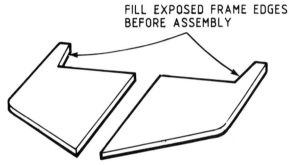

FILL EXPOSED FRAME EDGES BEFORE ASSEMBLY

Fig. 5.1.

The bottom of the hull is made from thin ply which needs only the minimum of coercion to pin and glue in place. The sides are planked, and provided that the edges of the formers have been bevelled to follow the shape of the hull, they go on fairly well. Having ensured earlier that the building board was absolutely flat, and because the accuracy of the pre-stamped parts is so good, the two halves of the hull fit together really well. Because the central false keel is of plywood the edges are still exposed after the two hull halves are brought together. I chose to fill these edges prior to sanding to provide a sound base for the later painting. It only remains to fit the side strakes and rails around the top edge of the hull and it is ready for painting.

A couple of coats of Humbrol primer undercoat is well worthwhile, with a final rub down with some fine wet-and-dry before applying colour. Matt paint with a final covering of satin varnish gives a nice finish, but this is a matter of personal choice.

The craft is relatively flat-bottomed and sits fairly well

but a simple stand — not provided in the kit — will help a lot from now on (see Fig. 5.2).

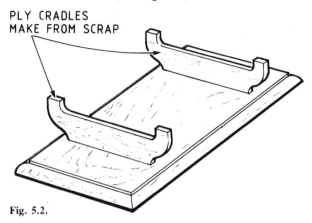

PLY CRADLES MAKE FROM SCRAP

Fig. 5.2.

Deck fittings

The drying time for these successive coats of paint is an ideal time to start making the various winches, cabins etc. The cabins are made from ply and again benefit from undercoating and a good rub down before painting. The bulk of the deck fittings are either turned brass or plastic mouldings, and very nice too. The majority of the plastic parts are better painted on the sprue before assembly. Cyanoacrylate gel is ideal for joining the metal to plastic parts, but have a dry run first to make sure everything goes together square and true.

Many of the shafts for the winches are cut from brass wire. A small point that makes all the difference to the final appearance is the finishing off of the ends. Take time to file the ends square rather than leave them with that 'pinched' look that comes from the use of side cutters or pliers (see Fig. 5.3). When assembling fittings to the previously painted deck, don't forget to scrape paint away from areas to be glued or you will not get a good bond.

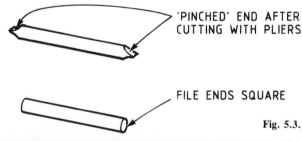

'PINCHED' END AFTER CUTTING WITH PLIERS

FILE ENDS SQUARE

Fig. 5.3.

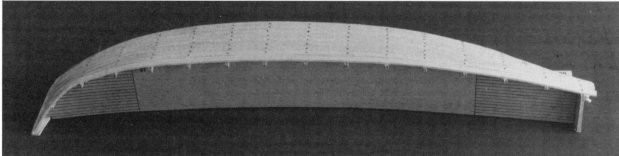

Starboard hull half finish planked ready for trimming. Remove all pins before rubbing down. Note curve of deck across the beam and fore and aft.

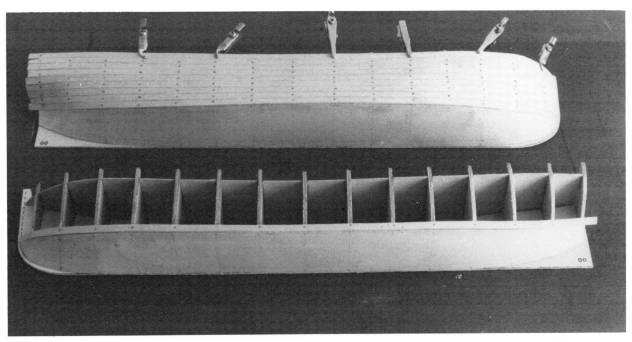

Lower, bulkhead in place on central false keel with deck and bottom pinned and glued. First plank in place with finished fit to stem and overlap at stern. Stern trimming is best done at planking completion. Top, planking completed. Planks above deck level should be clipped in place whilst glue sets; bulkhead 'ears' are not strong enough for pins.

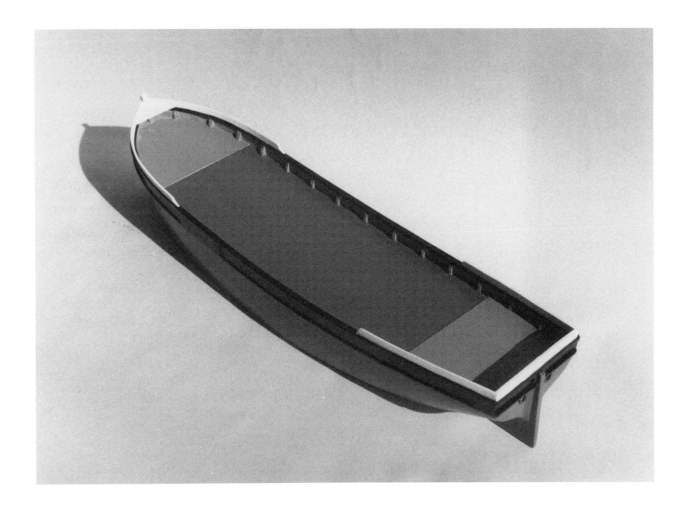

The two halves of the hull brought together and rails added. The hull has been primed, filled and painted at this stage.

Masts and spars

A real boon for beginners here; the masts come already turned and tapered, only needing the bottom ends squared off to sizes provided. However, do check that spider bands and collars all fit before painting and when assembling, establish a sequence to ensure that everything goes on in the right order. For instance don't fit the eyes to the main mast before the spider band or you won't get it on!

On the main spar it is required to fit three collars, one at each end and one positioned some way towards the middle of the spar. Each collar has four cross-holes and it is important that these line up axially or the eyelets fitted in them will not be positioned correctly for the subsequent rigging (see Fig. 5.4). The drawings of the masts and spars show exactly where eyebolts and blocks should be placed. It is good practice to assemble these before fitting masts to the hull — it certainly is more convenient and much easier than later when other rigging features may get in the way.

Tying on blocks is relatively straightforward but for best-looking results the following process is to be recommended. Take the required block and trim off any flash. A short length of thread is tied to the eye of the block and then both ends knotted about 2 mm from the

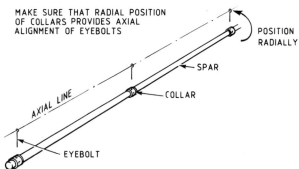

Fig. 5.4.

eye. The free ends are then tied in a single hitch around the mast or spar and secured with a touch of superglue (see Fig. 5.5). The ends can finally be trimmed close to leave a very neat job with the block hanging free to take up its correct alignment when rigging. At this stage it is worth ensuring that the decorative 'transfers' are applied and over-varnished before proceeding with putting the masts up. Again it is a matter of simpler handling and less chance of accidental damage.

Stepping the masts is straightforward enough but the bowsprit needs quite a bit of care. The drawings conflict somewhat in this area and no information is given as to what, if any, preparatory work is needed to the starboard forward rail to locate the bowsprit.

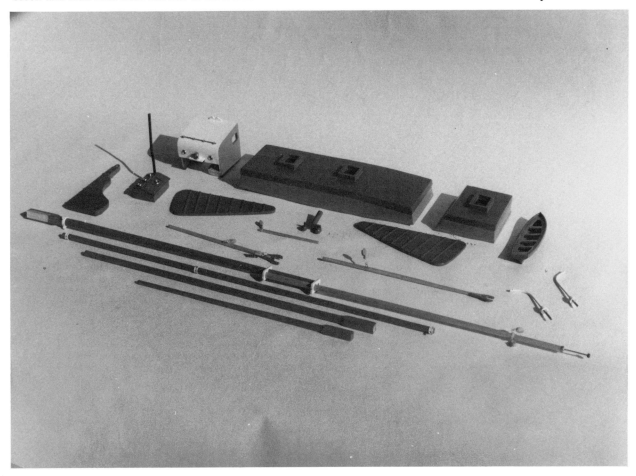

Deck fittings, mast and spars ready for assembly. Blocks should be fitted to spars where necessary at this stage rather than leave until proper rigging commences. Masts come tapered and it only remains to file the butts square and finish off.

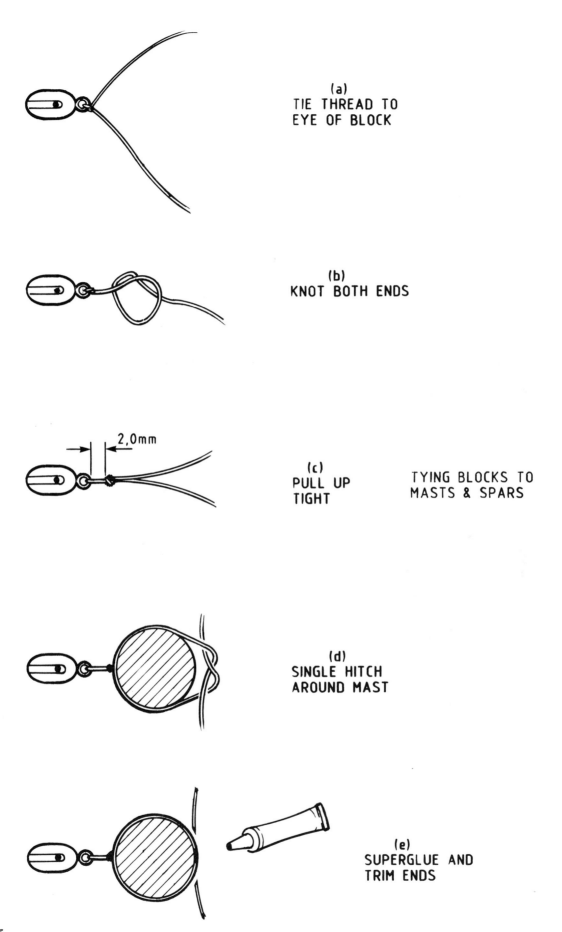

(a)
TIE THREAD TO
EYE OF BLOCK

(b)
KNOT BOTH ENDS

2,0mm

(c)
PULL UP
TIGHT

TYING BLOCKS TO
MASTS & SPARS

(d)
SINGLE HITCH
AROUND MAST

(e)
SUPERGLUE AND
TRIM ENDS

Fig. 5.5.

All deck fittings and main mast assembled. Note that the bottoms of all pieces sitting on the deck should be adequately curved to match the surface of the deck. Don't forget to remove print in areas to be glued, particularly on plastic winches, windlass, etc.

Rigging

Not too much to do on such a small model of course, but careful study of the drawings is required to get it right. Several lines terminate on winches and it is at this time you will find out how well you have fixed them to the deck! All ends were secured with a small dab of superglue and trimmed close.

The one feature in the rigging that it is worth taking extra care with is the ratlines. At this scale they are somewhat easier to apply and I think that if they are evenly spaced, and not pulled up too tight so as to distort the shrouds, you won't go far wrong.

Sails

Here is a model that for once looks better with sails, mainly because they show to greater advantage the rig almost unique to this type of craft. However, to make up the sails needs considerable time and needlework skill. The material supplied in the kit is fairly stiff and you really need access to a sewing machine (and an operator if possible)! The ongoing comments are based on re-marks made by my wife during the sailmaking process whose craftsmanship in this field is undoubtedly far superior to mine.

The sail cloth provided is clearly marked out with the various shapes required which, after cutting out, have

first to be tacked, then hemmed all round. All stitching on the sails was done with red cotton and all ends tied off and sewn in. Expect to take about six hours to make up the complete set properly before dyeing to the correct dark red colour. Having well pressed them with a hot iron, it remains to fit booms and rings and rig them to their respective masts and spars. An alternative way to make the sails is to machine the seams in a continuous manner as described for the *Royal William*. This avoids the need for all the sewing in of ends.

Conclusions

Apart from the sails, which definitely require some needlework expertise to make well, the kit produces a very nice little model within the scope of the beginner, but be prepared for quite a few hours' work. There are several books devoted to the history and construction of the Thames barges and reference to these would undoubtedly permit this kit to be made up into something a little bit special.

RECOMMENDED READING

A Handbook of Sailing Barges by F. S. Cooper and John Chancellor (Adlard-Coles, London).

CHAPTER 6

The *Faroes Yawl* F.D10

FD10 *Faroes Yawl*. **The finished model.**

The Kit

The Billings kit for the *Faroes Yawl* is another put together with the less experienced in mind. The quality of timber and the accuracy of pre-cut parts is excellent, as is the standard of brass and plastic fittings.

The hull

The hull is built on the two-halves principle where each half of the hull is constructed separately on a flat board and finally brought together for decking and railing. It is essential that the board be absolutely flat and that all frames are square and matched side to side. The latter is extremely well taken care of by the quality of the pre-stamped parts, and it is not difficult to set the frames up square on the false keel.

Planking the hull is not easy due to the complex shape under and around the stern, and I must say that some clearer detail in these areas for the novice would be most welcome. Planks need to be tapered both longitudinally and on the edges to follow the natural curvatures of ship and plank. The shape at the ends of each plank needs careful cutting to match the stem at one end and the false keel and baseboard at the other (see Fig. 6.1). I persevered with the method right through to the bitter end, but in the case of this particular model I am sure it would be better to apply one plank at deck level and another at approximately waterline level whilst the frames are still pinned to the building board, and finish the planking after bringing the two halves together.

Fig. 6.1.

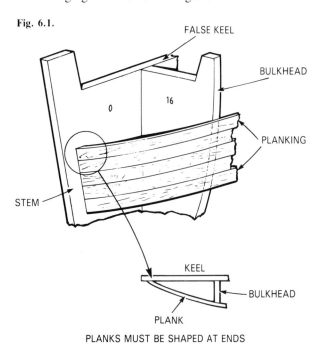

PLANKS MUST BE SHAPED AT ENDS
AND CONTROLLED TO LENGTH

The tops of the frames support the deck planking and before laying the deck you should make sure that there are no high or low spots. Note should be taken of plank lengths and the relative position of the joints. I chose to simulate this by making a small jig and using a razor saw cut about a third through the thickness at intervals along the length of the plank (see Fig. 6.2). Make sure that the first two planks (either side of the centre line) are

straight and true and firmly glued before adding further planks. These should be stuck not only to the tops of the frames but edge to edge to each other. If this approach is not adopted there is every likelihood of the deck finishing up uneven and planks springing between frames.

Having got the basic hull completed, before fitting pin rails and rudder I applied two coats of Humbrol white primer undercoat with a rub down between coats. The deck was treated with two coats of satincoat varnish, and for convenience, the inside of the bulwarks and the waterways were finish painted with the required colours. The pin rails and rudder can now be assembled and the hull painted.

The deck fittings

While the paint on the hull is drying you can progress to the deck fittings, although many of these also need painting before assembly, particularly the plastic parts. The winches are fairly detailed and worth taking time over, remembering to square off the ends of all shafts with a file and not to leave the 'pinched' end resulting from cutting the brass wire with pliers or sidecutters (see Fig. 6.3).

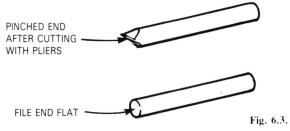

PINCHED END
AFTER CUTTING
WITH PLIERS

FILE END FLAT

Fig. 6.3.

The main anchor winch is best assembled in conjunction with the bowsprit to ensure correct alignment. It is also wise at this point to drill as necessary to fit the large cleat into the deck just forward and to the starboard side of the mizen mast. The large single block should also be

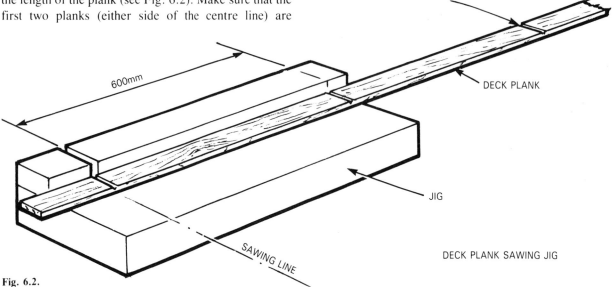

SAW PLANK ⅓ THROUGH

DECK PLANK

600mm

JIG

SAWING LINE

DECK PLANK SAWING JIG

Fig. 6.2.

fitted via a ring to the deck on the port side of the main mast. These items in particular will be more difficult to fit once the masts have been stepped. I used superglue gel adhesive to fix the deck fittings, remembering of course to scrape away the deck varnish as necessary to ensure a good bond.

The masts and spars

In their usual manner, Billings provide material for the masts already tapered and all that is required is to cut to length and finish off ends. Assembling the upper to lower main mast is quite straightforward and the drawings are particularly clear with regard to the position of rings and blocks etc. Careful study of all views on the drawing is required to make sure that nothing is missed and that pieces are assembled in the correct sequence. For instance, the sliding rings for fixing the mainsail must be assembled before the lower boom pivot ring and, before either, it is better to paint and varnish as required (see Fig. 6.4).

Fig. 6.4.

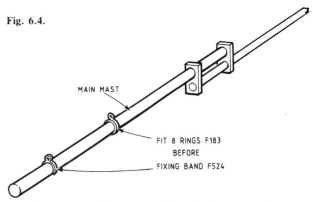

MAIN MAST

FIT 8 RINGS F183
BEFORE
FIXING BAND F524

I chose to step the masts without the booms and spars at this juncture, mainly to keep things as uncluttered as possible for applying the rigging. In fact, all spars are better attached to their relevant sails before assembly.

Rigging

Much of the information is spread around the various views on the drawing which, being doublesided, makes

Hull construction showing the starboard frame ready to start planking. The planking on the port side is finished. Note the plank formation around the stern, which I am not sure is as intended, however it worked out OK as can be seen from the accompanying photographs.

The nearly completed hull with exterior 'in white'. It is important when planking the deck to ensure that all edges are glued together or planks will spring between bulkheads and cause an uneven deck surface. With such movement between planks it would be impossible to sand the top surface smooth and even.

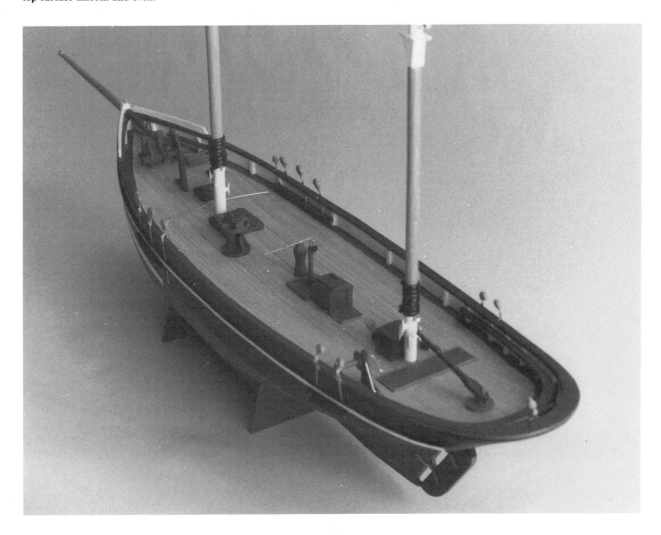

Ready to start rigging. Not too many deck fittings to get in the way but make sure that they are well secured by scraping varnish from the deck before gluing. Note gap between rudder and post is too big, rudder fittings supplied should either be severely modified or replaced altogether.

life a little difficult. One extra plan view showing all rigging tie-off points would be invaluable, but it is not too difficult to extract all the information and compile a rough diagrammatic sketch for oneself.

Apart from these particular comments, the rigging is really quite straightforward. There are not too many ratlines to do — always a tedious job that is good to get finished — and provided the shrouds are pulled up nice and tight they are fairly easily applied without distortion.

The sails

Sails come ready marked out on a sheet of fairly stiff material. Having cut them out, all edges have to be tacked and hemmed. If you haven't used a sewing machine before it is as well to put in some practice in order to be able to sew in straight lines. Operating the machine itself is not too difficult, it is purely the handling of the material at the needle point that needs care. Lines of stitches up and down or across the sails should be applied where indicated and the ends tied off and sewn in (see Fig. 6.5). Once all the sails have been made up comes the messy job of dyeing them to the colour required. Incidentally, I chose to use thread for the stitching near enough to the finished colour in case the dye had a different effect on it to that of the sail material.

A word of warning about the dyeing process. Don't use your best cooking utensils and do wear rubber gloves. (I found an old pair of my wife's but, too late, I discovered they had a hole in them! People were not too keen to shake my hand for a few days.)

You may find it easier to use the description of sail-making in the section of this book devoted to the *Royal William*. There are one or two alternative ways of stitching the seams which may suit you better.

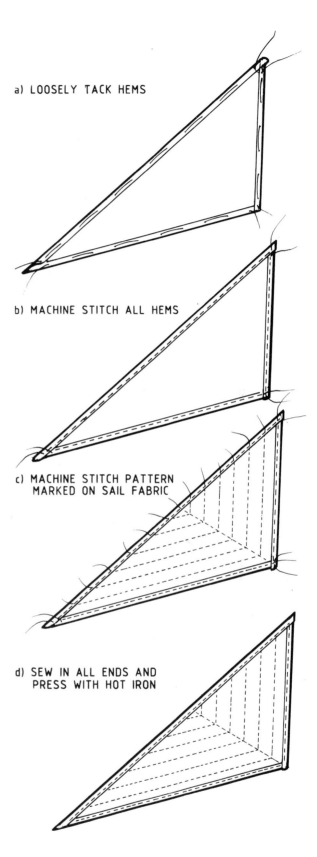

a) LOOSELY TACK HEMS

b) MACHINE STITCH ALL HEMS

c) MACHINE STITCH PATTERN MARKED ON SAIL FABRIC

d) SEW IN ALL ENDS AND PRESS WITH HOT IRON

Fig. 6.5.

Conclusions

This kit makes up into a very nice model about 685 mm long. There is really no part of the construction that should be beyond the skills of the less experienced modelmaker if a little bit of research and homework is done.

CHAPTER 7

The American Raider
Hannah

The *Hannah*. The finished model.

The *Hannah* was the first vessel commissioned by the Continental Army under George Washington in 1775. Originally a topsail fishing schooner, after purchase it was armed and used to raid British ships for supplies and stores, particularly arms and powder.

The Kit

The Artesania Latina kit makes up into a model nearly 30 in long, or 750 mm to be precise and, what appeared at first sight to be a pretty much run-of-the-mill enterprise, turned out to be quite an absorbing project.

The kit was well presented with a good standard of fittings and reasonably high quality timber. The drawings were clear and accurate, although the instruction manual suffered from several misprints. It was, therefore, important to study the drawings and photographs at length. However, I suspect that these misprints have by now been corrected.

In addition to a very comprehensive parts list, listing each and every item, the manual also includes instructions for the preparation of those parts which have to be cut to size from the materials provided in the kit. It clearly states that it is very important to cut each part as indicated and in the order listed. They kid you not. Failure to do this could result in not having sufficient material to meet the requirements, so be warned. The instructions also advise that the modeller takes time to read through the various stages of construction and identify the relevant parts.

Building the hull

A false keel/frames assembly with moulded bow and stern blocks make for a simple, but strong, basis for planking the hull. The fit of frames to false keel needs a little attention to make sure that the joints are not overtight thus distorting the assembly but, other than that, this stage of the project is very straightforward. The decks and deck planking follow this, prior to fitting the bulwarks and transom.

The first layer of planking can now be applied, using 5 mm × 1.5 mm strips of samba. The lines are fairly kind to the modeller and, apart from tapering each end of every plank to about half width over a length of approximately 90 mm, you just need patience and care to work your way down from bulwarks to waterline. Planking then resumes from keel upwards. The second layer of planking is from 5 mm × 0.6 mm sapele and mukali which really show off the lines of the hull to advantage. Walnut keel, stem and stern post are then added followed by transom planking and rubbing strakes. The framing of the transom needs considerable care to ensure a 'continuous' look to stern and side woodwork, but nothing that is too difficult if you do not rush. The stanchions on the inside faces of the bulwarks are fitted and spaced with reference to the relevant part of the plans.

The one-piece rudder needs heavy scribing to simulate a composite assembly prior to fitting the hinges and hanging on the stern post. On the other hand, you could actually make the rudder as a composite assembly for more authenticity. The gunwales need care and attention

The after deck. Note pump and gratings.

Three stages in hull construction. The basic hull frames before planking, planking and almost completed hull.

to ensure proper seating and adhesives left to completely cure before cutting the four gunports. Don't be tempted to cut them prior to fixing the gunwales or you will probably find that they spring out of shape. After lining them, the channels, culverin supports and the remainder of the hull fittings can be shaped and assembled.

Now is the time to varnish the hull and paint the main strakes black. On this occasion matt varnish was selected and on this model with contrasting woods, it proved a good choice. No subtle reflections detracted from the lines and shape, and the wood colours were enhanced beautifully. A word about deck gratings; ensure that all the grating strips on each unit run the same way. An odd one stands out like a sore thumb.

The brass strips provided for making up the chain-plates are too brittle to bend around the deadeye retaining rings and so a small lip, sufficient to locate a ring, was used and the ring soldered in place (see Fig. 7.1).

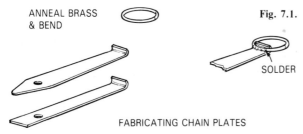

ANNEAL BRASS & BEND

Fig. 7.1.

SOLDER

FABRICATING CHAIN PLATES

All the deck fittings can now be made and put in place to complete the basic hull construction. Incidentally, the culverins are best left in the box until the model is completely finished since they tend to catch up the various lines as rigging is carried out.

Masts and spars

All masts and spars are made from the well matching dowel rod supplied. Tapering has to be applied to all pieces and the process involving reducing sections to first square, then octagonal shape prior to spinning, proved to be quite adequate (see Fig. 7.2). Do make sure that all holes are drilled before stepping masts and, further ensure that all blocks and eyes are fitted. It is much easier to rig them at this stage. A small drill run through all blocks before assembly enhances the later rigging work.

It is worth carefully checking which blocks need to be rigged with an eye. Reference was necessary to both drawings and photographs so as to not miss any. A little bit of precision woodwork on the ends of the booms (see Fig. 7.3) and gaffs is necessary to make a nice job of

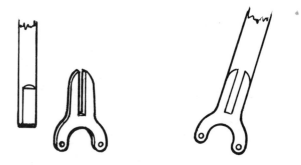

Fig. 7.3. Fitting jaws to booms and gaffs.

fitting the jaws supplied in the kit. Remember to varnish before assembling to the hull, taking care not to clog up any eyebolts or blocks.

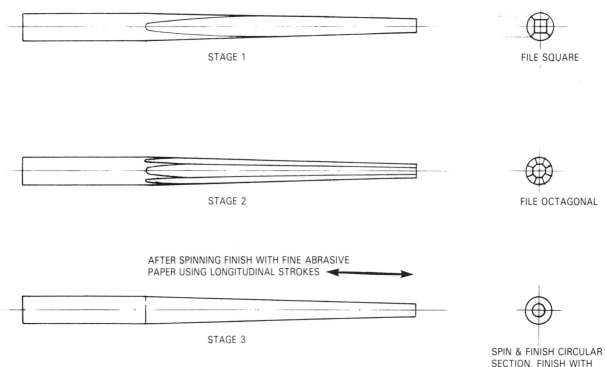

STAGE 1

FILE SQUARE

STAGE 2

FILE OCTAGONAL

AFTER SPINNING FINISH WITH FINE ABRASIVE PAPER USING LONGITUDINAL STROKES ◄━━━━►

STAGE 3

SPIN & FINISH CIRCULAR SECTION. FINISH WITH FINE ABRASIVE PAPER

SHAPING MASTS & SPARS

Fig. 7.2.

The foredeck.

View of the stern which reveals rudder arrangement.

Rigging

The drawings provided are extremely good and lay down a sequence of rigging which should be followed for ease of working. Each line is numbered and tying off points are clearly identified. Getting hands and fingers amongst the spars is not too much of a problem in this particular case since there are only two yards to contend with. Nevertheless, it is always helpful to smear the end of each length of rigging thread with just a smidgeon of superglue. It stiffens the material and it is like working with a built-in bodkin.

The standing rigging is set up first (Figs 7.4, 7.5 and 7.6), including the ratlines. Fortunately, not too many on this model, but do try to keep them equally spaced (see Fig. 7.6). The sails involve quite a few hours' work to get them properly stitched up and looking right. See the section on sailmaking in the chapter concerning the *Royal William*. Check particularly, that the shapes of the two spankers match the set up of the booms and gaffs — if you don't it is very easy to finish up with too much sail.

The remainder of the running rigging is straightforward. Correct tying off points being clearly shown on the drawings.

Fig. 7.5.

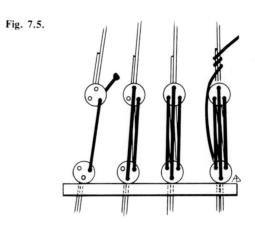

SEQUENCE FOR RIGGING LANYARDS.
NOTE RELATIVE POSITIONS OF DEADEYES.

Fig. 7.6.

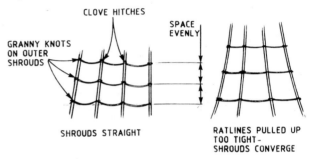

RATLINES

Fig. 7.4.

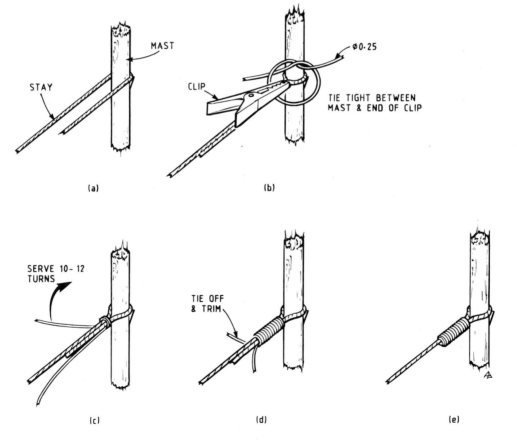

FIXING STAYS

The starboard bow. Enough detail to keep the project interesting.

The rear view of the fore mast. Sails are laced to yard and boom.

Conclusions

The kit makes up into a surprisingly attractive model built straight from the box as was the review model. It would undoubtedly also form the basis for a more detailed model should one wish to do a bit of research into the original. I have to say that it provided a lot of pleasant working hours and can be considered good value for money.

107

The French Goelette
La Toulonnaise

La Toulonnaise. The finished model.

The *Toulonnaise* was launched in Toulon during August 1823. Armed with eight, 18 lb carronades, it saw plenty of active service, particularly in the Franco-Spanish war, when it took part in the bombardment of the harbour at Cadiz; major repairs were found necessary and carried out at Brest in 1832. Four years later, further repair work was carried out at Fort Royal, Martinique. In 1843, the cost of work then required to put the vessel into serviceable condition was found to exceed two thirds of the cost of a new vessel and regulations decreed that the *Toulonnaise* was removed from the fleet.

The French chose to refer to this small type of craft as a Goelette, named after the smallest member of a family of marine birds found in Lower Brittany. The vessels were seen predominantly along the American coasts in the early years of the design, but later also became quite common in European waters.

The Kit

During the last few years, Artesania Latina have done much to improve their image; better representation, higher quality materials and, certainly, a more comprehensive instruction manual and set of drawings. The kit for the *Toulonnaise* follows the same trend and provides a manual comprising a 252 item, descriptive and numbered, parts list, together with 75 photographs illustrating the various stages of construction for a model 720 mm long. Included also is a cutting list which, I have to say, needs to be carefully adhered to if you don't wish to run out of material. In fact, it works quite well, but you have to cut parts in the sequence listed and, I would suggest, label the pieces when cut for later identification to ensure success.

I had no serious criticism of the materials supplied, although the diecast anchors exhibited considerable die offset, which made for very flimsy parts when corrective action was taken. The drawings were good, excellently draughted and totally unambiguous.

Building the hull

The hull is constructed around eleven bulkheads, cross-halved into a false keel. The slots of these joints should be gently eased to ensure that they are not too tight, then glued squarely in place. Overtightness in the fit between the false keel and the bulkheads can cause distortion of what is the main spine of the vessel. The mast support blocks are then fixed in place and the prefabricated bow and stern blocks added. This basic framework should then be set aside for the glue to thoroughly cure before tidying up the top surfaces preparatory to fitting the deck.

Pinning and gluing the deck in place stabilises the hull structure longitudinally, thus permitting the edges of the bulkheads to be suitably chamfered ready for planking. In spite of having been supplied with pre-shaped bow

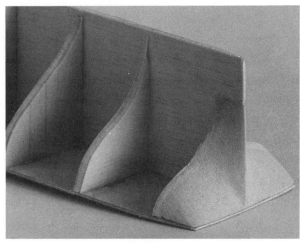

Close-up of the stern construction.

and stern blocks, you should be prepared for considerable shaping at these points to attain adequate seating, and alignment, of the ends of the planks. A simple, but effective, way of checking that the maximum area of contact between plank and bulkhead is achieved is to frequently monitor the situation using a spare planking strip. Particular attention should be paid to the area adjacent to the stern post, remembering that the combined thicknesses of the port and starboard planking together with that of the false keel, has to basically match the thickness of the stern post itself. Patience is also needed to get a good line across the edges of the last three bulkheads and on to the stern block. Again, constant checking with a piece of planking is as good a way as any to achieve this (see Fig. 8.1).

Fig. 8.1.

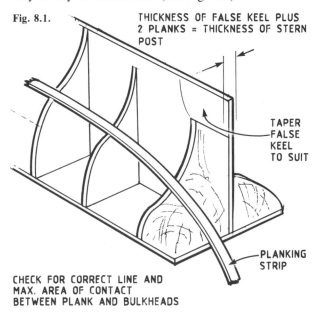

THICKNESS OF FALSE KEEL PLUS 2 PLANKS = THICKNESS OF STERN POST

TAPER FALSE KEEL TO SUIT

PLANKING STRIP

CHECK FOR CORRECT LINE AND MAX. AREA OF CONTACT BETWEEN PLANK AND BULKHEADS

Planking starts 3 mm down from the deck line and continues for five strips down towards the keel. The remaining planking is carried out from the keel upwards. It will be found better to taper the width of most planks, particularly at the bow end, and fit stealers at the stern. I found that the amount of taper for best results was over a distance from the bow to the fourth bulkhead.

The width of the plank was determined by measuring the length of the edge of the second bulkhead and dividing this figure by fifteen. Each plank was marked with the position of second and fourth bulkheads. The second was also marked with the reduced width and the plank tapered from full width at the fourth, through the determined width at the second, and on to the end of the plank. The strip can then be offered up to the hull, using the fourth bulkhead position as a datum line. A little bit of extra fitting here and there may be found necessary, but in general the tapering procedure described will give the basic requirement. As to the magic 'fifteen' as a divisor, this is the number of full plank widths required to go from deck to keel at the deepest part of the vessel (see Fig. 8.2). The instructions recommend that you now lightly sandpaper the hull to a smooth finish. I would strongly suggest that this be left until after the bulwarks have been fitted, so that these and the hull planking can be finished smoothly together, thus forming an uninterrupted base for the second hull planking.

which to do the second planking layer. Unless you want to risk tearing your fingers, I would suggest that you remove all the planking pins first. The 0.6 mm thick strips should be tapered and laid in the same sequence as was used for the first planking, but this time using contact adhesive only. A final sanding leaves the hull ready for the fitting of the keel, stern post and stem. The pre-shaped stem needed quite a bit of work doing to it before a satisfactory fit with the hull was attained. The stern post should now be fitted followed by the keel. The alignment of these three parts is not easy and I pre-drilled each before gluing to permit a light tacking to get everything right. Once satisfied, the pins could be driven fully home and the heads underflushed and stopped.

The rudder and tiller can now be made and assembled. The rudder itself is required to be scored to represent an assembly of several pieces of timber. Quite frankly, it is much simpler to use three pieces of surplus material and do the job properly. Once the poop deck planking has

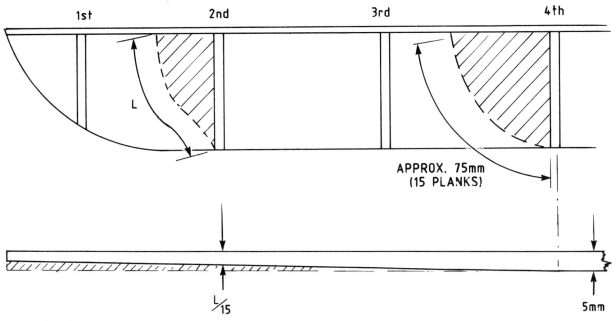

Fig. 8.2. Tapering planks.

The next step involves the planking of the deck with 0.6 mm thick mukali strips. The use of a contact adhesive for these thin materials is usually much better since a white PVA will tend to soak through and warp the planking before it is dry. Incidentally, the same size strip is used for planking the outside of the bulwarks later on and I found it worthwhile to lay out all the strips to determine the best choice of grain pattern and colour for each feature. The deck should then be sanded smooth and the waterways fitted. Before proceeding further, and because the very light wood is prone to marking as work continues, using a soft cloth, I rubbed in some matt varnish to seal the surface of the deck.

The first hull planking should now be well sanded to blend with the bulwarks to provide a smooth surface on

been laid, you can consider the fixing of the transom. It is imperative that this be done using the stern quarter gallery castings as a positional guide. It also ensures that all the angles are right or, at least, are capable of being corrected in wood, rather than having to try and alter the castings. Superglue is ideal for fixing the galleries and the head rails, but make sure that the position is exactly right or the line of the main rubbing strakes will be affected. All these items have to line up with the intersection of the two different types of planking material at the lower edge of the bulwarks.

One of the items usually guaranteed to raise the blood pressure is the fitting of the gunwales, and this kit is no exception. The gunwales at the fore section are pre-shaped, but it is always very difficult when raising the

111

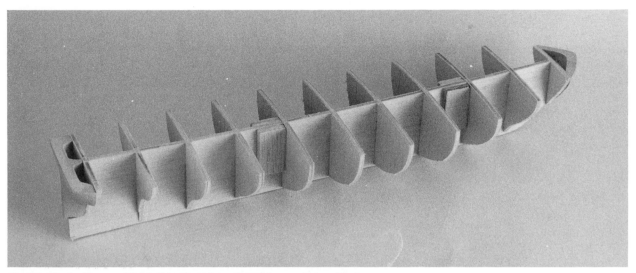

The false keel with assembled bulkheads and pre-shaped bow and stern blocks.

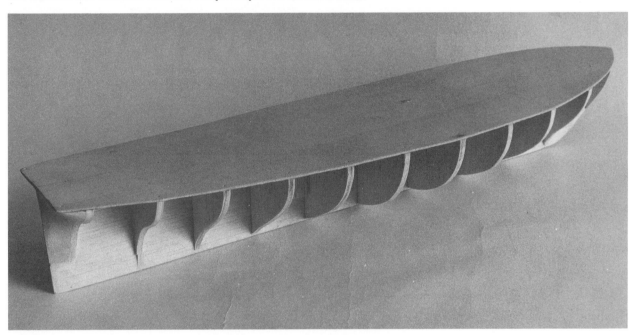

The false deck is pinned and glued before chamfering the edges of the bulkheads.

Hull and deck planking completed.

The Finished Models in Colour

The *Royal William*
(see also front cover).

The Thames Barge *Will Everard*.

The *Faroes Yawl* F.D.10.

The American Raider *Hannah*.

The French Goelette *La Toulonnaise*.

Above: The American *U.S.S. Constellation*.
Left: The Brandenburg Frigate *Berlin*.
Below: The Spanish Man-of-War *San Juan Nepomuceno*.

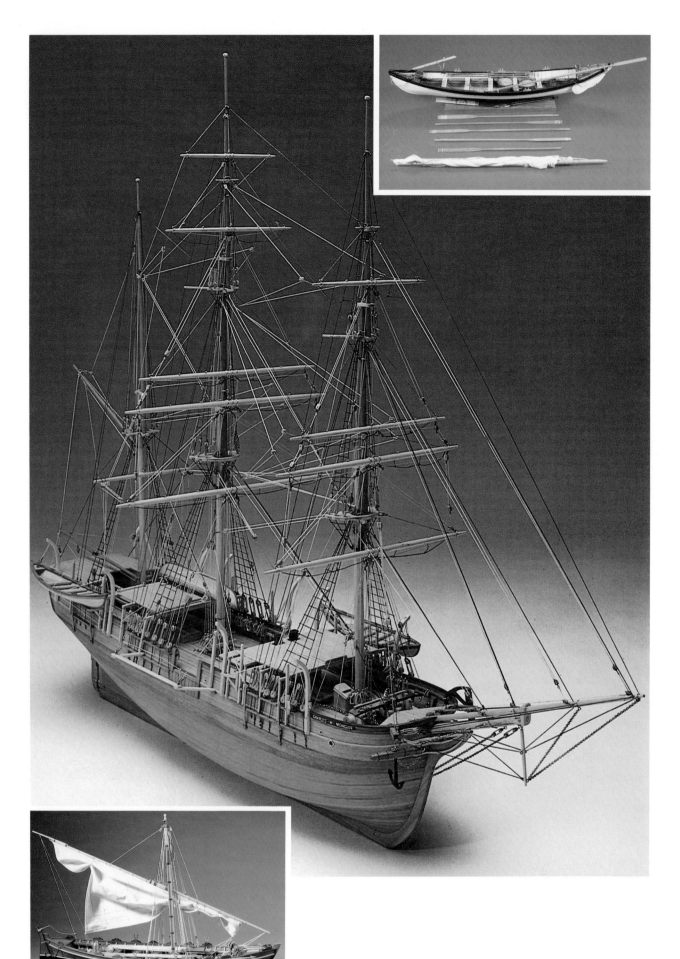

Main picture: The American Whaling Ship *Charles W. Morgan*.
Inset top: A New Bedford Whaleboat.
Inset left: A Square-Sterned Whaleboat.

bulwarks to match the top edge curve to that of the pre-shaped gunwale. In this particular instance, it was fortunate that things lined up quite well, but I must admit that with the type of construction used by kit manufacturers for this feature, the fit is somewhat in the lap of the gods. The problem lies in the fact that the line at gunwale level is reliant on the curve resulting from bending the ply bulwarks in two planes, rather than following a positive shape given by the tops of frames extending above deck level — the method that the scratchbuilder would almost certainly adopt. The aft gunwales do not have such a pronounced curve on them but, even so, you could take advantage of the fact that there are hinged portions above each of the gunports. Separate pieces can be fitted, rather than using a fine saw at a later stage to cut through a single piece as described in the instruction manual (see Fig. 8.3).

The outline of the gunports is scribed into the bulwark planking. Having already drilled the openings for the carronade barrels, it is important that the scribed outlines be symmetrical about them. Any small deviation does tend to stand out. In order to achieve the required symmetry, a simple marking gauge should be made (see Fig. 8.4), which fits snugly into the hole and locates between the underside of the gunwale and the top of the main rubbing strake. A finely pointed HB pencil can be used to accentuate the scribed lines produced by a sharp scalpel.

The fitting out of the hull is, for the most part, quite straightforward. One or two features do, however, call for comment. I have already mentioned the amount of die offset found on the diecast anchor parts which, with considerable care, is correctable. A similar situation was found to exist on the davit castings and whilst it was nowhere nearly so bad, the very fine nature of the items leads me to suggest that no attempt be made to use the file on them. A couple of coats of matt black paint does

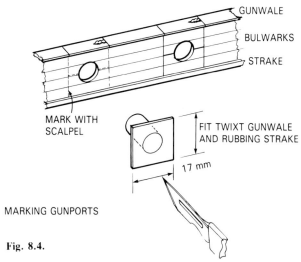

MARKING GUNPORTS

Fig. 8.4.

much to hide the problem, but it is a pity that they were not better cast. Unfortunately, the detail involved makes it most unlikely that the average modelmaker would be able to replace them from scratch.

The gunwales need to be drilled to take the culverins but, I strongly suggest that, having done the drilling, the actual fitting is left until the model is virtually complete. This eliminates four points at which rigging can get caught up and, in retrospect, I'm not sure that it would not have been wiser to have also left the davits off until later. The gratings are also worthy of comment. Do make sure that the grating strips all run the same way on each of the gratings, an odd one certainly stands out (see Fig. 8.5).

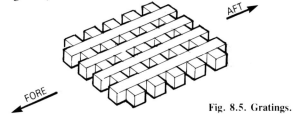

Fig. 8.5. Gratings.

The entire hull assembly can now be given a couple or so coats of matt or satin varnish according to taste.

Fig. 8.3.

AFT GUNWALES ONE PIECE CUT TO SIMULATE
HINGED RAILS OVER GUNPORTS

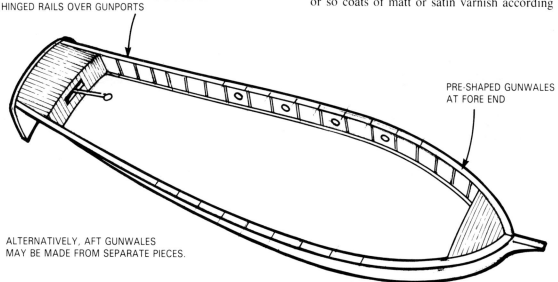

PRE-SHAPED GUNWALES
AT FORE END

ALTERNATIVELY, AFT GUNWALES
MAY BE MADE FROM SEPARATE PIECES.

Bulwarks and gunwales fitted.

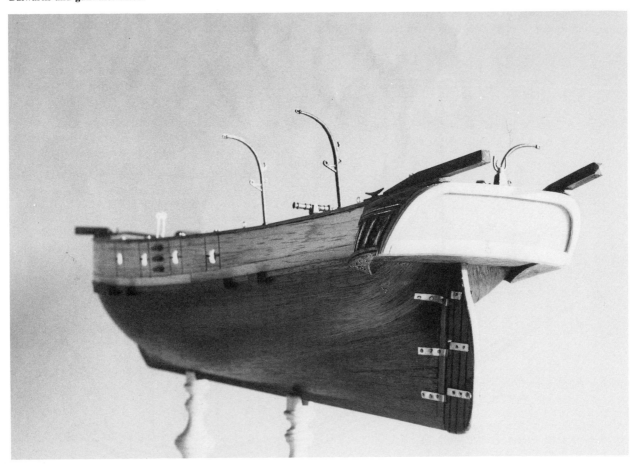

Underside view of rudder and transom.

Masts and spars

The quality of the five different diameters of dowelling provided for the making of masts and spars was excellent and well matched in colour. All pieces required tapering to drawing and this was done by filing the sections first with four flats, then with a further four to produce an octagonal section at the small end. This was then reduced to the required round and tapered section by spinning and sanding in the chuck of an electric drill.

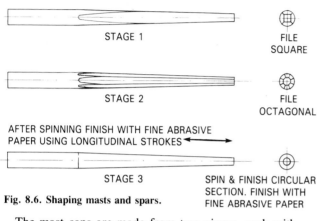

STAGE 1   FILE SQUARE

STAGE 2   FILE OCTAGONAL

AFTER SPINNING FINISH WITH FINE ABRASIVE PAPER USING LONGITUDINAL STROKES ←——→

STAGE 3   SPIN & FINISH CIRCULAR SECTION. FINISH WITH FINE ABRASIVE PAPER

Fig. 8.6. Shaping masts and spars.

The mast caps are made from two pieces, each with two half-round cutouts which, when brought together, form holes for the lower and upper masts. These holes are not large enough for the size of the mast and require opening out. However, the majority of this operation is best carried out before fixing the two pieces together, remembering also that the caps sit parallel to the deck on masts that lean back at 8½° and 10° on the fore and main masts respectively. To prevent splitting, only the final sizing should be done after bringing the two parts permanently together (see Fig. 8.7). The single piece boom support rings also need careful fitting to ensure that they also sit on the masts parallel to the deck. The masts and bowsprit only, having been varnished, should now be stepped, leaving yards and booms until later in the rigging process.

Fig. 8.7.

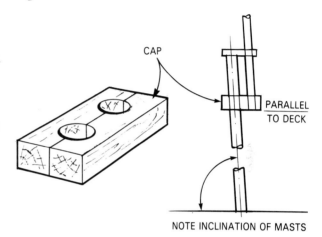

CAP

PARALLEL TO DECK

NOTE INCLINATION OF MASTS

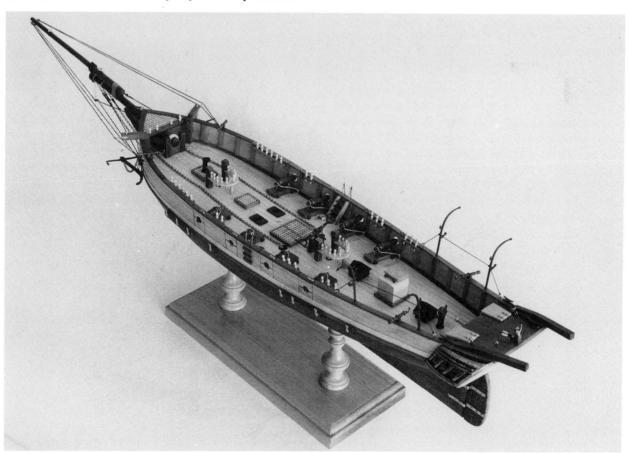

The model ready for stepping the masts.

Detail of the foremast top. Rigging details are clearly laid out in this kit.

Rigging

The sequence for rigging is most clearly laid out on the drawings provided in the kit. Every item of rigging is numbered sequentially in order of application and a belaying plan, similarly numbered, gives clear indication as to where every line terminates.

A few words of advice to those readers who may be building a model ship for the first time. It is well worth opening out all holes in blocks and deadeyes provided as it definitely permits easier rigging. Smearing a drop of superglue on the first 10 mm or so of each length of rigging thread tends to provide a built-in bodkin, and helps the thread through blocks and other small tackle. In fact, pulling each thread through gluey fingers (PVA

glue of course, not superglue!), does much to enhance the rigging process and, because it lays down the surface hairs on the thread, also helps prevent the adhesion of dust particles after the model has been completed.

Look at the mast and spar drawings very carefully to identify those blocks which need an eye or hook on their outgoing side. These are rigged with soft wire which both forms the eye and fixes the block to mast, spar, deck, etc. It is very difficult to add the eye at a later time if the requirement was overlooked in the first place (see Fig. 8.8). Make up your mind whether or not you are going to fit sails so that you rig the yards in the right place on the masts. Remember that the upper yards will be almost down on the caps if no sails are to be rigged.

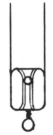

a. FORM LOOP IN CENTRE OF WIRE

b. FIT AROUND BLOCK

c. TWIST ENDS. USE TAILS FOR FIXING.

Fig. 8.8. Eyeing blocks.

Some models take to sails; some do not, but in this case the extra work involved is very worthwhile.

The shrouds were not tensioned via the usual deadeye/ lanyard facility at gunwale level, but by the use of turn-buckles. These are simulated on the model by lengths of brass wire with an eye formed at each end. It is worth making up a simple little jig to make sure that all twelve required are the same length. When rigging the shrouds, do try and get them as tight as possible — not so tight as to distort the alignment of the masts, of course, but the tighter they are, the easier it is to fix the ratlines without pulling the shrouds out of line (see Fig. 8.9).

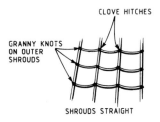

Fig. 8.9. Ratlines.

On the *Toulonnaise*, you will probably find it easier to lash the sails to the yards and to the gaffs before rigging the latter to the masts. This is purely a personal choice which, apart from simplifying the actual lashing, also helps rig the spars in the right place and at the right angle. If the spars are rigged first, it is essential to check that the sails are tailored to the correct size and shape. As I say, purely a matter of choice.

Making the sails

You will definitely need the use of a sewing machine and, if your sewing is anything like mine, a fairly large piece of material to practice on. I would refer you to that section of the *Royal William* where, I trust, you will find enough information and guidance to make yourself a very acceptable set of sails.

More rigging

A further point about the running rigging. In many cases the lines are not meant to be taut and would hang slack under their own weight. Many models are spoilt by the failure of the modelmaker to simulate this condition. One way that I have found to be reasonably successful is to not only glue the threads as described in *Rigging* p. 116, but to also apply tension to the thread whilst the glue is drying. This permits the thread to be persuaded into the desired curve without the kinks that usually result from using untreated thread.

Finishing off

The kit provides a nameplate but, as usual, no stand to fix it on and so, to finish off you need to make one. In fact, to build one much earlier in the kit construction

Close-up of upper stem.

La Toulonnaise **ready for a show case.**

can be very useful if you don't employ a building jig. A flag is also supplied but, in my opinion, tends to turn the image of what can be a very acceptable standard of scale model into that of a toy. Flags are usually quite awful, not in their printing, but in the material used. Like sail material, only more so, it is often too thick or too stiff for its area and simply refuses to hang in a manner anything resembling a flag. Thus it will be seen that I chose to rig the flag halliard to the block at the end of the mainmast gaff and omit to fly the flag.

Conclusions

La Toulonnaise is not too difficult to build and you should attain a very attractive result with very little effort. In fact, with a bit of research and some changes in material for some of the deck fittings, you could use the kit as the basis for a very desirable model indeed. Although not really a *first time* model, the less experienced modeller could still anticipate a creditable result.

CHAPTER 9

The Brandenburg Frigate
Berlin

The finished model of the *Berlin*.

The *Berlin*, built in 1674, is an attractive vessel and one which provides the modelmaker with something between the 19th-century clippers and the more highly ornate vessels of 17th-century France and Spain. There are features in hull construction which call for different techniques and, of course, the rigging has its own peculiarities.

Corel provides a potted history of the vessel outlining its somewhat chequered career as part of the Brandenburg war fleet, largely under the command of a Dutchman, Captain Reers. Further research into naval actions in the Baltic during the 17th century and against Sweden in particular, have all the potential of a most interesting project in its own right.

The Kit

The Corel kit for a model 830 mm long comes in a fairly hefty box and you cannot avoid being impressed by the presentation. The strip-wood is separately boxed and fittings are contained in a sealed partitioned tray, later found to be even more useful during the rigging process. The brass-plated ornamentation was also well presented, although several items did not conform strictly to the detail shown on the drawings. Sail material was also supplied, but as always seems to be the case, the weight, weave and stiffness of the cloth does not permit that natural 'hang' and thus demotes a scale model into just another ship ornament. Similar comment is made of the flags, nicely printed, but somewhat artificial looking. In general, the quality of materials was extremely high, although in a kit of this class, one should not have any cause for seriously adverse comment.

The 40-page instruction booklet contains instructions in four languages, Italian, English, French and German, supported by a dozen line sketches and two photographic reproductions. A large part of the manual is devoted to the identification of individual elements numbered on the drawings and specifying the materials from which they are made. A section giving translations of the Italian notes on the drawings was found to be most useful. The assembly instructions are quite understandable, but perhaps a little inadequate for the less experienced modelmaker in spite of the fact that, from the comments in the manual, Corel anticipate that *Berlin* will be attempted by the beginner.

Tools and equipment

A list of equipment required is contained within the instructions, all items being almost essential in the building of this particular model. In a general sense, and most useful for the construction of any rigged sailing vessel, I can recommend in addition the use of various size crochet hooks, a few small electrical crocodile clips and a handful of wooden sprung clothes' pegs which can be shaped to order. For the really dedicated, a pair of

Detail of the fore-top.

small pedicure side cutters and long-handled nail clippers are great for getting in amongst the rigging to trim ends. The sharp scalpel is alright, but one slip in the closing stages could radically alter the attitude of the rigging!

The hull construction

Before taking knife or saw in hand it is absolutely essential to study the drawings *together with* the instruction manual. This may seem an unnecessary comment to make to those who have made model boats before, but in this case it is imperative because of the limited detail in the instruction notes, and the fact that some details are not shown on all sheets of the drawings. I would strongly recommend that above each of the notes of the drawing, you write in the translation contained at the back of the manual. This helps in the familiarisation process and avoids the constant reference back and forth from drawing to book. Of course, those who have a command of Italian are home and dry!

It is a good idea to unspool the rigging thread supplied, hank it up and wash it. Cut out enough for the standing rigging and dye it dark brown or black, although in this day and age I would have thought thread could have been provided ready coloured. Once washed and dyed, hang the hanks to dry with weights to take out the natural stretch. This will take most of the time taken for the building of the model so now is the right time to get this chore done.

Some of the 'extras' that make life a little easier.

The basic framework of the hull is fairly straightforward and the frames were found to be very accurately cut with little work needed to attain firm and square joints with the false keel. Corel very loosely describe a building board which locates and supports the skeleton framework while planking, and their suggestion is very sound provided one has room to physically move around

the model under construction. The weight of the 800 mm × 400 mm particle board, plus support blocks, would prove a bit of a handful if it had to be turned around each time when fixing planks on alternate sides. A much lighter work holding fixture that could be held in the vice and worked over was found to be more than adequate with the added advantage of not restricting

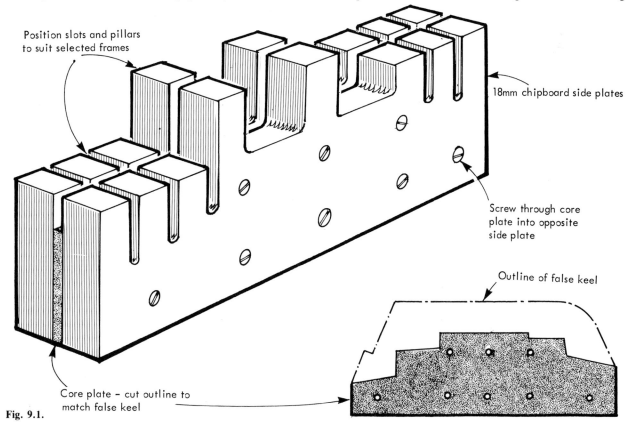

Position slots and pillars to suit selected frames

18mm chipboard side plates

Screw through core plate into opposite side plate

Outline of false keel

Core plate – cut outline to match false keel

Fig. 9.1.

123

access for shaping, filing, or sanding in the later stages. A sketch showing a diagrammatic arrangement is seen in Fig. 9.1. The centre slot, of course, accepts the false keel and each of the cross-slots is cut to depth to suit the particular frame it locates. The main support is along the top edge of the false keel with packing glued in at salient points to attain final squareness and alignment.

Having glued the frames and left them for at least 24 hours for the adhesive to harden off, it is then necessary to prepare the edge of each frame for planking. For convex areas, a strip of 3 mm ply faced with a fairly coarse grade of garnet paper will permit each frame to be correctly formed relative to its neighbour. Aim the strip against the edge from which the most material has to be removed to avoid too much breaking out of the trailing layer of ply frame (see Fig. 9.2). For the hollow or concave edges of frames, a short length of broom handle or dowelling about 25 mm similarly wrapped with garnet paper is ideal. Use one of the planking strips to constantly monitor progress until such time as it makes contact across the entire thickness of all the frames concerned.

When all frames have been so treated, the blocks between the forward frames can be glued in position

and, when set, correctly shaped. At this stage it should be remembered that the planking above deck level is double planked, and that the upper section of several of the frames has to be removed after the first outer layer of planking has been applied. It is therefore necessary to prepare those pertinent edges of the frames to ensure that the planking does not stick to them, also to pack out the mouth of the slots across the frames to prevent the structure distorting during the planking process (see Fig. 9.3). Sellotape is ideal to prevent the planks sticking to that part of the frame that will subsequently be removed.

We are now ready for planking. With this particular model it is not an easy task. The bending of 4 mm × 2 mm short grained walnut strips around the very tight radii in the bow area is quite a hazardous operation. There are known continental methods involving the use of fairly high wattage soldering irons, and well soaked planks, but the use of electricity and water together in the home workshop is something to be treated with care.

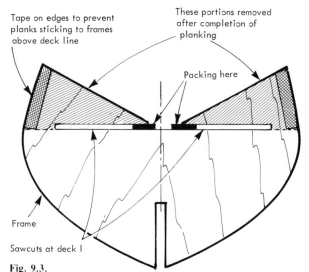

Fig. 9.3.

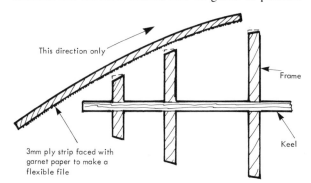

Fig. 9.2.

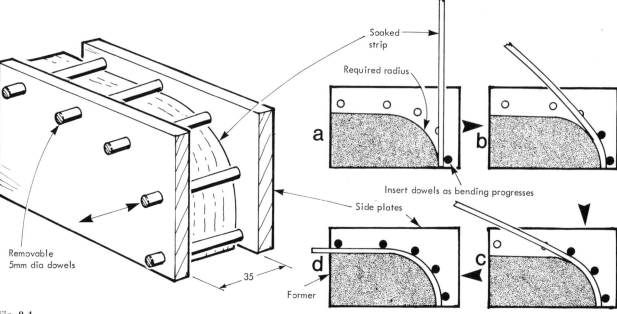

Fig. 9.4.

The method I used is a little more time consuming, but successful; I think I snapped only four strips in the total operation. First, of course, you must prepare the strips by tapering and bevelling edges as determined by the shape of the hull and as indicated in the instructions. For the actual bending, an electric kettle, a 1 metre length of 32 mm diameter plastic waste pipe and a bend retaining fixture made specially for the job, is required (see Fig. 9.4). Put the pipe over the spout and fill the kettle with water. Slide a half dozen strips of wood down the pipe and hang a damp cloth over the end to retain the heat and steam. Boil the water, and keep the water near boiling point by switching the kettle on and off periodically over about an hour. Don't use an ordinary kettle on a gas ring, the heat coming up the sides from the source below will melt the plastic!

When the strips have had a good soaking, put the end into the fixture and gradually pull round the block holding the strip in place by inserting the retaining dowels one by one. Leave to thoroughly dry out before removing the dowels when it will be found that the strips have kept more or less the radius of the block — certainly near enough to successfully apply to the frame. For extreme curves, a second soaking may be necessary. When fixing the strips, using both pins and glue, remember to drill before pinning to avoid splitting the wood and also ensure that not only are the strips adequately glued to the frames but also to each other edge to edge. This is most important, particularly in those areas where the hull has to be double planked. Also, don't forget to apply planking alternately side to side, to avoid distortion. This is a good point to make the stand, from now on it will become most useful.

Once the planking has been completed, the outer surface can be finished by filing, scraping, and the use of various grades of sandpaper. At this stage it is not a bad idea to give the hull a coat of thinned varnish. This will protect the surface from marking while work proceeds. The upper supporting section of the frames can now be removed and the inside surface of the planking smoothed off. This needs to be done properly as it forms the base onto which the inner planks are laid. The stern, keel and stern post can now be fixed in position using screws and glue, and the three pieces rubbed down to blend at the two butting joints.

We now come to the decks, the part of the construction which prompted the first serious criticism. The instructions recommend that the plywood decks are scored with a steel point to simulate the planking, the scoring accentuated with a lead pencil and the surface then varnished. Corel considerately tell you it is not easy to prevent the grain pulling the steel point away from the edge of the guiding rule, and they are right. I tried the scribing process recommended but was not in any way pleased with the results, so I purchased some strips and did the job properly using the ply decks as a base. Button thread was used as a spacing medium between planks, this being stripped out after the glue had dried. Fitting the lower decks was straightforward and, having done so, one could proceed with the inside planking up to the forecastle deck level.

It is important at this point to fit the anchor bitt and make provision for the knight. The latter should be dry-fitted only and, for adequate strength, dowelled into the deck. Permanent fixing should be done later when rigging the foreyard halliard. The gunports should also be cut at this stage before fitting the forecastle and other higher level decks. I chose to cut the ports a little larger than finished size and then line the insides with scrap strip. Such a boxed port looks infinitely better than one with the exposed layers of double planking.

The remaining stages of hull construction are straightforward until it comes to fitting the bulwark railings. Remembering the difficulties of bending the 4 mm ×

The planked frame. Note the severe bending required in the bows area.

Ready for putting in the decks. The upper parts of the relevant frames have been removed.

Fig. 9.5.

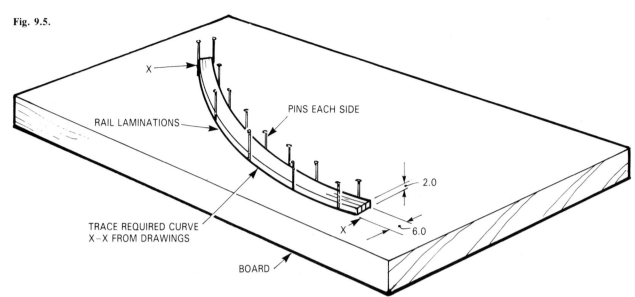

X

RAIL LAMINATIONS

PINS EACH SIDE

2.0

TRACE REQUIRED CURVE
X–X FROM DRAWINGS

X

6.0

BOARD

2 mm hull planks I decided to approach the bending of the handrails in a different manner. On the basis that it is easier to bend against the 2 mm thickness rather than the 6 mm width, three thicknesses of 2 mm × 2 mm were laminated together and bent round a jig until dry. The procedure is illustrated in Fig. 9.5. Having fitted the rails it only remained to make and position the rest of the facings and upper woodwork.

The stern area is worthy of mention if for no other reason than to say that its apparent complexity belies the ease with which it was built. The only pieces with which to exercise extra care are the extreme outer knees, which need to be individually fitted on each stern corner. The Corel leaflet advertising their range of model kits show the hull of the *Berlin* with a broad lighter band from stem to stern. Bleaching walnut is not a nice proposition to consider and so one must resort to double skinning with a light wood to give this attractive longitudinal band

down the hull. Regrettably this is not provided, and if your stock cupboard can't help, you are faced with a visit to your stockist for a supply of 0.5 mm thick strips. Of course, you could consider a paint job of some sort, but to me, it seems almost sacrilege to cover the beauty of the natural wood. The only concession I would make to this is the dark blue background on the transom, where the colour enhances the ornamentation of the stern elevation — see later.

The fitting of the rudder needs special attention in the alignment of the hinges. Careful marking is required and provided that the inside surfaces of the hinges are carefully scraped and cleaned, they can be initially held in place by a spot of superglue while the holes are drilled prior to inserting the shortened brass pins. The tiller passes through the top of the rudder and its appearance benefits from the simulation of the drawn mortice and tenon joint (see Fig. 9.6).

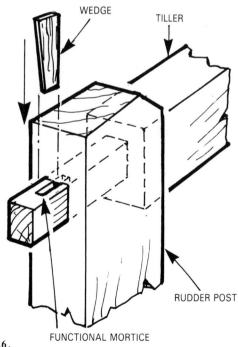

WEDGE

TILLER

RUDDER POST

FUNCTIONAL MORTICE

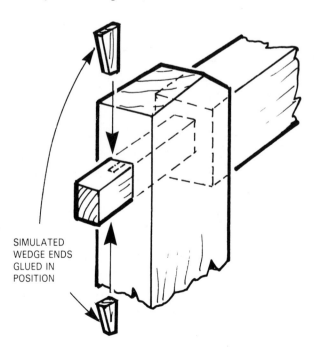

SIMULATED
WEDGE ENDS
GLUED IN
POSITION

Fig. 9.6.

The facing at the front of the quarter deck and poop deck require little comment, but careful fitting of the individual planks is needed if no unsightly gaps are to be left at the ends. In the case of the poop deck, it was found best to fit the metal ornamentation piece before doing the facing. Because of the rather severe casting line in the metal, I chose to apply a 0.5 mm thick capping strip on top of the casting right across the front of the poop deck.

We now come to a part of the structure guaranteed to stimulate the vocabulary to new heights — make sure you are alone and keep the workroom door shut. Head rails and timbers, beak-head rails, call them what you will (and you probably will), are those lovely curved pieces that decorate the prow area of the vessel. I gave much thought as to which way to tackle them, not helped by a lack of, and indeed, confusing detail on the drawing. The strip material has to be bent in two planes and, of course, one side has to match the other. Bearing this in mind, I decided to make the rails in pairs, soaking and bending in one plane at a time. I traced the required curve from the side view on the drawings, tightened it up to provide some over-bend and transferred the shape to a simple pin jig, similar to that shown in Fig. 9.5. The soaked strips were pulled round the inner pins, one on top of the other, and held in place by the outer lines of pins. They were left to dry out for at least 24 hours. When released from the pins, the overbent strips opened out to the required curve.

The bending in the second plane called for a different approach. By chance I found that a large empty paint tin provided just the right radius. Having again soaked the strips, I clamped them with toolmakers' clamps to the outside of the tin, first in the middle then at each end (see

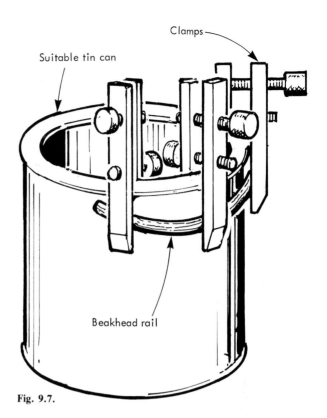

Fig. 9.7.

Fig. 9.7). It is essential to use at least three clamps or the strip will twist rather than bend in two planes. When thoroughly dried out, the ends can be shaped for fixing to the forecastle and prow. Some may argue that the timbers should be fitted first and the rails applied to their ends, but with the inherent uncertainties involved in the bending process, I decided to fix the rails first and fit the timbers secondly. This also has the advantage of giving a little scope to balance up the structure side to side.

The hull ready for fitting out.

127

To finalise the main hull construction, the channels can be fitted. These take quite a strain once the shrouds are tightened up, so it pays to ensure that a maximum area of contact on the glued edge is attained. Having established this condition, further strength should be obtained by cutting short a couple of brass pins and using them to dowel each channel to the hull side.

At this point the upper sides of the hull were stained with a Jacobean Oak finish and the transom painted medium blue, the whole then given a further coat of satin varnish.

Fittings and fitting out

The quality of fittings was extremely good, particularly the pump and capstan. The metal ornamentation was also pretty good, but several pieces contained a considerable residue of what appeared to be mould release agent. This was not too easy to get rid of and needed quite a lot of work with probes and an old toothbrush.

Gun barrels, carriages and wheels needed very little work done on them but axles had to be made from scrap. Whilst on the subject of guns, Corel go to some length to illustrate the correct installation but make a point in the manual to say that the necessary blocks are not provided in the kit. However, having set the guns in position, I have chosen to include the gunport lids as part of the fitting out process, in the main because the pro-truding barrels provide a convenient base for a packer to support the lid while the glue sets! The lids are simply two squares cut from appropriate size strip, metal hinges stuck in place with superglue, and brass pins cut short to simulate the heads of the fixing bolts. The rope for lifting the lid passes through the hull above the gunport and is belayed inside adjacent to the gun. This, of course, also gives support during the setting of the adhesive.

The grating in the forecastle deck should not be fitted at this stage but during the rigging of the foreyard ties and halliard at which time, of course, the permanent fitting of the knight can be made, by gluing and dowelling. The doors and frames cut from the photo-etched brass sheets were given a light brushing with an oak varnish-stain after fitting the doors with ring handles. Carefully mark their positions and stick them to the facings with a general purpose cement.

The remaining task is to fit the cast metal decorations. These were found to need a little preparation and cleaning. Due to either mould flash lines, or surface contraction, those areas to be stuck to the hull needed to be filed flat. The coat of arms to be mounted on the transom is best painted before mounting. The two Roman soldiers that stand on the corners of the stern gallery each hold a spear. The casting supplied would, when scaled up, have a haft some 75 mm in diameter. The spearheads were therefore cut off and mounted on

Main deck detail.

The capstan and pump area.

wire of more suitable size, and the hands of the figures drilled accordingly. The spears were put to one side for assembly at the very end of the project. The lion figurehead needs considerable work on the area between the hind legs (you have to be a veterinary as well??) in order to make it fit the prow and assume its correct attitude. (Note, the lion no longer roars.)

The two-part epoxy resin and hardener is probably the best adhesive for fixing all these metal parts. The hull is now ready for masting.

The masts

The masts are provided as square-sectioned but tapered lengths of timber which, of course, have to be converted to round section over the majority of their length. Whether or not you have the use of a lathe, it will be necessary to knock the corners off first to give an octagonal section. A fairly coarse file is ideal for this and, if you don't have a lathe, take the process a stage further to reduce the octagonal section to nearly the round section required. A useful alternative to the lathe is an electric drill in a horizontal stand. Place one end of the pre-shaped mast in the chuck, ensuring axial alignment and rub down to final circular section with varying grades of abrasive paper. Fold the paper to double thickness to protect the fingers from the heat generated. Also make sure that the fold is in the correct relative position to the rotation to avoid 'snatch' (see Fig. 9.8). A few words of warning. It creates a hell of

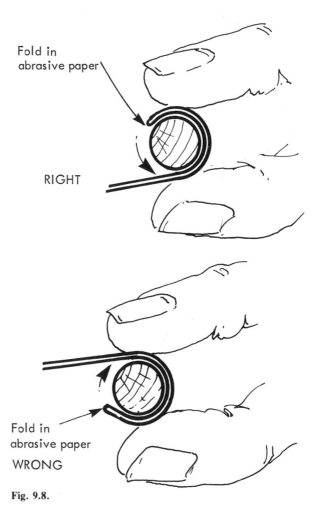

Fold in abrasive paper

RIGHT

Fold in abrasive paper

WRONG

Fig. 9.8.

129

A view of the ornate stern.

a dust which gets everywhere — particularly in your eyes and breathing equipment. So please, if possible, wear protective glasses and a mask. Better still, on the basis of safety in the home, use a vacuum cleaner to apply the wide carpet cleaning nozzle immediately below the work area. It is surprising the amount of dust generated by a few masts and spars.

Once the mast proper is finished to shape, apply the woldings as shown on the plan and fix the cheeks, trestletrees and crosstrees. Follow this procedure for all three masts and bowsprit, give a coat of varnish and assemble in the appropriate holes in the deck, fitting the combings where necessary. It is important at this stage to ensure that the masts are correctly aligned — they cannot be adjusted once fixed. Now that the masts have been correctly stepped, the lower deadeyes can be assembled to the channels. The sketch in the manual is very clear and really needs no further comment except to say that a spot of superglue will adequately fix the deadeyes into the chains which are made from fairly soft brass and will tend to unwrap once the lanyards are tensioned up. Also the attitude of the deadeye holes is important (see Fig. 9.9).

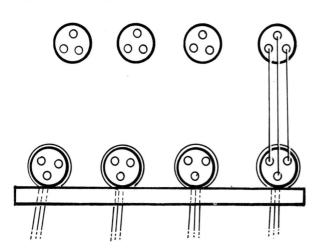

Fig. 9.9.

Standing rigging

Now rig the stays to all three masts — without over-tensioning. It is worth mentioning that the rigging is the biggest accumulator of dust on the finished model and whilst a proper case is hopefully going to be used, every precaution should be taken to minimise the dust problem. If the situation is analysed, it will be found that the surface of the thread is covered by thousands of upstanding fibre ends, just right for the dust particles to hang on. You cannot get rid of the fibres, but you can make them lay down. So after cutting a piece of thread to the required length, pulling it through gluey fingers a few times will do just that. Use white PVA and you will find the effort well worthwhile. A wax block is preferred by some modelmakers, but it can sometimes inhibit the performance of the touch of superglue used to seal off knots.

A close-up of the shrouds and standing rigging.

Another 'chore' well worth undertaking is the opening out of all holes in blocks and tackle. There is nothing so frustrating as trying to rig a block and find that the end of the thread only goes halfway through the hole. So, in addition to drilling out the blocks, when rigging the more inaccessible blocks, and particularly when using the finer thread sizes, a smear of superglue on the first 10 mm of thread end will stiffen it up into a useful built-in 'bodkin'.

Back to the masts. Having set up the stays we move on to the shrouds. There is a formal order for rigging the shrouds, first the starboard forward pair, then the port forward pair, second starboard pair, second port pair, and so on. The drawings show the correct loopings but don't make the order quite clear. There are all sorts of favourite ways of setting up the deadeyes and getting a reasonably similar distance between the upper and lower. The one I find most successful is to make up a small jig (see Fig. 9.10). One pair of pins is placed in the lower deadeye fixed to the channel, and another deadeye placed on the top pair of pins making sure that the third hole is uppermost. Take the relevant shroud and pull the end round the upper deadeye until reasonably taut and clamp in place with a spring clip close to the deadeye. Seize the threads together with a couple of turns between the clip and the deadeye, remove the clamp, finish the seizing as required, seal off with a spot of superglue and trim. Remove the shroud from the fixture, and the fixture from the lower deadeye, and repeat the process for

131

the remaining shrouds. Having assembled all of the deadeyes, the lanyards can now be rigged. The drawings show the procedure very clearly, but note that the view is from outboard the vessel and that the starting knot is inboard. Do not tie up the free end of the lanyard above the upper deadeye until all of the lanyards have been rigged. The tension can then be taken up and the spacing between deadeyes adjusted as required before the final tying up. The tension of the stays can now be finalised.

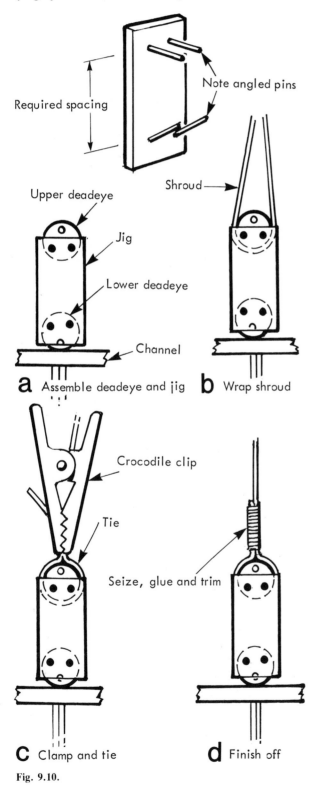

a Assemble deadeye and jig   **b** Wrap shroud

c Clamp and tie   **d** Finish off

Fig. 9.10.

When all lower masts have been so rigged, the tops and upper masts can be made and assembled.

Corel provide a turned stepped former around which one is invited to make three turns of 3 mm × 1 mm walnut strip, after soaking of course. That's a challenge for masochists only! I chickened out and used the fretsaw to cut rings from suitably thick material. Do a bit of forward checking at this point to determine how many holes are going to be needed in the floor of the top — it isn't too easy to put them in after the mast has been completely assembled. You need to jump about a bit from one drawing to another to determine what blocks are going to be needed where, and if indeed, holes are needed. The crowsfeet are, of course, taken from the main and foretops to their respective stays, and holes will be required for these, as well as fixings for the topsail and topgallant yard rigging. It will also be found easier to tie on blocks as you go, but do study the drawings carefully, one can be easily missed.

The lower mainmast and foremast caps have to be drilled and grooved to take the lower yard ties. This must be done before assembling the upper mast elements and tops to the lower mast assembly. It was found best to assemble the topmast and topgallant parts together as a unit, apply a coat of varnish and then bring together with the top and cap at the head of the lower mast.

The upper stays and shrouds are fixed in much the same manner as the lower ones but utilising a smaller pin jig for spacing the deadeyes.

The yards

These are made from dowel rod and, of course, have to be tapered. Mark the centre of the yard and the point at which the taper starts. The length to be tapered is then filed to first square, then octagonal, section. The yard can then be placed in the electric drill for finishing down to a tapered round section — an almost identical procedure to that adopted for the mast elements. When finished, apply any binding necessary and give a coat of varnish. It is safer to do this before hanging any blocks. Having gone to the trouble of clearing holes it would be a pity to inadvertently fill the hole with varnish.

Now is the time to finally make up your mind whether or not you are going to fit sails. The decision has to be made at this stage because it affects the positioning of the yards on the masts. If no sails are to be used, the yards are rigged in the lowered position almost down to the caps. Otherwise, as shown on the drawing, they are hoisted into their working position. Starting with the lower yards, I 'jury' rigged them in place in order to fit parrals, ties and lifts. Particular attention should be paid to rigging the foreyard jeers. You will remember that the knight or forecastle bitt was only temporarily fitted to the lower forecastle deck and should now be unshipped. Having fitted the ties and block, the jeers should be rigged from block to knight, the thread passing through the opening in the unfitted grating.

When this has been done, carefully avoiding any 'cross-over', the knight can be glued to the deck and when set, the halliard can be correctly tensioned. Only then, should the grating be fixed in place on the forecastle deck.

Ratlines

The ratlines are a right pain, but the agony can be lessened with a bit of thought. The application is relatively straightforward, a simple hitch around the left-hand outer shroud, a clove-hitch on all intermediate lines, and another simple hitch around the right-hand outer shroud. A touch of superglue on the two outer hitches finishes each step. It is important not to pull things up too tight or the shrouds will be pulled out of line. Incidentally, this is the one time it is not recommended to glue up the thread, it makes it too stiff to get the right tension. Also try not to induce any twist to the thread as you work, it will result in a deformed ratline (see Fig. 9.11). Not the easiest of things to avoid and not simple to correct. The only way I have had any success is to apply the inevitable superglue to the offending thread and very smartly stroke it into shape with a piece of polythene, but this is a case where prevention is definitely better than cure.

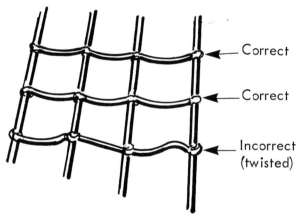

Fig. 9.11.

The planning aspect concerns the sequence in which you choose to do them. For most models, I reckon to complete the standing rigging, then do the foremast ratlines. The running rigging is then applied to the spritsail, the spritsail topsail and the foremast assembly. This gives a welcome break before going on to the mainmast ratlines. After the mainmast rigging is complete the same procedure is repeated for the mizen mast. The spacing between ratlines should be even, and this can be accomplished by a grid drawn on a piece of card which is then gently sprung in place behind the shrouds.

The recommendations regarding procedures and methods are a matter of personal choice. The main thing is to be adaptable, the best method is the one you are happiest with, and provided it gives the required result, there is no argument.

Sails

A brief word about sails. Brief, because I chose not to fit them and cannot therefore comment on any problems associated with their preparation or rigging. The various materials I have come across in the past have one failing — they don't hang right and look very artificial. The material supplied in the kit, alas, has the same out-of-balance weight/stiffness ratio. Even when furled, the folds are just not authentic in size and shape. To stiffen the sails into a 'wind-filled' shape results in an even more contrived appearance.

Running rigging

Not only the position of the yards alters if you choose to not fit sails, but the way some of the running rigging is fitted is also different. For instance, the sheets were normally shackled to the clewlines and hauled up to the blocks on the underside of the yard if the sails were taken down or furled and, in fact, the box art shows this quite clearly. Slack or hanging lines can also prove troublesome in making them look natural. Again, it helps if you avoid inducing twist when rigging them and certainly take trouble to properly seize the fixings rather than tie them. Provided that they are not too far away from a natural curve, they can be wiped with PVA adhesive and stroked into shape. The anchor ropes are typical offenders, being of heavier size thread they tend to have a mind of their own when it comes to which way they want to hang.

Once the rigging has been completed, all the belaying points should be provided with rope coils or 'falls'. If you make plain coils of thread, on a simple four-pin jig for instance, when you hang them they won't look right.

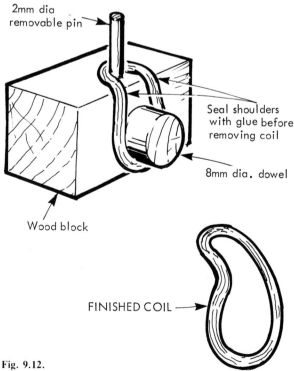

Fig. 9.12.

133

It is much better to make a jig that enables the coils to be pre-shaped for dropping over the tops of the belaying pins (see Fig. 9.12). Wind the thread haphazardly for the 'natural' look and finish off at the bottom with a touch of superglue, and another touch on each of the shoulders. This helps retain the shape of the finished coil. Whilst the sketch shows a jig for only one coil, in practice it is easier to make provision for say a dozen coils on the same jig. When you are finally satisfied that everything else has been done, the final task is to give the Roman soldiers their spears.

It is a good idea to look at the model carefully and regularly over a period of 7 to 10 days. It is surprising what will have been missed; an unvarnished area, a thread end untrimmed etc. The major omissions are, of course, mostly discovered when showing the model to a visitor.

Conclusions

Time and care can result in a very satisfying and attractive model. Corel have provided a high quality kit which, in today's market place, must be considered good value for money. Not a model for building on the dining room table, and probably not the wisest choice for the absolute first-timer, but certainly a project to give many hours of enjoyment and reward to the patient modelmaker.

CHAPTER 10

The Spanish Man-of-War
San Juan Nepomuceno

The *San Juan Nepomuceno* finished model.

The *San Juan Nepomuceno* was a 2700 ton Spanish man-of-war built in Santander in 1765. It carried 74 guns and a crew of 500 men, acquitting itself well at the battle of Trafalgar under the command of Brigadier Don Cosme Damien Churruca. The Brigadier yielded only under vastly superior fire from the English fleet and having sustained over 400 dead and wounded. He had continued to command even though he had lost a leg earlier in the engagement.

The Kit

Artesania Latina have packed everything into a compartmented styrene box fitted with four individual trays to accommodate the various brass, wood and diecast fittings for this 910 mm long model. Frames are routed out and it is only necessary to cut through small linking tabs to separate the parts from the boards. Thinner ply parts are diestamped in the more conventional manner. Dowel rods for masts and spars are not ready tapered, but it was nice to see that the colour of the various pieces matched throughout. The dowelling, and indeed all strip material, was bagged in clear plastic.

Prior to starting construction, it is well to check the contents, at least as far as the unique fittings are concerned, just in case an odd item is missing.

Building the hull

Having cut out all the frames and false keel, it is absolutely essential to relieve all slot widths for assembling the frames to the keel. The ends of the slots should also be squared out to ensure that the tops of the frames can line up with the deck levels on the keel. Note that if the slot fits are too tight the result could be considerable distortion of the final hull assembly. The internal corners of some frames should be squared out to facilitate later deck planking.

Before making the final assembly, three significant points should be noted. Firstly, Artesania do not provide materials or design for a stand. It is therefore quite useful to trace the lower shape of the appropriate frames to form the basis of a cradle design. The longitudinal strips need a certain amount of coercion to slide through the slots in the frames. A short 30-degree lead in on the ends of the strips helps a lot, but even so, a light mallet to drive them through makes life a lot easier.

Before proceeding further, it is as well to check that the top edge of the lower strip is not above the main deck level. Should that be the case, it should be pared down at this stage before starting to lay the second gun deck planking. The quality of the strip wood supplied is very high, but there are inevitably some very small variations in thickness, probably no more than 0.15 mm. Before planking the lower decks, it is wise to select material of the same actual thickness, because even a small amount like 0.15 mm can take some getting off in the restricted space available.

Procedures for deck laying and edging are quite straightforward and, after fitting the ply bulwarks, you can consider starting to plank the hull. The edges of the frames should, by this time, have been bevelled and shaped to follow the longitudinal lines of the ship. There is quite severe bending to cater for, particularly under the stern moulding, and considerable care should be taken in this area to ensure that the frame edges do have the correct contours. You should not lose sight of the fact that the quarter galleries also locate here and it is essential to provide adequate seating for these pieces, particularly at the lower scroll end. Obviously, it is as well to periodically check this point as planking proceeds.

The planking starts immediately below the bulwarks and continues for eleven planks downwards towards the keel. The first seven are relatively easy to apply, although some extra attention must be paid to those that curve around the bow moulding. Having said that, I did not find it necessary to soak or steam the planks, although the radius concerned must have been on the borderline of severity for a broken plank. If you don't wish to take the risk, then the following procedure may be adopted for the last four planks which have to sustain a very severe bend under the stern.

First I selected the actual thinnest of the 2.0 mm strips supplied. As I mentioned earlier, a 0.15 mm variation does not seem much, but it represents a 7.5% reduction in cross-sectional area, which is quite helpful when bending. The ends of the strips were soaked for a couple of hours and then a series of half-depth saw cuts were made 4 mm apart over a strip length of about 60 mm. White PVA adhesive was rubbed into the saw cuts before pinning and gluing to the hull and strengthened the whole assembly in the 'bend' area.

At this point, I have to say that too late, I was given an Amati plank nipper which, in fact, does put a cut to about half a plank thickness. Having tried quite a number of these so-called modelling aids over the years, I have found the majority to be gimmicky and a waste of money. However, in this case, this particular tool works very well and I am sure that it will prove most useful in projects to come. Although I had by now got over the worst of the bending problems, those bends remaining were better accomplished using the Amati tool. The remaining basic planking is done from the keel upwards to the bottom of the eleventh plank previously laid. Several triangular areas needed to be left for the later fitting of 'stealers' so that not too much distortion of plank is necessary. It is helpful if the width of these triangular gaps is arranged to be just a little less than the 5 mm strip width. When planking, I find it useful not to drive the pins fully home in order to make their removal that much easier before rubbing down. Having once ripped the pads of my fingers during this task, I take no chances on a repeat performance.

The second planking of 0.6 mm × 7.0 mm wide strips is put on with contact adhesive. For the most part this

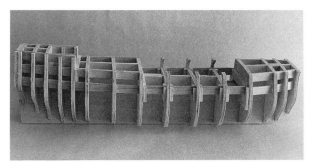

The completed basic structure prior to mounting the stern and bow mouldings and shaping the edges of the frames.

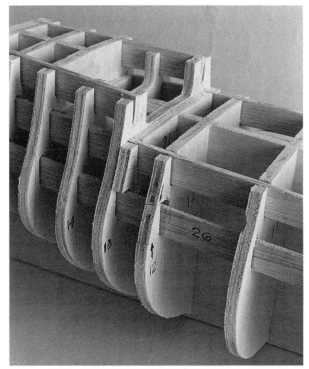

The slot in frame 12 was one width out of position. The arrows indicate where the frame had to be cut to rectify the problem in order to correctly assemble ply strip No. 26.

The bow moulding in place. Note the extensions of frames above the planked lower deck. These are very vulnerable during the ongoing hull construction and care should be taken not to break them off.

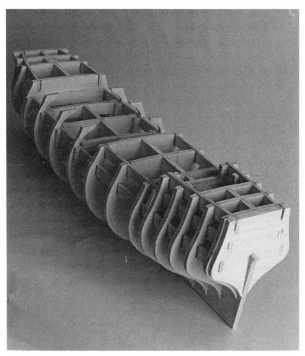

The completed basic hull framework. The design provides an extremely strong structure with minimal risk of distortion during the planking process.

The stern moulding in position and planked prior to shaping the edges of the frames.

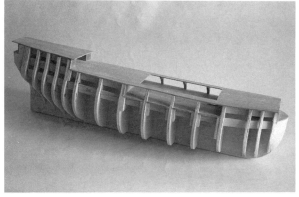

The framed hull with decks laid and ready for planking.

137

follows the line of the original planking, but beware, the 0.6 mm thick strips don't take the bends quite so well at 7.0 mm width and some cutting and spiling was found to be necessary. Railing up the bulwarks is relatively problem-free, although you should realise that the pillars that support the forward rail have two holes in them. These are not referred to in the instructions and certainly should be drilled before assembly.

Opening out holes for gunports can be a bit tricky. Firstly, they must be positioned in the right place, so accurate marking out is essential, particularly for those ports on the second gun deck adjacent to the arched upper deck supports. A 9 mm square hole cut in a piece of thick plasticard makes an ideal template, the actual marking out can then be confined to one corner of each port and the template used to draw the square in the right position. Probably the easiest way to make each opening is to drill all round with a 1.5 mm diameter drill and cut through with a heavy duty scalpel. Some ports will be found to coincide with the basic hull frames. Here it is necessary to chisel the frame away back to a sufficient depth. As to the ports themselves, the frames nearly all needed some doctoring in order to freely assemble the port lids prior to mounting in the hull.

The castings for the quarter galleries and transom should be checked for a good close fit against the hull. The transom needs to be curved and I found this was best done by supporting the outer edges using a couple of matchsticks and gently rolling the back face with a rolling pin, remembering to put a piece of greaseproof paper between the casting and the rolling pin. These parts are best painted before assembly and the 40/60% gold/black paint mix suggested in the instructions is just right. When thoroughly hardened off, the raised details can then be dry-brushed with gold to highlight the ornamentation.

The head timbers and rails are represented by 2 mm square brass section which makes this usually difficult part of the building process comparatively simple. It is

Planking at the stern demanded the insertion of three stealers each side.

The curve around the bow is on the borderline of severity for a broken plank.

The basic planking completed with rudder and stern diecastings assembled.

still a long and painstaking task, but at least you can keep adjusting the bends and overall shape until it comes right. Make port and starboard items simultaneously to achieve a balanced shape and don't forget to use the figurehead as a reference for positioning the lower rails. It is a good idea to make the channels in pairs to attain identical hole positions side to side, also to leave the outer edging off until after the chains and deadeyes have been assembled. The back edges should be shaped to provide total contact with the hull before fixing in place.

The hull is now ready for varnishing, but before you start beavering away with the bristles or airbrush, a word of advice. If the hull is turned upside down, all the gunports drop open and a shower of dust, chips and shavings fall out. A judicious application of the vacuum cleaner using the smallest nozzle attachment will suck out the remainder of the muck and dust. Putting the hull the right way up, use a small paint brush to disturb the remainder of the surface dust, again using the vacuum cleaner to take it away. Having got the hull totally clear of dust and dirt, you are now posed with a real major question. On what do you support the hull? Answer, you have to build some sort of stand.

Making and assembling the deck fittings provided a pleasant change from the heavier carpentry of building the hull proper. Do remember, however, to remove varnish from those areas on deck to which fittings have to be glued. For added strength, I pushed pins into the bottom of the bowsprit knightheads and the pin-rail supports. A hole, 0.75 mm diameter, in the deck to accept the pins when fixing in place gives a much stronger joint, and one that you will be grateful for when you start rigging (see Figs 10.1 and 10.2). I deliberately chose to leave the assembly of the chainplates and deadeyes until later. It always seems easier to get the

correct angle on the chains after you have stepped the masts and can run a false shroud from the tops down to the channels.

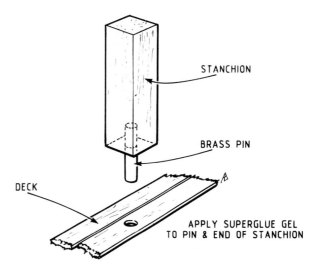

Fig. 10.1.

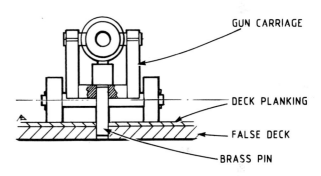

Fig. 10.2.

The completed hull ready for the assembly of deck fittings.

A small point about the hatch gratings. Some of the combed strips are thinner than others, so it is a good idea to go through them all and grade them with regard to their thickness. Any drastically thin pieces assembled alongside normal ones stand out like a sore thumb.

Masts and spars

It is most important to refer to the cutting list in the instruction manual before cutting the dowel rod supplied to the required length. If you don't you will be in danger of not having enough timber. To avoid confusion, I found it simplest to take each piece of dowel in turn and cut it to make up the lengths of the masts or spars specified for that piece, labelling each length for later identification. The rods are not tapered in any way, so considerable filing is necessary before spinning and sanding. I keep an old stand-mounted electric drill for this and it works very well. One point to watch, however, is that the sanding is thus obviously across the grain. After removing from the drill, the mast or spar should be longitudinally sanded for final finishing. It will be realised at this point that it is not wise to use a sandpaper with too coarse a grade whilst spinning as the resultant 'rings' are very hard to remove (see Fig. 10.3).

The photographs in the instruction manual are very clear as to the assembly of the various masts and spars, but even so, there are a few points to watch. The central yard reinforcements can be a bit awkward to fit, and I found it easiest to fit the initial strip on every yard first then the second on every yard and so on. Each strip was fixed with superglue gel along one edge to attain position and then with PVA under the remainder. The 0.6 mm planking can be taped or bound round the spar until dry which, I found, was just about the time the last spar had been planked. Each main top features a rear handrail and supporting pillars. The assembly needs to be done using

superglue gel, but it is essential that the length of each pillar in the assembly be absolutely identical or a weak joint will result.

Once the masts have been stepped, the chains and deadeyes can be assembled. A false shroud run from the relevant top to the channels will provide a correct line for fixing the chains. Make sure that the three holes in each deadeye are properly cleared out and positioned in the correct attitude (see Fig. 10.4). A spot of superglue will fix the chain to the notch in the edge of the channel until chains have been assembled and the outer edging strip fixed in place.

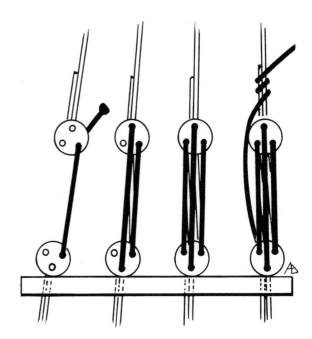

SEQUENCE FOR RIGGING LANYARDS.
NOTE RELATIVE POSITIONS OF DEADEYES.

Fig. 10.4.

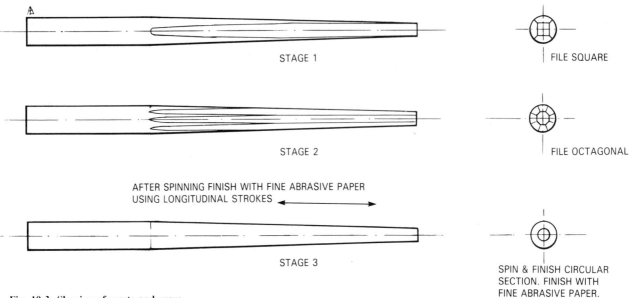

STAGE 1

STAGE 2

AFTER SPINNING FINISH WITH FINE ABRASIVE PAPER
USING LONGITUDINAL STROKES

STAGE 3

FILE SQUARE

FILE OCTAGONAL

SPIN & FINISH CIRCULAR
SECTION. FINISH WITH
FINE ABRASIVE PAPER.

Fig. 10.3. Shaping of masts and spars.

The mizen shrouds, deadeyes and lanyards.

The main and mizen tops.

The standing rigging

The bowsprit is assembled and rigged first, and the main point to watch is that the bobstays are not pulled up too tight. In fact, the lanyards can be left slack until the forestays are rigged and the tension balanced out to avoid distorting the bowsprit. The sequence of rigging on the plans suggests that the lower shrouds be set up next, before the various stays. I chose to reverse this sequence because the width of the shrouds on this particular model severely restrict access to the centre regions between the masts. Even with small hands or long fingers, the task of rigging the stays is easier if done first (see Fig. 10.5).

The shrouds should be set up starting with the forward starboard pair on the foremast, then the forward port pair and so on. This permits a constant balance of tension and helps avoid pulling the mast out of line. I

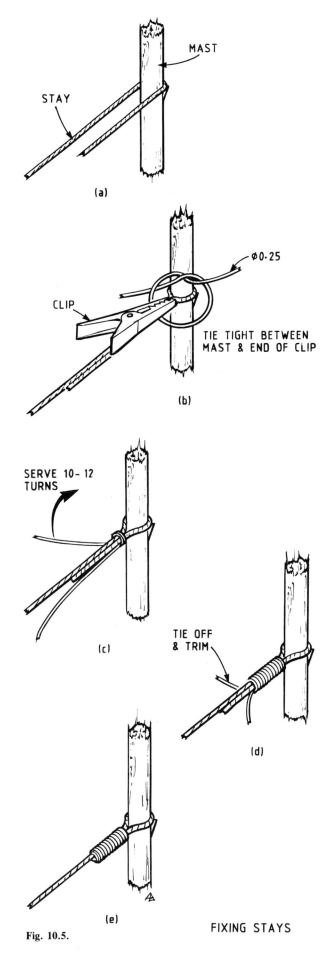

Fig. 10.5.

FIXING STAYS

141

like to apply a fair tension to shrouds, to first give strength to the overall system and secondly, to make the application of ratlines more straightforward. The ratlines do have to be rigged I'm afraid, and this is the time to do them, before any other rigging gets in the way. It is quite a formidable task on this model involving some 1500 knots and quite a few hours' work. In spite of several 'aids' to rigging ratlines, and I think I've probably tried most of them, I have to say that the best, and the most effective, way is to rig them on the ship, one at a time (see Figs 10.6 and 10.7). Use the natural twist of the thread to try and simulate the sag between each shroud and apply a touch of superglue or acrylic varnish to each knot as you go. Constantly check to ensure that the outer shrouds are not being 'pulled in' by overtightening the ratlines. A useful tool to trim the ends off is a pair of nail clippers, they permit a very close cut to the sealed knot at each end.

The back stays can now be rigged and the mizen mast boom and gaff assembled.

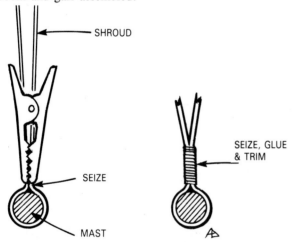

Fig. 10.6. RIGGING SHROUDS TO MASTS

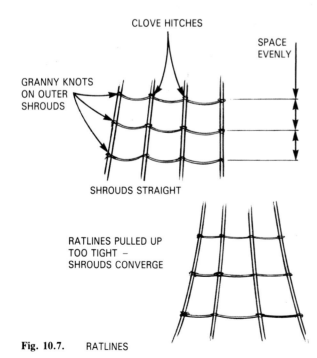

Fig. 10.7. RATLINES

Note the three arrows indicating the arched deck supports. These must be considered when marking out the position of the gun ports. They should be sufficiently clear to enable the gun to centralise within the port.

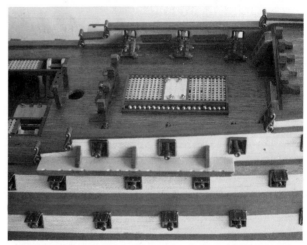

The main main bitts and pin rail. Note spacing of guns between shroud positions.

The stern and quarter galleries are painted before assembly. Raised decoration is dry-brushed in gold.

The figurehead and head rails. The 2mm square section brass used for the rails are more easily persuaded to shape than wood.

The quarter galleries.

The forecastle deck with capstan and belfry.

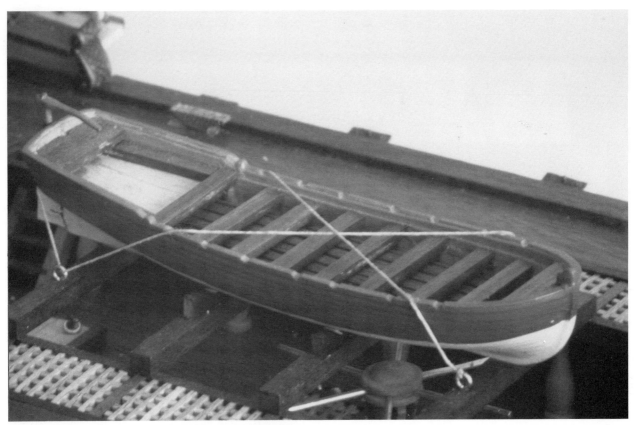

The ship's boat. A diecast shell with wooden interior fitting out.

Sails

It is a personal thing with me, but I feel that sails on some static full-hulled models look wrong. The material is often not of the correct area/weight ratio and therefore never hangs right. This is not a criticism of Artesania — in fact, the sail plans and methods of making them are as good as I've seen in a kit. But it does raise a point for consideration by all kit manufacturers; why not show correct rigging details for both conditions, with sails and without? I would guess modelmakers fall about fifty/fifty for and against sails, so why not try to please us all?

Conclusions

A kit full of good quality materials and excellent manual instructions and photographic guide. Drawings are exceptionally well draughted and everything is there to produce a most satisfying model.

CHAPTER 11

The American
U.S.S. Constellation

The finished model

The Kit

Artesania have put a lot of thought into the way they market their products. The packaging is basically a compartmented polystyrene box and with removable trays for supplying and storing the many smaller items.

Three double-sided sheets of plans support two extremely well-printed instruction manuals. The smaller booklet contains the instruction text in four languages

and, by the use of graphic symbols and a conventional numbering system, indicates which part is being considered, whether it is to be made, or is supplied in the kit. It also advises the tools to be used and the type of adhesive to be employed. The larger of the two manuals contains a parts list, again in four languages, a list of those pieces that have to be cut from strip stock, how long, how many and from what basic size and, most helpful to the novice and experienced builder alike, a series of 123 stage-by-stage photographs each cross-referenced back to the instructions and parts list. The overall length of the model finishes up at 1010 mm.

Building the hull

The first stage is to assemble the 'frames' to the false keel. Each of these twenty frames have been routed to shape in 6 mm ply and a fretsaw is needed to separate them from the boards provided. The routed shapes were very good and a minimum of cleaning up was required. The frames are halved into the false keel and it is most important not to have the joints too tight or, on this length of false keel, a bend will be induced. However, once the lower decks have been assembled and the inner midships section fixed into place, the whole structure is immensely strong. (Fig. 11.1).

It was at this juncture (stage 8) that if I had used a little more foresight, I could have saved some later problems. It is not until stage 52 that you are advised by the instructions to cut and line the gunports. I can tell you that it is far from easy to cut and finish the six midships ports and starboard ports, particularly those below the forward and aft main decks, at that later stage. It is even more difficult to secure the guns themselves (stage 81) and certainly, if I ever make this model again, my records will remind me to try and fathom out a method whilst still at stage 8, even to the point of fitting further gun bases and assembling gun barrels only, similar to the means already adopted at stage 15 (Fig. 11.2).

The hull is double-planked, first in pine and then secondly, after fitting bulwarks, in walnut with a band of mukali. Planking is very straightforward with a minimum number of stealers to fit. The curves of the hull are, for the most part, fairly gentle and whilst it was necessary to well soak the planks to flow around the semi-circular stern, steaming was not needed. An Amati nipper would be really ideal. Preparing the hull for

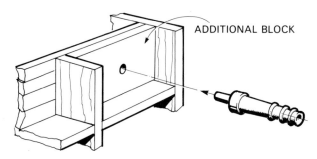

Fig. 11.2. Alternative method of fixing midship guns.

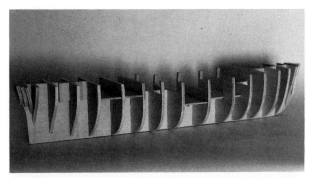

The basic structure: the frames assembled to the false keel together with the lower decks.

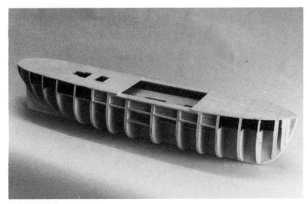

The fore and aft decks in place. It is at this stage thought should be given to the later assembly of the midship guns.

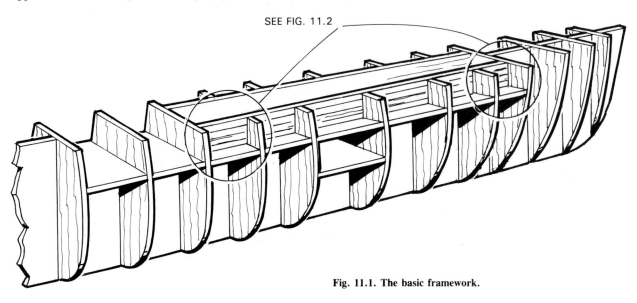

Fig. 11.1. The basic framework.

The hull construction complete ready for the second planking. Care is needed to attain a good curve around the stern to match the segmented rails supplied.

fitting of the stem, stern post and keel needs care and patience if the stem, particularly, is to fit well. When satisfied with the fit, each part was both pinned and glued to the hull.

Lining the edges of the decks, fitting hatchcombings and rails followed. The rails around the stern comprised several sectored pieces cut from semi-stamped board (Fig. 11.3).

Getting a smooth inside curve to match into the longer side rails, and match for thickness, is quite a task. Success at this point is also very dependent on how good a radius the upper edge of the stern has adopted. I found

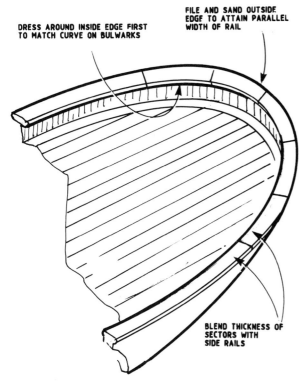

DRESS AROUND INSIDE EDGE FIRST
TO MATCH CURVE ON BULWARKS

FILE AND SAND OUTSIDE
EDGE TO ATTAIN PARALLEL
WIDTH OF RAIL

BLEND THICKNESS OF
SECTORS WITH
SIDE RAILS

Fig. 11.3. The stern rail.

that a small cylindrical grinding wheel in my electric hand drill was most useful to blend all the pieces together. I found it better to make the assembly adjacent to the anchor bitts before fixing to the hull, rather than as directed in the instructions (Fig. 11.4).

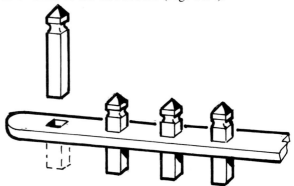

Fig. 11.4. Make sub-assembly before fitting.

At this stage it is as well to paint the white band around the hull, also the two quarter galleries with at least one coat of paint. To apply paint, after fitting the rubbing strakes would have been a far more delicate job, whereas the strakes themselves would now clearly define the white band. Making the head timbers and rails was probably the most taxing part of the whole project. The timbers were pre-cut parts and did not present too much of a problem. The rails, however, are specified to be made from 2 mm × 2 mm walnut strip and bending these to shape proved nigh on impossible and ultimately I cut them from larger stock.

We come now to stage 52, cutting and lining the gunports as mentioned earlier (Fig. 11.5). There are three major points to consider here. One, be extremely accurate with the marking out. Two, make sure that all tools used are properly sharpened and three, ensure that all ports are finally the same size. Considering each point in turn; the marking out is self explanatory, but a medium sized pair of dividers is a most valuable aid. Cutting the gunports obviously has to be done from the outside, thus tools need to be very sharp so as not to cause breakout as they penetrate the inboard surface. The instructions recommend the use of a 1.5 mm diameter drill to cut out the ports. Do not be tempted to use a larger drill to save time; consider 1.5 mm to be an absolute maximum size.

Having fitted the hand rails to the tops of the bulwarks, the white band is painted *before* fitting the strakes around the hull sides.

147

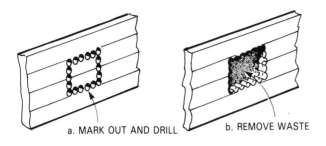

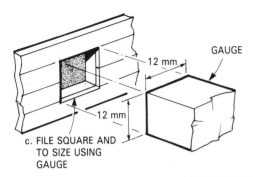

a. MARK OUT AND DRILL

b. REMOVE WASTE

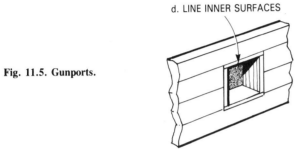

GAUGE

12 mm

12 mm

c. FILE SQUARE AND
TO SIZE USING
GAUGE

d. LINE INNER SURFACES

Fig. 11.5. Gunports.

Having removed the bulk of the material by joining up a series of 1.5 mm diameter holes all round each port, it now comes to filing to final shape and size. The bottom edge of each port has to be level with the waterways running round the edges of the deck and particular attention needs to be paid to the midships section mentioned earlier, where you are bridging what is, in effect, a cavity wall. To get all ports the same size I used a piece of wood cut to 12 mm square as a plug gauge, constantly offering it up until the required shape and size was attained. After I had lined each of the gunports, I applied a second coat of white paint, steering marginally away from the rubbing strakes. When this was thoroughly dry, the entire hull was given several coats of satin varnish.

To keep the hull steady in order to work on it in the fashion described above, it was necessary to hold it by clamping the keel in the soft jaws of the vice. (This will test just how good you have fixed it to the bottom of the hull!) From now on, though, it really does need a stand, or protruding pieces like boat davits and braces will soon get knocked off. As can be seen from the accompanying photographs I kept my stand fairly plain and simple, and made it to comprise a rectangular base and a pair of turned pedestals. Two screws from the underside of the base through the pedestals and well into the false keel were more than adequate for the job.

Deck fittings

I find that the making of pin rails, hatches etc., a very relaxing interlude after the 'heavy' construction of the hull proper. There really is not too much to say about this stage of the project except that it is far more convenient to fix the eyebolts each side of the gunports before fixing the deck fittings in place. The gunport covers are designated to be made by joining edge-to-edge three pieces of 5 mm × 2 mm each 16 mm long. I found it much easier to take three lengths of 5 mm × 2 mm × 500 mm long and glue them together to make

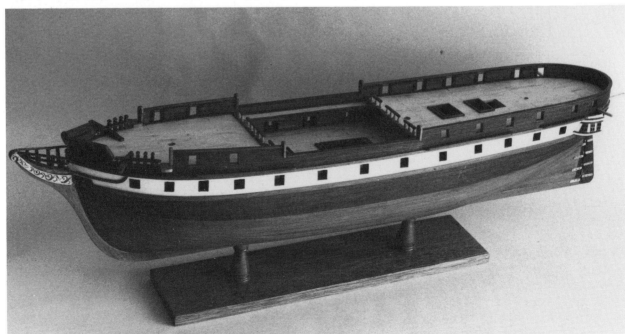

Strakes in position and the gunports cut and lined. Once the stem, stern post and keel have been fitted, the stand can be made to support the hull for further work.

a strip 15 mm × 2 mm × 500 mm long. Both wide faces were then sanded smooth and 16 mm lengths cut off to make each cover. (Fig. 11.6).

Fig. 11.6. Gunport covers.

The ship's boat is made from three diecastings, the hull shell, the seating and the rudder. I was not too happy with the seating piece and chose to discard it in favour of fitting the boat out in wood. Purely a personal choice and not meant to be a serious criticism.

Masts and spars

The drawings of each mast and its associated spars, supplemented by the photographs in the manual, were first class, showing clearly the position and type of blocks to be used. One word of warning though; pay particular attention to the 'Preparation of Parts' listing in the manual to ensure that you cut the various pieces of dowelling from the correct length of stock supplied. Failure to do so may well mean a trip to your local model shop. There is ample dowelling supplied in the kit, but you must cut it as instructed.

The mast caps are made in two sections, each with half holes to take the masts. These need adjusting both for size and position before assembly. I am in two minds about the use of two pieces to make these caps. On balance I think I would prefer to make them in one piece, although I would agree that without sharp drills you can easily finish with two bits anyway when the wood splits!

All masts, yards and spars have to be tapered and I used the well tried method of first filing the section square, then octagonal towards the smaller end, finally spinning them in my electric drill to finish them off to a tapered diameter (Fig. 11.7). It is not necessary to use a chuck key, the parts can be held quite satisfactorily just nipping them up by hand. That way you don't leave marks on the parts being finished. All yards are fitted out with stirrups, foot-ropes, pendants, blocks etc.,

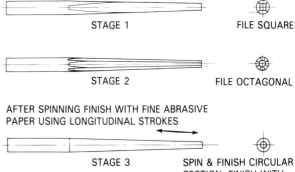

STAGE 1   FILE SQUARE

STAGE 2   FILE OCTAGONAL

AFTER SPINNING FINISH WITH FINE ABRASIVE PAPER USING LONGITUDINAL STROKES

STAGE 3   SPIN & FINISH CIRCULAR SECTION. FINISH WITH

Fig. 11.7. Shaping of masts and spars. FINE ABRASIVE PAPER.

Deck fittings all in place and ready for masting. Whilst a little vulnerable at this stage, the gunport covers are more easily aligned now than later.

before assembly to their respective masts. This makes for much easier rigging later on. The actual assembly of the yards and masts is not difficult, but one or two points are worth mentioning. File flats on to masts and spars where it is necessary to fit hounds etc., this makes for a much stronger joint. At the outboard ends of several yards there is a hole drilled through to take subsequent running rigging. Such rigging will look better set up if these holes are relieved (Fig. 11.8). The same thing will apply to the holes through the upper masts.

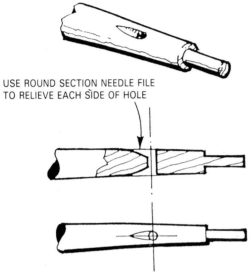

USE ROUND SECTION NEEDLE FILE TO RELIEVE EACH SIDE OF HOLE

Fig. 11.8.

Having completed all of the mast/spar assemblies give them a couple of coats of varnish before stepping masts to the hull, although it is better to leave the yards off until the ratlines have been rigged.

Rigging

The rigging is fairly extensive on this model, but with the aid of the rigging diagrams provided, the procedures are simplified, both with regard to where everything goes and, in what order. In fact, in my experience, the presentation of rigging information is as good as I have seen in any kit. Bearing in mind it is the rigging that deters many people from attempting this type of model, if Artesania were to extend this feature to their entire range, maybe more modellers would be tempted to have a go.

As mentioned previously, all the cordage provided in the kit is white and needs to be dyed before use, that for the standing rigging either dark brown or black and a lighter brown or tan for the running rigging. Washing and dyeing is a chore but it does have the advantage of providing a convenient opportunity to remove much of the natural stretch from the material. I usually wind the thread into a skein some 300 mm long and after the dyeing has been done I hang it up to dry with some weights on the bottom. This will take most of the stretch out of the thread and make it less 'lively' when actually rigging. Of course, you can always chicken out and buy

thread already coloured — but it will be a lot more expensive than a pot of dye.

The parts list tells you how long to cut each piece and the excellent diagrams show you where and when. Having cut a length I usually give it the PVA treatment which involves nothing more than pulling it through fingers modestly coated with PVA adhesive. This stiffens the thread, making it hang with a more natural look. It also lays all the ends of those very fine fibres to which dust particles like to cling. The initial rigging sets up shrouds and stays to the lower masts (Figs 11.9 and 11.10) and of course, ratlines, the main cause of 'Rigger's Remorse'. They have to be done at some time and to start at this stage at least gives a break whilst you later rig the upper masts.

It is the most tedious part of rigging and, being faced with twelve sets of shrouds to rattle down, many will be tempted (a) to put it off until later or, (b) try and evolve a quick way of doing them. The first option is definitely a mistake, the more rigging there is, the more it gets in the way of fingers and forceps. As to the second option,

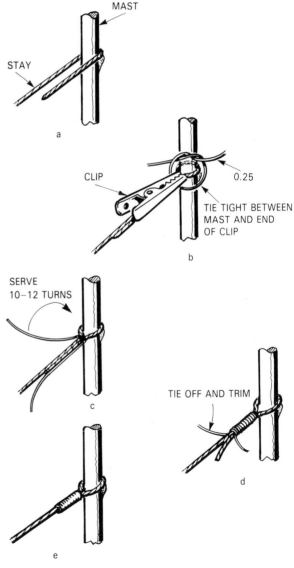

MAST

STAY

a

CLIP

0.25

TIE TIGHT BETWEEN MAST AND END OF CLIP

b

SERVE 10–12 TURNS

c

TIE OFF AND TRIM

d

e

Fig. 11.9. Fixing stays.

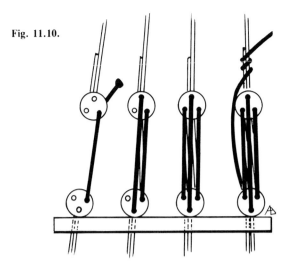

Fig. 11.10.

SEQUENCE FOR RIGGING LANYARDS.
NOTE RELATIVE POSITIONS OF DEADEYES.

many have tried to find a quick way and they, like myself, always come back to doing it properly, by tying them on. Not difficult, just a lot of knots, nearly 1500 in the case of the *Constellation*!

Space them out using a pair of dividers, a simple hitch or granny knot at each shroud, sealed off with a touch of superglue and the ratline is on. Trim very close at each end; a pair of nail clippers is ideal to make a neat job (Fig. 11.11).

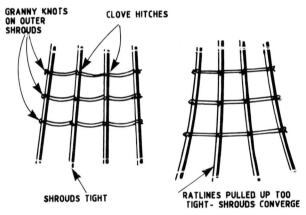

Fig. 11.11.

Once the lower shrouds have been completed, you have to move on to the shrouds for the upper masts. The futtock shrouds are rigged first since they secure the lower deadeyes on the tops for the lower mast shrouds. To make a neat job of this it is acceptable to lash a small spar or shear pole behind the lower shrouds and rig the futtock shrouds to it (Fig. 11.12). The upper shrouds are then rigged in a similar manner to those on the lower masts. Now you come again to the dreaded ratlines, not so many this time of course, and once they have been done, the standing rigging can be completed.

Your mind has to be made up at this juncture as to whether sails are to be fitted. The yards will be lowered to their respective tops if you decide to leave them off, as I did, rather than elevated to the position shown on the drawings (Fig. 11.13). Purely as a personal choice,

Fig. 11.12.

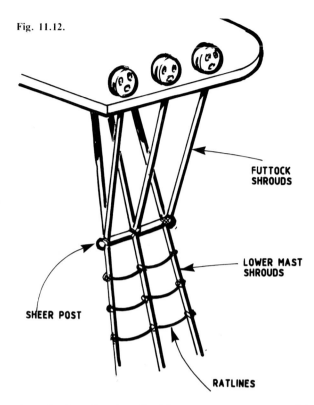

I rarely rig sails, since I seldom come across a material in a kit that looks or hangs right for my taste. Nonetheless, the kit does include material and comprehensive sail plans should your choice differ from mine.

Fig. 11.13. Yard positions on mast.

The yards can now be rigged to the mast and a start made on the running rigging. Again, follow the diagrams contained within the plans and, what at first appears to be a bit of a maze, will soon reveal itself to be quite straightforward and sensible. In fact, much can be learnt about rigging by studying the step-by-step diagrams laid out in the plans. Obviously, when tying off the deck end of any line, there will be considerable spare rope to be coiled up and hung on the belaying pin concerned (Fig. 11.14).

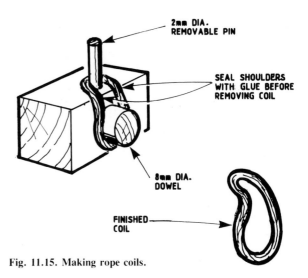

Fig. 11.15. Making rope coils.

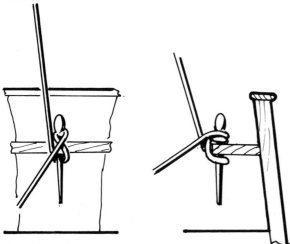

Fig. 11.14. Tying off.

It is equally obvious that it is not practical to do this as one would on the full-size vessel. Much better to tie off, trim close and make separate coils to hang on afterwards. To give the coils some semblance of hanging

right, I use a simple jig and make about a dozen at a time (Fig. 11.15).

Once the rigging has been completed, it only remains to rig the anchors and the ship's boat across the stern.

Conclusions

Artesania Latina are to be congratulated on their presentation, content and overall quality. It was a delight to build and I can't help feeling that I will be looking for similar standards in any future kit that I build.

Not a beginner's kit, but with a little experience one can make a very impressive model. Excellent value for money.

CHAPTER 12

The American Whaling Ship
Charles W. Morgan

The finished vessel, shown from the starboard side.

Designated a National Historic Landmark in 1967, the whaling ship *Charles W. Morgan* is the sole survivor of the great 19th-century whaling fleets of New Bedford and Nantucket.

Built at the Hillman brothers' shipyard on the Acushnet River at New Bedford, Massachusetts, the *Morgan* was launched in July 1841. Few could have foretold the success and reputation she would achieve during her lifetime, and none could have foreseen that over one hundred and forty years later she would be lying in retirement at Mystic Seaport, Connecticut, annually attracting thousands of visitors who look on her in much the same way as the British look on the *Cutty Sark*.

She was named after her launch for the principal owner Charles Waln Morgan, a Quaker businessman, who was deeply involved in whaling and who owned several other ships. The *Morgan* cost over 50,000 dollars to build, but it is interesting to note that the value of cargo from her first voyage far exceeded her cost. She returned home for the last time in May 1921 having completed her thirty-seventh voyage, some of them lasting as long as four years. A remarkable working life by any standard for a wooden ship, having survived everything the seas could throw at her around Cape Horn and the grip of the ice in the Bering Sea. Her crew, on two trips, defied the traditional 'Jonah' of having a woman on board when Lottie Church, the Captain's wife, signed on as assistant navigator. Also on these voyages, and several previous ones, the Second Mate was one George Parkin Christian, the great-grandson of Fletcher Christian who led the mutiny on the *Bounty*.

Strangely, not much is known about the vessel's appearance during the early years and certainly there is no pictorial record as to what she looked like when new. Changes that took place during her lifetime are documented in the various ship's logs but unfortunately, the handwriting and spelling is so poor as to make the entries indecipherable. Nonetheless, a grand old ship, whose every timber oozes history, legend and drama.

The Kit

This kit by Artesania Latina is one of the older items in their range, but this does not detract from the possibility of building a very high standard of model. The six sheets of plans are based on restoration drawings provided by the Mystic Seaport Museum and in terms of detail and clarity it would be nitpicking, generally speaking, to offer criticism. The strip material was of high quality and there was plenty of it. Fittings were of a good standard with blocks and deadeyes made of boxwood. There are only just enough, so keep them safe until actually needed.

The rigging thread supplied has a nice 'lay' and does look pretty much like rope. However, it is very white and should be dyed dark brown or black for the standing rigging and a lighter shade for the running rigging. Previous experience leads me to advise doing this fairly early in the project. Wash all thread anyway, regardless of whether it is dyed or not, and hang it somewhere out of the way to dry.

Before washing, rewind into skeins about 250 mm long. This helps prevent tangles and makes it more convenient to hang weights on whilst drying to stretch the natural 'give' of the thread out before use.

The parts list and instruction booklet provided are very good and I would recommend that the sequence of working is followed fairly closely. Artesania have obviously done their homework when building the prototypes and ironed out the assembly pitfalls. Every detail is numbered and cross-referenced and I found identification and building most straightforward.

Here then is a kit that will provide many hours of rewarding modelmaking, resulting in a model of a subject just a little bit different. At 780 mm long, it is large enough to get down to fairly fine detail without causing too much eyestrain, yet not so big as to be a domestic embarrassment. The completed model will obviously benefit from a dust-free environment and a formal glass case or an enclosed cavity amongst built-in furniture is really a must.

One final point before I get on to other matters; there is no stand provided in the kit. Whatever means of mounting you decide upon for the final presentation, one thing is certain — you will definitely need support for

Masts up and standing rigging completed.

the model during construction. I used a drawer front and handle described later — my wife's brilliant idea.

The construction of the hull

The construction of the basic hull is extremely simple and straightforward, but care must be taken to ensure that the frames are assembled squarely to the false keel with the top edges of all parts in line. In my kit, the frames had been very accurately cut and no shaping prior to assembly was necessary. The slotted joints were a bit sloppy and several needed a little packing to maintain squareness while the glue dried. The addition of the reinforcing blocks at this stage strengthens up the entire structure. Make sure that all the parts are well glued and that nothing has moved before putting the assembly to one side. The instructions recommend that it be left for at least four hours to dry out. A lot depends on the adhesive used of course, but some of the later stages involved fairly arduous working and I took no chances, letting it lie for a couple of days.

Fitting the false deck requires a bit of care to attain symmetry and the recommendation to dry-fit the deck before using glue is a good one. Draw a line centrally down the deck, line it up on top of the frame assembly and temporarily secure it in position with three or four pins into the top of the false keel. Turn the whole thing over and, with a sharp pencil, mark the position of the keel and frames on to the underside of the false deck. Now remove the deck (and pins), and turn it over so that the pencil lines, now on top, become an excellent guide for alignment and placing of pins. The frames being of plywood, tend to soak up the glue. So, before permanently fitting the deck, I coated the edges of the frames

Off the starboard bow.

with adhesive and let it dry off for an hour.

Now apply glue to the top of the keel and to the frame tops on one side only, line up the deck and pin it as instructed. Because of the camber across the top of the frames, there will now be a gap between the frames on the unglued side and the underside of the deck into which you can introduce glue prior to completing the pinning. Again, it is worth letting the whole thing dry out before proceeding further.

The next stage is decidedly messy. The shaping of the edges of the frames and the reinforcing blocks at stem and stern is fundamental to successful planking and final shape. I removed the bulk of excess material with various shaped craft knives holding the hull in my lap. This was the only way that I could safely stabilise the model to work on it. Having got rid of most of the unwanted bits with the knife, the remainder can be sanded to shape. A short length of broom handle wrapped with coarse abrasive paper is a most useful tool. Generally, the instructions explain very well the finished requirements, but I would emphasise the need to keep a constant check on shape and symmetry. A short rule and a pair of dividers are ideal for this. By this time, you, and everything else, will be absolutely covered with wood shavings and dust and your partner's tolerant attitude to modelmaking will be tested to the full.

So to the planking. The first covering is in limewood and the method described in the instruction book is quite comprehensive. I would add a few comments which I feel may be of help to those who haven't done too much planking. Having laid the top two planks each side starting 10 mm down from the edge of the false deck, it is then necessary to lay the 'master plank'. The position of this is described as being about halfway down the hull. Bearing in mind its importance to the rest of the planking procedure, I found it paid to be a little more precise in deciding on its placing (see Fig. 12.1). To keep the run as natural as possible, I measured five planks' width from below the first two strips at frame number six and set the top of the master plank in this position. It is worth gluing five short pieces of strip edge to edge as a gauge to ensure that the plank on the opposite side of the hull is on exactly the same level. It also means that when the space above each master plank is filled in, there are no awkward gaps left.

As to the shape of the planks themselves, it will be apparent that the distance along the edge of the frames from deck to keel is different at the bows and stern to what it is amidships (see Fig. 12.1). To assess the amount of taper that should be applied to each plank, measure the distance along the edge of frame No. 6 from the underside of the master plank to the keel and divide this by the width of the planking strips. This obviously tells you the number of planks needed for this part of the hull. Now measure the edge length at frames No.3 and 11, divide these lengths by the number of planks previously determined, to give the plank width at frames 3 and 11. Assume that the

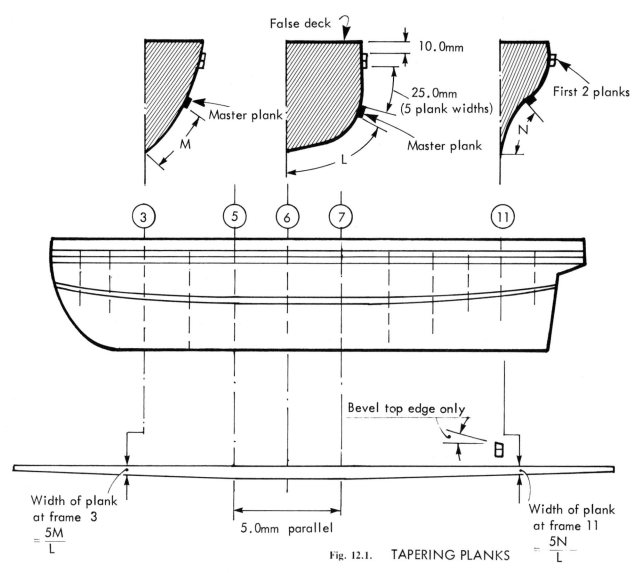

Fig. 12.1.   TAPERING PLANKS

width is constant between frames 5 and 7, and, as shown in Fig. 12.1, you now have a good guide as to the shape of each plank. Use the razor plane to bevel the top straight edge only, for good edge-to-edge abutment. Prepare and fit one plank at a time, checking the length of the remaining edges at frames 3 and 11 and adjusting the tapers as necessary. Inevitably, if the planks are not to be overstressed and twisted as they follow the shape of the hull, you will finish up with several triangular gaps at stem and stern. Fill these in with 'stealers' after careful measurement and dry fitting.

A good rub down with fairly coarse grade garnet paper, followed by a couple of coats of sanding sealer, prior to finishing with finer grades of sandpaper, will provide a good surface for laying the top layer of planking later on. The instructions for planking the deck tend to be a little vague and pass the buck to the builder. Certainly, to get the best effect, one needs to cut each plank as a separate piece and as far as the caulking goes, my own preference is an extension of the thread method. But first, it does help if all the planks are the same length and to that end I made a simple jig as shown in Fig. 12.2, a piece of ply for the base and offcuts of limewood

from the hull planking are more than adequate. For use in conjunction with this, I made a 'plank' from 0.5 mm brass shim, again see sketch, with six holes each 0.5 mm diameter. Held in place on top of the wooden plank in the cutting jig, the hole positions can be transferred and marked with a sharp HB or B grade pencil onto the plank below.

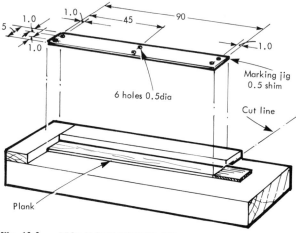

Fig. 12.2.   DECK PLANK MAKING JIG

Off the starboard quarter.

thread. Make sure that the thread is stuck firmly down to the deck all the way along, because if it isn't and you decide to leave it in place, when you come to sand the deck you will fur up the thread and it will look horrible.

If you decide to use the thread purely as a spacing aid, then the planks can be laid using a contact adhesive. The procedure is exactly the same as for leaving the thread in, but of course it isn't wise to glue it in. At this scale, I think the shadow cast by the gap that is left after removing the thread gives a more natural appearance than the more contrasting effect of the thread left in. Just a matter of personal choice. The other method mentioned using a felt-tipped pen is one that is fraught with danger. One unsealed grain fibre in the edge of a plank will permit the fluid to spread itself with disastrous results. If you don't have the patience for either of the thread methods, you would be better to consider the soft sharp pencil rather than the felt-tipped pen.

I managed to progress with no major problems to the second planking, which, because of the thinner material, is a little easier than the previous planking process. Carried out using contact adhesive, the pieces should be cut and tapered exactly as before, with the exception, of course, that it is not necessary to bevel the edges. The next stage to cause a bit of concern was the preparation of the rails on the bulwarks. The curve around the bows is quite vicious and no amount of soaking and heating had the required effect. To get around the problem, I took three lengths of 3 mm × 1 mm and carefully slit them down the middle to give me six lengths of 1.5 mm × 1 mm. Turning the boat upside down I traced around the tops of the bulwarks, transferring the curved shape onto a piece of paper. Placing this on a convenient offcut of floorboard, I arranged a series of panel pins 3 mm inside and parallel to the line (see Fig. 12.3). Taking three of the aforementioned strips, I glued the 1.5 mm wide edges, laminated them together and bent the whole around the pins, adding a series of pins to the outside of the curve to hold position while drying. Released after 24 hours, the result was excellent.

The use of thread for the caulking is, in my opinion, an effective way of producing a good result. You can either leave the thread in place or, as I did, remove it after the planks have all been positioned and the glue has dried. If you choose to leave the thread in place, I would recommend that you use white PVA to fix the planks. Position one entire row, coat a length of button thread (not cotton) with glue, lay it against the edge of the fixed row of planking and lay the next row tight up against the

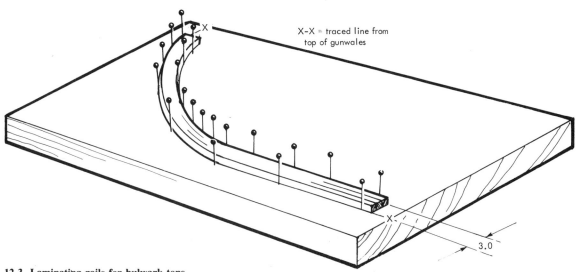

X-X = traced line from top of gunwales

3.0

Fig. 12.3. Laminating rails for bulwark tops.

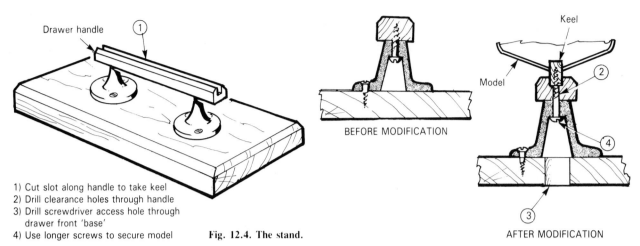

1) Cut slot along handle to take keel
2) Drill clearance holes through handle
3) Drill screwdriver access hole through
   drawer front 'base'
4) Use longer screws to secure model

Fig. 12.4. The stand.

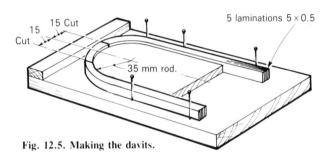

BEFORE MODIFICATION

AFTER MODIFICATION

The fitting of the stem, keel and rudder post is worthy of mention, not so much because of the difficulties involved technically, but to stress that patience in shaping and dry-fitting until a perfect match with the hull is attained is essential if these features are not going to appear as three separate pieces just stuck on. Because of the method I chose for making a stand (described later), I reinforced the fixing of the keel by introducing three 1 in × No. 4 countersunk brass woodscrews, equally spaced down the length of the hull. Now is the time to give an all-over final rub down prior to varnishing. Avoid the use of sanding sealer which, being a cellulose preparation, might adversely affect the contact adhesive used for the final planking. A wipe over with a piece of rag *dampened* with white spirit is adequate to pave the way for the first coat of matt varnish. I applied five coats in all, lightly rubbing down between coats. The result is a very attractive eggshell-like sheen. It is very convenient to use the drying time between coats to make the stand.

As stated earlier, one of the shortcomings of the kit is that no stand is provided. Certainly some means of stable support is necessary for the continuation of building, and a visit to the local DIY store solved the problem. One fancy drawer front for a kitchen cabinet, one handle, wooden, of reasonable quality, suitably modified (see Fig. 12.4) and voilà, one very acceptable stand.

Having got the hull mounted, it is now possible to proceed with the remainder of the posts, stanchions and channels. But first, those davits. I quickly decided to discard those supplied with the kit due to the fact that none of them were of adequate width and made my own from odd lengths of mukali strips from the scrap box. As it happened, there was enough deck planking material left over in the kit, but it was an ideal way to use up some shorter lengths left from a previous project. I made a former jig similar to that used for making the bulwark rails, but in this instance, formed a complete arch from which could be cut two davits (see Fig. 12.5). Although, as can be seen from the sketch, the initial curve over the top of the arch is a radius, when cut to make the two items, the natural spring in the wood, although

laminated, opens the radius out to form a curve that is just right.

Fig. 12.5. Making the davits.

The bowsprit

Artesania suggest a novel way of tapering masts and spars. A carpenter's plane is wedged between the knees or thighs and the dowel drawn across the upturned sole of the plane in order to produce a taper of the size required. I gave it a try, but it soon became apparent that the method was not for me. I was going to be in need of a large supply of plasters and the *Morgan* was going to feature a somewhat bloodstained bowsprit. I returned, therefore, to my own preferred system of using a file to first quarter the section over the required length of taper, then 'eighth' it. Having left an extra 12 mm at the thick end, I then placed this in the chuck of an electric drill which is lightly but firmly gripped in the soft jaws of the vice. The mast or spar can now be rotated and with a piece of sandpaper (a quarter of a standard sheet), suitably folded and held between thumb and the first two fingers, the section of the mast can again assume circular shape. I have a gauge made from 0.5 mm brass sheet which has fifteen holes drilled in it, ranging in diameter from 1.0 mm to 8.0 mm in steps of 0.5 mm. This easily lets you see how much, and where, more material needs to be sanded off. Drawbacks to the method? Yes, you need to move the fingers along the rotating mast parallel to the axis or you could pull it out of the chuck. It is advisable to wear some sort of safety glasses, not so much in case of flying masts (or jibs), but the air expelled from the ventilation slots in the drill blows the dust around far and wide.

The next item to cause a little concern was the fitting of the anchor catheads. I found it easier to deviate from the sequence laid down in the instructions and wait until the forecastle was ready for fitting before putting them in place. Drill the hole for the spigots first, but don't fit the spigots until after the forecastle and catheads have been assembled.

Having done all this, I found that the hull could then be taken to completion with little trouble. Certainly, features like the hurricane house need careful fitting and not a little patience, but then, without those attributes you wouldn't be making the *Morgan* anyway.

The whaleboats

A little more research would have been in order; the boats portrayed in the plans are very basic and to my mind, spoil the ship for a ha'porth of tar. They offer a reasonable frame on which to build, so maybe a brief description of the traditional American whaleboat will help in deciding just how much detail needs to be put in to give some degree of authenticity.

In order to be able to quickly back off from the whale to avoid flukes or jaws, the boats were double-ended. Artesania have depicted the curve at each end admirably, but alas, no means of propulsion are mentioned. In fact, the boats were rowed 'single-banked', with two oars to larboard (port was not a term normally used amongst whalers) and three to starboard. Each oar was handled by one man who sat on the opposite side of the boat to the rowlock, to permit greater leverage on the very long oars. In order to equalise the pull, the oars were of differing lengths, varying from about 15 feet up to 23 feet for the mate's steering oar. The blades of the oars were often striped for rapid identification by the crew when first scrambling into the boat.

Although many of the earlier boats had no rudder and relied solely on the use of the long steering oar, later versions had rudders shaped specifically to suit the curve of the hull that had no skeg. The rudder was in addition to the steering oar and, when not in use, was stowed on the larboard quarter.

The stem of the boat featured a deep cutaway in which the whale line ran. Across the cutaway, and above the line, was fitted a wooden peg. This was to stop the line jumping out which could easily be broken in an emergency when it was necessary to clear the line. Most boats carried mast and sail usually rigged immediately in front of the number two rowing position.

Bearing all this in mind, the assembly was constructed in accordance with the instructions and shaped up ready for planking. I soon found that planking with 5 mm wide strips was not very practical and decided to start again, this time reducing the width to 2.5 mm. As when planking the ship's hull, tapering the strips on one side over a third of the length from each end was of considerable help. Once completed, the planking was reinforced with a coat of PVA and left to dry out. This

produced a very strong shell, but I quickly discovered that, if held up to the light, there were many gaps that my lack of skill had not catered for. I thus decided to use some spare mukali strip and double-plank the whaleboats, leaving a mahogany strip around the gunwales. Bearing in mind that there are three boats to make, this considerably added to the amount of work to do. However, in retrospect, it was the right decision to make and the results well worth the extra effort.

I removed one of the layers of ply from the gunwale tops before fitting to reduce thickness and also reduced the width considerably to match the width at the tops of the frames. At this stage, having made and fitted the thwarts, it is time to decide just how much, and what, extra detail you are going to include in the model. I chose to make a rudder and lash it to the stern quarter, a set of oars, the brace and strap for the steering oar, the cutaway and peg for the whale line, an eye for the painter, the crotch for the harpoons and the unstepped mast and sail. Most of these features are a little on the small side to make, but the result is a more authentic representation of a working boat rather than a cosmetic acknowledgement of something that hangs from the davits.

The main details of the whale-boat fittings are shown in Fig. 12.6. For the oars I cut some strips from 1 mm thick material and pulled it boldly through a 1 mm diameter hole in a piece of brass shim to form 1 mm diameter dowel. Cut to length and tapered to a point over the last 6 mm at one end, this is let into a similarly shaped notch (cricket bat fashion) in the oar blade made from 0.5 mm thick deck plank material.

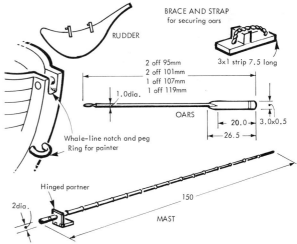

Fig. 12.6. Whaleboat details.

The mast was straightforward — a series of thread hitches run up its length and a small roll of soft tissue lashed on one side to hide the knots is all that is needed to simulate the mast/sail assembly.

Masts and spars

The tapering of these pieces is carried out in exactly the same way as that described earlier for the bowsprit,

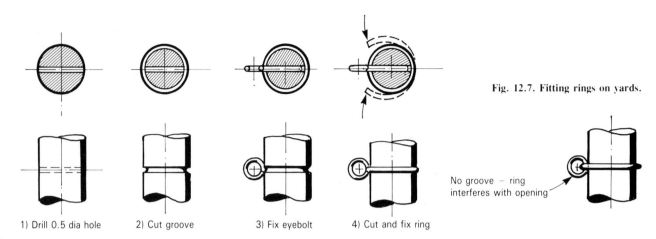

Fig. 12.7. Fitting rings on yards.

1) Drill 0.5 dia hole   2) Cut groove   3) Fix eyebolt   4) Cut and fix ring

No groove – ring interferes with opening

whichever method is chosen. There really isn't much to say about the mast assemblies, they are quite straightforward. However, the yards posed one or two problems which, after a little experimentation, I managed to get round in a quite satisfactory way.

The rings around the yards really need to be recessed in for best appearance. If this is not done, the ends of the ring can conflict with the opening through the associated eye-bolt (see Fig. 12.7). Having positioned and drilled the hole to take the shank of the eye-bolt, I then cut a shallow groove around the spar before gluing the eye-bolt in place. Then, using a suitable size ring from those supplied, I cut about a quarter of the circumference away, sprung it into the groove (like a circlip) then closed it up with fine-nosed pliers. It needs a little practice to determine the exact amount to cut from the ring, but when you get it right, the result is one that makes the ring and eye-bolt look like one piece.

The second problem area with the yard assemblies concerns the foot ropes and stirrups. It was going to be very difficult to get stirrups made from 0.25 mm

diameter thread to hang right, so I decided to use galvanised wire of the same diameter. I cut lengths of about 35 mm, formed an eye on one end by wrapping it around the shank of a 1 mm diameter drill and trimmed off the surplus. This leaves a reasonable length to handle, feed through the hole in the yard and bend over the top to retain the correct length of stirrup. The eye-bolt superglued in position holds the whole thing in place and when set, the excess wire can be cut off and the eye on the end of the stirrup twisted into the right attitude (see Fig. 12.8).

The problem with the footropes is to get them to look as if they hang naturally under their own weight. To do this, I find it helps considerably to cut off a length of thread, apply PVA and pull and stretch it between thumb and forefinger several times until it stiffens. After assembly, it can be stroked into a fairly realistic curve which looks infinitely better than the donkey's hind leg shape which untreated thread will take up. As indicated in the instructions, it really is better to rig the yards as far as possible before assembly to the masts.

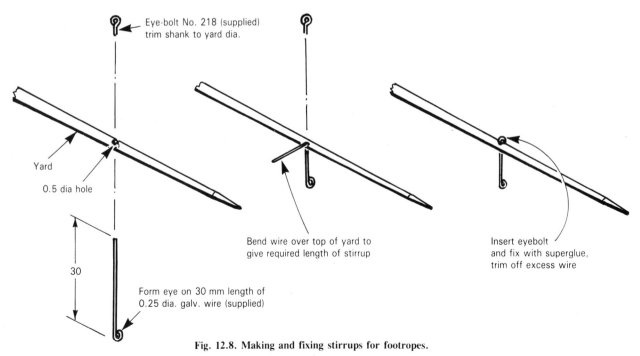

Eye-bolt No. 218 (supplied) trim shank to yard dia.

Yard

0.5 dia hole

30

Form eye on 30 mm length of 0.25 dia. galv. wire (supplied)

Bend wire over top of yard to give required length of stirrup

Insert eyebolt and fix with superglue, trim off excess wire

Fig. 12.8. Making and fixing stirrups for footropes.

The fitted hull with amidships shelter and try works shelter in place. A stand is essential from this point on.

Incidentally, I find it a good idea to re-drill the holes in all blocks before assembly, it makes the forthcoming rigging operation less taxing. Even the smallest block supplied in this kit will sustain opening out to 1 mm diameter.

Now we come to the part of model ship building which seems to frighten a lot of people away from this very satisfying field of modelmaking.

The rigging

It really is worth finding a book in your local library which describes the basics of sailing ship rigging to give just some understanding of what goes where, and why. It is true that the *Morgan* has quite a lot of rigging to contend with but, when you break it all down and appreciate the purpose of each line, much of it becomes a matter of common sense. I hesitate to recommend a suitable work to read — there are several good ones and it largely depends on your previous reading as to which one suits your own particular needs.

Earlier, I commented on the need to dye and stretch the thread provided for the rigging so I assume that this is now ready to be used. Before discussing particular difficulties, I think it is appropriate at this stage to suggest that as each length is cut off, it is run through the thumb and forefinger having received a coating of PVA glue. This serves two purposes, first, as with the footropes it gives a more natural 'hang' to the line and, secondly, it lays the hairs of the thread and minimises the adherence of dust.

Many lines are tied off at belaying pins and the residue hung in a coil. A 'flat' coil hung on a pin and which hangs out at about 45° doesn't look right at all. To give a more natural appearance to the coil, I use a simple jig as shown in Fig. 12.9. Again, the thread is well glued and whilst wet it is wrapped around the pins and dowels. My own jig has twelve positions, thus one long length can be continued along to form a dozen coils. When dry,

they are separated with a sharp blade, the top pins removed and the coils taken off the dowels. When hung on the belaying pins, they then look like rope hanging naturally under its own weight.

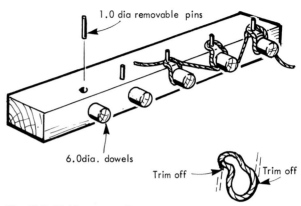

Fig. 12.9. Making rope coils.

The sequence of rigging indicated in the instructions, and as shown on the plans, is probably as good as it can be, in order to maintain the maximum access to tying off points. Nevertheless, there are some fixings at deck level where a bit of practice in tying knots with two pairs of tweezers will pay dividends. The stays and bob-stays are fairly straightforward and shouldn't present any difficulty. The shrouds, however, are a different proposition and if some thought is not given to how best to tackle them, things can become very difficult indeed. I offer my own particular method as one that works well and is as simple as possible. No doubt there are several others, equally good, since every modelmaker develops his own preferences with experience and hindsight. However, I feel that the less experienced modeller will find my system one that gives acceptable results with the minimum of tedium and frustration.

Prepare the lower deadeyes and galvanised wire chainplates and position them in the channels — DO NOT SECURE at this time. Mentally number the shrouds 1 to 5 (No. 1 to the fore and No. 5 aft), and cut a length of thread to make No. 1 and 2 starboard shrouds. Fit a deadeye to one end and seize correctly, pass the free end around the mast at the crosstree and fit a second deadeye on the other end, correctly determining for length and ensuring that the three holes in the deadeyes are in the correct relative position. The two shrouds should now be seized together at the mast. Take a suitable length of thread for the lanyard, knot one end and pass through the forward hole of the upper deadeye on No. 2 shroud FROM THE INBOARD SIDE, and proceed to rig the upper to lower deadeyes. Not having secured the chainplates, it is possible to raise the lower deadeyes to a level above the rails for ease of rigging. At this stage, of course, the lanyards are rigged with considerable slack and having dealt with the No. 2 shroud, the process is repeated with the No. 1. The chainplates can now be secured in position and the lanyards pulled up to give the required tension.

Fig. 12.10. The cutting stage.

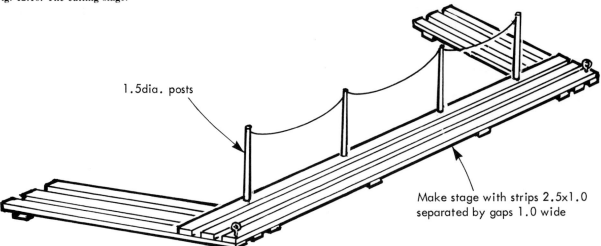

1.5dia. posts

Make stage with strips 2.5x1.0
separated by gaps 1.0 wide

The process is now repeated for the port side Nos 1 and 2 followed by the starboard Nos 3 and 4 and so on. This keeps a balance of tension in the rigging overall and maintains correct alignment in the masts. The sketches in the plans are extremely well detailed as to the way the lanyards are rigged although, of course, no sequence of application is given. Before proceeding to rig the backstays which, incidentally, are handled in exactly the same way as the shrouds — you should fit the ratlines. These are an absolute pain regardless of how you tackle them, they just go on, and on, and on. The reason for not rigging the backstays is simply one of access. Without them in position, you can at least get around both sides of the shrouds. Of course all these procedures have to be repeated on the main and mizen masts at both lower and upper levels — something more than a weekend's work, I might add.

The remainder of the rigging is relatively simple — plenty of it but not really requiring special comment — the main problem is, as mentioned earlier, one of access for deck level tying off. A special tool that I find quite useful is a pair of nail clippers whose length I have extended to enable me to get amongst the rigging to trim loose ends etc. A long slender scalpel is alright, but if it slips, or you lose your grip, it's easy to cut something you don't want cut. Having completed the rigging, the rope coils mentioned earlier can now be hung at the relevant points — a drop of superglue to hold them in place.

The whaleboats should now be rigged in position and the cutting stage made and assembled. I made my stage a little more elaborate than the one described in the plans. The sketch in Fig. 12.10 is based on a photograph at the museum at Mystic Seaport and adds a little more authenticity to the finished model.

Conclusions

It is a long time since I have had so much pleasure from a model boat project. The vessel itself is a different subject from the usual run of clipper ships, ships of the line and the like, and so much enjoyment came from the research before the model was even started. Whilst not a kit for a beginner, any reasonable craftsman should, with care and patience, produce a model of considerable interest and one that would form the focal point of any lounge or den.

The kit is, in my opinion, one that provides many hours of enjoyable, rewarding work.

REFERENCES

Ansell, Willets D — *The Whaleboat, A Study of Design, Construction and Use From 1850 to 1970* — Mystic Seaport Museum Inc. 1983.

Leavitt, John F. — *The Charles W. Morgan* — The Marine Historical Association Inc. Mystic Seaport, U.S.A. 1973.

CHAPTER 13

A Square-Sterned Whaleboat

The finished square-sterned whaleboat.

The development of the whaleboat as an efficient working vessel evolved over a long period of time and designs varied, particularly between the European and American boats.

A significant difference was in the shape of the stern. The Panart kit depicts a craft with a straight stern, whereas the boats used on the American whaler the *Charles Morgan*, for instance, were double-ended to permit a sudden backing away, or 'stern all' to avoid the flukes or jaws of an irate whale.

Whatever school of development one refers to, all whaleboats evolved into very elegant craft, extremely seaworthy and completely functional. Everything on board had its known place and everyone on board had their own responsibilities. A total team effort was required, where each relied on the other, often for the safety of their lives.

The Kit

The instructions come in four languages — Italian, English, French and German — but are extremely brief and really can only be considered a basic guide. The drawings provided are excellent and, although all annotation is in Italian, they are really very clear, the language difference not really being a problem.

The quality of materials throughout is excellent with many fittings provided in turned brass. However, there are many wooden items that have to be made by hand and thus a number of Swiss needle files and small drills are essential. Rigging blocks are supplied, so too are belaying pins but, as stated, most other wooden fittings have to be worked from the appropriate size timber. At 1:16 scale the model makes up to a length of 615 mm.

Constructing the hull

The hull is constructed on a basic stem, keel and stern post assembly, with one permanent bulkhead at each end. Bow and stern blocks are shaped and fitted to provide fixings for the subsequent planking. Seven further bulkheads slot into place on the keel and are held in position by three longitudinal bridges. It is most important at this stage to ensure that all joints are snugly fitting without being overtight, a condition which, if not watched, could lead to distortion of the total assembly.

The planking proper is carried out in three stages. The first stage, which provides the inside surface, is of 6 mm × 1 mm walnut strip, with the upper edge of the first strip in line with the top edges of the bulkheads. Fifteen planks each side are needed to go from top to keel, and it was found best to reduce the width at each end to about 4.5 mm for a length of about 30 cm. The edges of the temporary bulkheads should be covered with Sellotape to prevent the planks from being stuck at these points. Each plank in the first layer should be glued edge to edge, pinned at the ends and to each bulkhead. White PVA is entirely adequate for this layer and when this first stage of planking is complete, the assembly should be left for at least 24 hours for the adhesive to properly cure and harden off.

All pins should now be removed before starting on the second layer of lime planking. I chose to rub in a coating of contact adhesive to the first stage walnut planking, letting it dry before applying the 6 mm × 1 mm lime strips. They should be prepared as before with tapered ends, but this time I started half a plank width down from the top, so that the width of lime plank overlapped the joins between the first stage walnut strips (see Fig. 13.1).

Contact adhesive was used throughout the second stage of planking and no pins were employed. This stage was completed by applying the last strip around the top edge of the assembly and trimming it down to match the top edge of the first walnut plank.

The last, outer, layer of planking is again of walnut

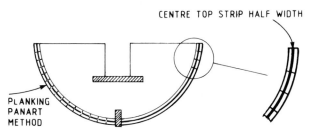

Fig. 13.1.   ALTERNATIVE PLANKING METHOD
STAGGERING THE LAYERS

CENTRE TOP STRIP HALF WIDTH

PLANKING PANART METHOD

and is applied in the same manner as the second layer, using contact adhesive. This time I started at the top edge as in the first layer. For this final layer there is one very significant difference in the preparation of the strips. While it is still required to taper each strip, it is also necessary to more precisely shape each end to correctly follow the curve of prow and line of stern post (see Fig. 13.2). It was also found to look more authentic if the strip thickness was pared down to about 0.2 mm gradually over a length of about 3 cm from each end. After the assembly is completely dry, the ends can be tidied up using a sharp scalpel.

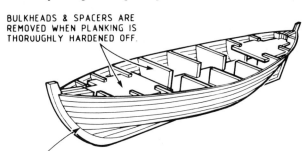

BULKHEADS & SPACERS ARE REMOVED WHEN PLANKING IS THOROUGHLY HARDENED OFF.

T. TRIM OUTER PLANK ENDS TO MATCH LINE OF STEM & STERN POST.   Fig. 13.2.

The seven temporary bulkheads are now removed, permitting total access to the inner surface, which should now be thoroughly cleaned up and smoothed. This is not a five-minute job and the time expended really depends on how well the first stage edge-to-edge joints were made. When finished to satisfaction two more bulkheads, one at each end, can be permanently fitted before sanding the outer surface of the hull. Eighteen ribs have now to be fitted in position on each interior side of the keel. Each rib must be in its right place, square and true to the centre line of the boat. The gunwale plank should be fixed in position using both pins and glue.

Probably, the most difficult operation in the building process is the bending of the 10 mm × 3.5 mm rails to match the top edge contour of the boat. The bend has a drop in arc of about 7 cm over a length of 56 cm and needs fairly sophisticated bending equipment to achieve such a curve against the 10 mm width. For modelmakers without this sort of bending kit, a very simple alternative is to use the lamination method. Trace the required curve onto a board and peg out with a line of panel pins.

Three strips of 4 mm square can now be laminated around the pins, glued and held in place with further pins around the outside of the curve until the adhesive has thoroughly cured. The width and thickness can then be reduced to 10 mm × 3.5 mm before fixing to the model (see Fig. 13.3).

Fig. 13.3.

ALTERNATIVE METHOD OF MAKING RAILS WITHOUT BENDING EQUIPMENT.

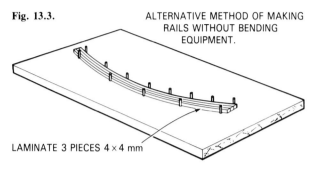

LAMINATE 3 PIECES 4 × 4 mm

A lot a care and patience must be exercised in applying these rails, since the ends must be shaped to fit snugly on the stem and the stern post respectively and, at the same time, take up the right curve around the top of the hull (see Fig. 13.4). Only when everything fits and lines up to satisfaction should the glue come into use.

The basic floor frame is pressed out of 1 mm birch ply and has to be stiffened, and surfaced, with strips of 5 mm × 2 mm beech. There are four apertures fore and aft into which gratings have to be framed and fitted. The gratings are constructed from multi-crosshalved strips

Fig. 13.4.

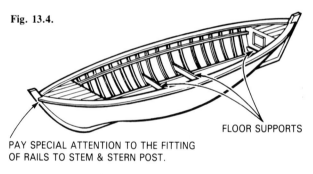

FLOOR SUPPORTS

PAY SPECIAL ATTENTION TO THE FITTING OF RAILS TO STEM & STERN POST.

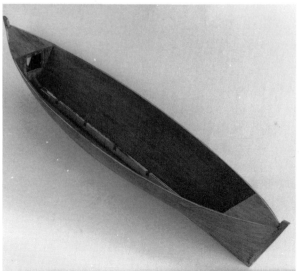

The hull shell with end bulkheads permanently fitted and the inside surface smoothed and finished.

The completed shell prior to removing the temporary bulkheads and bridges.

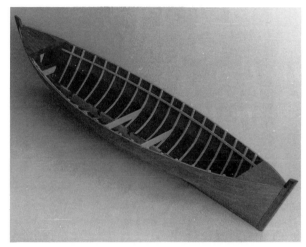

The ribs, gunwale plank and floor supports in place.

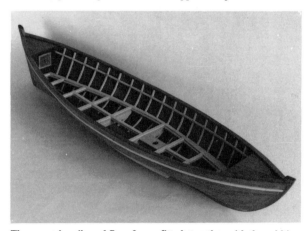

The gunwale rails and floor frame fitted, together with the rubbing strake and stabilizers.

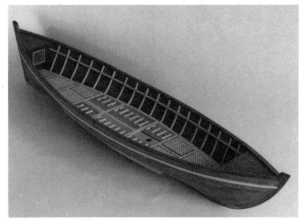

The completed hull shell ready for fitting out.

165

which slot together and are then framed on the outer edges with 3 mm × 0.5 mm walnut. You need to be careful here, because the 125 grating pieces supplied come from at least two different machine settings and have been cut from two slightly different thicknesses of material. They are readily identifiable and should be grouped so the pieces selected for each grating come from the same group. From a cosmetic point of view, it is also better to ensure that the line of hatching runs in the same direction on all assemblies (see Fig. 13.5).

Fig. 13.5.

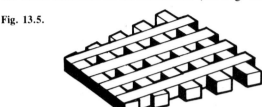

ASSEMBLE ALL GRATINGS WITH
LONGITUDINAL ELEMENTS ON TOP

I also found it easier to make the floor inserts before fitting the floor frame into the hull. This frame is supported by four pieces of 10 mm × 2 mm beech, fitted transversely across the hull. It was necessary to reduce the height of these supports to about 8.5 mm in order to attain a better fit between the edges of the frame and the inside of the hull. Getting everything just right can be a little time consuming and much will depend on how true to contour the first, inner stage, planking was done. The fit does not have to be absolutely perfect, because the final union between frame and hull is covered in by small inserts of 3 mm × 2 mm strip. The exposed edges of the prow, keel and stem should now be faced with 6 mm × 1 mm walnut strip, trimmed and sanded to width. This operation concludes the basic construction of the hull shell and, after fitting the rubbing strakes and stabilizers, one passes on to the making of the various fittings and ancillary equipment.

Fittings and ancillary equipment

The drawings show all necessary dimensions and these, coupled with the instruction booklet, are entirely adequate for making the various bits and pieces required to complete the fitting out of the boat.

However, I feel that one or two additional comments could be helpful. The bow cable blocks or cleats have angled apertures but you have to make sure that one right hand and one left hand are made (see Fig. 13.6). The various tubs or baskets are made from a series of staves arranged around a pair of ply discs and the instructions recommend that every third stave is tapered to bring the alignment back into order. A simple arithmetical calculation will establish the necessary dimensions to correctly shape every stave and the result is well worth the effort (see Fig. 13.7). Exact accuracy is not necessary but every stave tapered is definitely better than one in three.

Fig. 13.6.

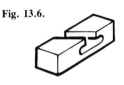

MAKE ONE AS SHOWN
AND ONE OPPOSITE HAND

The bow cable blocks, cleats and rowlock bases. Note that the cable blocks are handed.

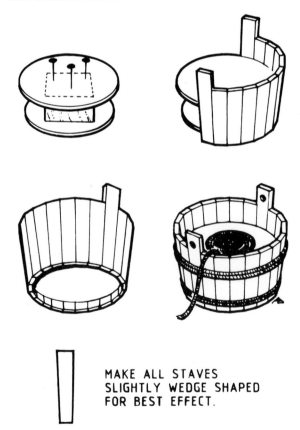

MAKE ALL STAVES
SLIGHTLY WEDGE SHAPED
FOR BEST EFFECT.

Fig. 13.7.

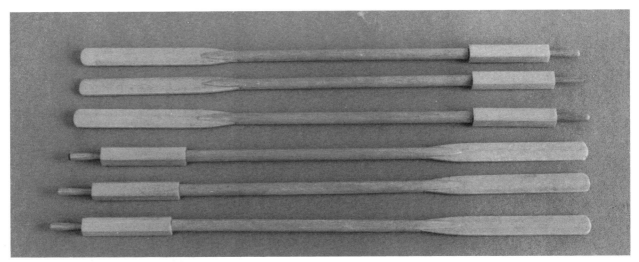

The oars are made from four separate pieces.

Metal castings are supplied for harpoons, boat hook and axe heads and these need trimming to remove risers or sprues. The shafts are made from various sizes of dowel rod which have to be correctly tapered before fitting the heads. Each of the six oars is made from four pieces, the blade slotting into the end of the shaft (see Fig. 13.8). The handle is undoubtedly more easily made by turning, but if you are not blessed with a lathe, spinning the dowel in a drill chuck together with the application of a half-round file will do the trick.

The mast has to be tapered by 2 mm on diameter over a length of 330 mm — a fairly slow taper which is not too difficult to attain. The mast head, however, needs more careful working. Made from 10 mm × 10 mm stock it requires a 7 mm square hole cut right through to house a pair of shafted brass pulleys. Well sharpened chisels are the order of the day plus, of course, a fairly steady hand.

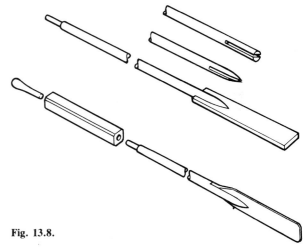

Fig. 13.8.

The lateen yard is made up from three pieces, suitably tapered, the two longer pieces being semi-halved and lashed together.

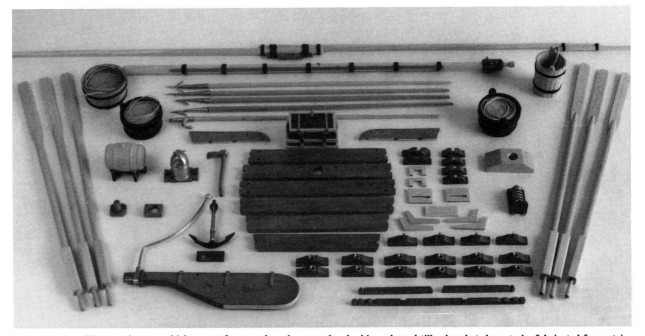

Fittings and ancillary equipment which, apart from anchor, harpoon heads, binnacle and tiller bracket, have to be fabricated from strip or block material supplied in the kit.

Rigging

Having stepped the mast, you can start on the standing rigging. At this larger scale, greater attention should be paid to the making of proper lashings etc., and probably one of the most difficult jobs is to make hanging coils of rope look natural. Judicious application of cyanoacrylate or acrylic varnish can work wonders.

The sail is a simple shape, but not too simple to make if, like me, your woodwork is better than your needlework. First the material should be cut leaving about 8 mm extra on each edge for 'piping' the thread in. Before doing this, the thirteen vertical and two horizontal rows of stitching should be applied and the ends tidily sewn in. The piped edges can now be done. The heavy thread has to be covered by the 8 mm surplus material, the material then turned under and the stitching applied through three thicknesses of material (see Fig. 13.9). It is, of course, much easier if a sewing machine is available as three thicknesses can soon result in sore fingers if sewing by hand, plus with the machine two hands are free to hold and guide the seam.

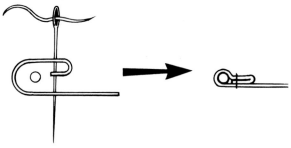

Fig. 13.9. Piping the edges of the sail.

I found it simpler to lash the sail to the yard before rigging the yard to the mast. The running rigging should not be permanently tied off until all lines have been rigged. This is to attain correct attitude of the lateen yard relative to the mast and also ensure the right degree of tension in each line.

The model is depicted with a black bottom and 3 mm white band at the waterline. Having used a chisel-edged carpenter's pencil to mark the upper edge of the white band position, the hull can be painted to within a millimetre of it. The lower edge of the white band can now be marked in, masked off and painted in. I chose to cheat and bought a coil of 3 mm wide white 'Go-fast' striping from my local car accessories shop. This was applied to the hull using the upper of the pencil lines as a guide. The hull was then given a couple of coats of satin finish varnish to seal everything up.

Conclusions

It is difficult to find serious fault with this kit, apart from asking the same old question, 'why no stand?'. The drawings are very clear and, although all notes are in Italian, there really isn't a problem deciphering their meaning. The instruction booklet is rather sparse in the English language section, but then there isn't too much in the Italian section either.

Materials throughout were of very high quality and a pleasure to work with. Maybe not a model for a first venture into model boat building, but an extremely pleasant change from the more usual man-of-war project. It makes a very attractive model.

CHAPTER 14

A New Bedford Whaleboat

The finished New Bedford whaleboat.

Having had the opportunity to visit some of the whaling museums in the New Bedford area of the USA, I have, over the years, developed a more than passing interest in the history of whaling. Thus, it was with particular anticipation that I opened the box of this kit from Amati.

The Kit

The picture on the box had me a little worried at first, since the combination of a clinker-built hull and forged rowlocks was, I suppose, just about a possibility, but not one I thought that would have been chosen for the subject of a kit. However, much was put to rights when the historical detail in the box was read, as it describes the model as being of a New Bedford whaleboat typical of those used *up to* 1860. More significantly, the drawings provided, correctly show thole pins rather than

forged rowlocks and my assessment is that the model is of a craft built around the late 1840s, after which time clinker construction was largely replaced by the smoother carvel planking, often combined with a couple of lapstraked planks at the gunwales.

Having got that little worry out of the way, I looked more closely at the kit contents. The drawings looked pretty good and the quality of the timber appeared to be OK. Quite a few whitemetal fittings for things such as lances and harpoons and, I noticed, for the loggerhead, wooden tubs and water keg! I particularly liked the robust rudder hinges. All major wooden parts are laser cut in 4 mm ply and the external 'clinker' planks are ready spiled and shaped from 0.8 mm ply. All dowelling appeared straight and well matched for colour. The instruction manual is reasonably illustrated with Italian text and a separate translation in English cross-referenced to it.

The size and weight of the box had led me to hope, mistakenly, that at last we had a kit with a stand supplied. However, one doesn't have to know too much Italian to realise that there is a note on the box lid that states that the stand illustrated is not provided. The model finishes up at a length of 560 mm.

Hull construction

The illustrations within the instructions are very clear and with a reasonable amount of common sense you can follow the procedures quite well, albeit that the English text is somewhat sparse.

The hull is constructed around a false core, Fig. 14.1, which is removed once the main shell has been built. Everything is quite straightforward but the main thing to realise is that some parts are temporarily pinned, rather than glued, in order to facilitate the final removal of the core. The core is essentially a false keel to which a number of bulkheads are jointed. At only 21 in long, the main member was surprisingly in two pieces, to be joined with a large central dovetail, Fig. 14.1. This laser-cut feature was a poor, sloppy, fit and needed to be packed to make the strong, sound joint required for this major load-bearing part. The glued joint should be left to thoroughly cure before assembling the bulkheads, the edges of which need to be protected with adhesive tape to prevent the bonding of the inner planking to be built around them.

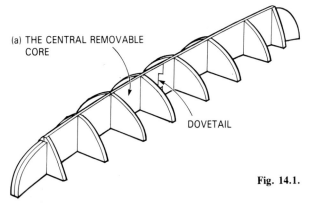

(a) THE CENTRAL REMOVABLE CORE

DOVETAIL

Fig. 14.1.

The prow and stern post pieces are pinned in place on this assembly together with the keel, after which the internal layer of planking can then be applied, Fig. 14.2. This needs to be done very carefully, remembering that the inner surface is, in fact, the visible floor of the boat. The ends of each plank have to be chamfered and glued securely to the inner prow and stern post pieces. Reference to the drawings is essential to establish the line of the top inner plank.

Fig. 14.2.

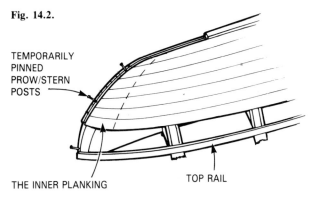

TEMPORARILY PINNED PROW/STERN POSTS

THE INNER PLANKING

TOP RAIL

Once the inner planking has been completed, the frames proper can be added, Fig. 14.3. To assist in getting the right curve to these frames a rail, at gunwale level, is fixed to the top edges of the core bulkheads. I think, at this stage, I would say that the material for the frames was insufficiently flexible — a softer, more pliable strip would make life a lot easier and without detriment to either strength or appearance. However, whatever choice is made, the use of the Amati plank nipper, or similar bending tool, is to be recommended. Each frame needs to be correctly bent to lay snugly around the inner planking and the aforementioned top rail before gluing in place. It helps considerably to leave the frames overlength to the rails, thus allowing the natural curve to be better attained. Small crocodile clips are handy to hold the end of the frames to the rail while the glue dries.

We now come to that part of the construction that you just have to get right or foul up the whole model! I would like to have seen in the manual a little more advice on

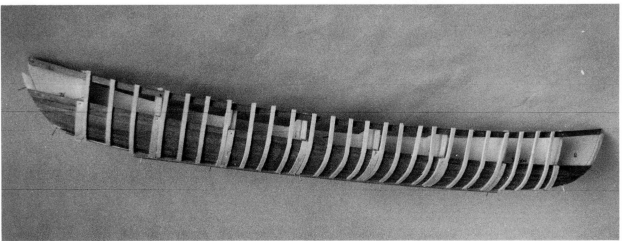

The frames fitted around the inner planking.

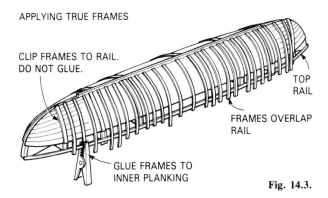

APPLYING TRUE FRAMES

CLIP FRAMES TO RAIL.
DO NOT GLUE.

TOP
RAIL

FRAMES OVERLAP
RAIL

GLUE FRAMES TO
INNER PLANKING

Fig. 14.3.

the correct application of the clinker planking, Fig. 14.4. No mention is made of 'chamfering' the edges of the frames to provide maximum adhesion area for the outer planking. After some consideration, I decided that this was the right course of action and could only provide a little more excess in length of plank relative to stern and prow pieces. Having read the manual several times previously, I was aware that the ends of the outer clinker planks had to be trimmed to form a slot to accept the outer prow and stern posts. This needs to be borne in mind when positioning the outer planks longitudinally. You are also quickly made aware that the numbering of the planks is in reverse order to that shown on the drawings — not too much of a problem since you really would have to be a bit dumb not to spot it when fixing the first plank. Taking all these points into consideration, the outer planking proceeded remarkably well with judicious use of crocodile clips, elastic bands etc.

A razor saw is most helpful in the creation of the slot to house the prow and stern posts. They should be cut a little on the narrow side and trimmed very gently with

a scalpel to provide the very close fit required. Once everything has been fitted to satisfaction, the central core can be removed. This, of course, is entirely re-usable should you wish to scratch-build a second model.

The hull shell was now ready for the building in of the gunwales, keel capping, carlings and rubbing strips. There was ample material in the box to fabricate these parts and the hull finished up a very commendable assembly. The inside of the first planking needs to be cleaned and smoothed before fitting the fore and aft flooring, both of which should be on a common level. The box at the front end and the cuddy board at the stern can then be added. Patience is required when fitting the five thwarts and their supporting knees. Although the business part of the knees are laser cut, they do have to be trimmed for a precise fit against the inside of the hull.

Making the thole pin assemblies (an earlier form of rowlock), the peak cleats and the remainder of the hull fixtures, was found to be quite straightforward (see Fig. 14.5). I did, however, replace the diecast loggerhead

Fig. 14.4.

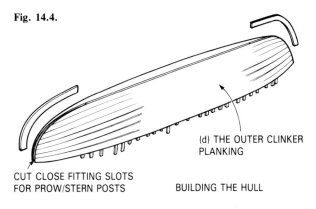

(d) THE OUTER CLINKER
PLANKING

CUT CLOSE FITTING SLOTS
FOR PROW/STERN POSTS

BUILDING THE HULL

Basic hull complete.

The basic hull painted and with harpoon support fitted.

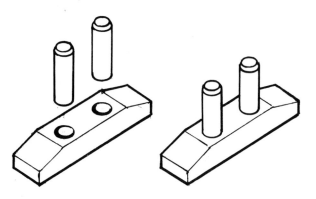

Fig. 14.5.   THOLE PINS

with a wooden one for the sake of authenticity, this item normally being made from oak or hickory.

The rudder is an assembly of four pieces plus the hinge fittings. Again, no problem, but watch that the inner curve of the assembly matches that of the stern post. This will become particularly important if you decide to fit the rudder and sails, rather than stow them as when proceeding under oars.

Before fitting rings and tabernacle, the finishing should be considered. The colour scheme shown on the box art is typical of the period, but it should be remembered that there is no *right* scheme. Whaleboats were painted for a variety of reasons; preservation, identification and, in some cases, camouflage. In fact, some builders left the finish painting to the whaleship, whose officers might have had their own preferences, or colour code, for identification. It was not unusual to see port hung boats with the sheer strake of one colour and the starboard boats of another. Early in the 19th century boats were certainly more colourful having white sheer strakes and the hull painted the predominant colour, sometimes even to the point of having red bows, the red

ending in a diagonal slash with the rest of the hull white. However, it is wise to do a bit of study before going too far, there is always some 'clever clogs' who will say 'They were never like that'.

Fitting out

Whilst the diecast tubs are extremely well detailed and, no doubt, with the correct dry-brushing techniques, look very good, I decided that I would make them, and the water keg, in the traditional manner (see Fig. 14.6).

CONSTRUCTION OF WOODEN TUBS

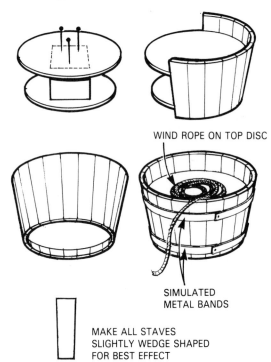

WIND ROPE ON TOP DISC

SIMULATED
METAL BANDS

MAKE ALL STAVES
SLIGHTLY WEDGE SHAPED
FOR BEST EFFECT

Fig. 14.6.

Thus, I made two circular discs separated by a block of suitable thickness, around which I glued a series of tapered staves. Once the glue had set, the top and bottom edges were trimmed and sanded flat and level. The metal restraining bands were simulated by strips cut from the black pages of a photograph album. The upper disc provided an ideal platform on which to coil the rope that leads from one tub to the other, then on around the loggerhead and forward up to the harpooner's position. A point of accuracy here. Tubs were usually the same size on boats without a centre board. Fitting a centre board restricted the space available for the forwardmost tub and thus it had to be of smaller diameter.

The oars and paddles were made by fitting a tapered handle into a similarly tapered slot in the blades (see Fig. 14.7). The blades were specified to be made from 10 mm wide material but, with no such width provided, I used two 5 mm wide strips glued together, edge to

edge. I'm still not sure whether this is what was intended, but it does have the advantage of making the tapered slotting of the blade easier — just do it in each half before gluing the pieces together. Whilst the paddles are all the same length, it will be seen that the oars are not. This is an absolutely essential feature of whaleboat design and reflects the severe curvature of the sides of the boat. Oars used in American whaleboats were the longest in general use, the midship oar often having a length of eighteen feet. Another small detail, but one which adds that something extra, is an additional handle on the steering oar for the boatsteerer's left hand. This was fitted a short way down from the end of the oar and in the same plane as the blade. When you consider that the steering oar could be as long as 23 ft, you will understand that this extra handle could make a life a lot easier for the boatsteerer. Each oar, except the steering oar, should be identified by a number of white bands

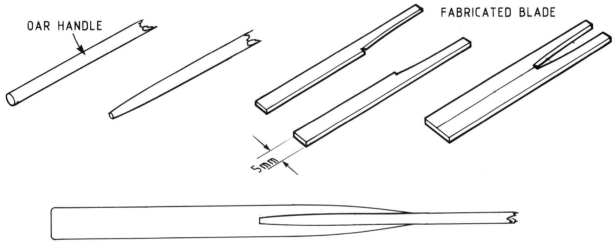

Fig. 14.7.   MAKING THE OARS

All the bits and pieces laid out prior to assembling on to the hull.

This is a second model, built on the same removable core. A later version, carvel built with sail and rudder rigged.

painted around the blade. An alternative, but very effective, way of doing this is to use self-adhesive 'Go fast' stripes of suitable width obtainable from the local motorists' centre. Varnish the oars first, apply the stripes, then varnish again. Cheating? Yes it is, but it gives a pretty good result!

The harpoons and lances, because of their small cast diameter, need careful handling. They have to be lashed to wooden stocks and the nature of the lashing involves quite a bit of twisting and turning to get it right. Prior to making up these assemblies, I painted the metal castings a dark blue/grey. After the lashing was completed, the heads were scraped back to bare metal and the whole thing given a coat of matt varnish.

The mast and sprit have to be tapered and the bottom end of the mast provided with a plug to permit it to be stepped into the plate fixed to the bottom of the boat. You should now decide whether the mast is to be up with sail set, or, stowed in the boat. In the former case, the rudder and tiller should be rigged in place or, in the latter instance, stowed on the port quarter. Choosing to stow the mast, it became apparent that there was a need

for a mast rest to be mounted on the cuddy board just to starboard side of the loggerhead.

The sail needs to be made up whether it is to be set or stowed, otherwise it will look exactly like a piece of material wrapped against the mast — not very inspiring. Remember too, that the blocks will still be rigged to the top of the mast and the lower stern corner of the sail. Rigging the mast and sail in the 'up' position is very straightforward, the drawings and instructions being entirely adequate so as not to require further comment.

Fitting everything in the boat is quite a task and quite a lot of detail is covered up in so doing. I therefore chose to lay some of the harpoons and other equipment on the base. When running the line from the tubs and loggerhead forward up the centre of the boat, it should pass over the roller mounted in the upper stem and back to a coil on the front, or box of the boat. This was called the box warp and contained three or four fathoms of line, its purpose to provide adequate slack when the harpoon was thrown.

Having taken the trouble to make up the boat compass, I decided to fix it in the open position where it could be seen. It would be equally correct to house it under the cuddy board, a position often favoured by some boat-steerers.

Conclusions

It is certainly possible to build a model to exhibition standard using this kit. While it is a doubtful choice for a beginner, it is a most worthwhile challenge to the more experienced modeller who knows a few of the wrinkles and has a wider range of specialist tools at his disposal.

I enjoyed building it immensely and I am very pleased with the result. There is plenty of work to do, even though the clinker planking is already pre-formed (thank goodness!).

REFERENCES

Ansell, Willets D. — *The Whaleboat, A Study of Design, Construction and Use From 1850 to 1970* — Mystic Seaport Museum Inc. 1983.
Leavitt, John F. — *The Charles W. Morgan* — The Marine Historical Association Inc. Mystic Seaport, U.S.A. 1973.

CHAPTER 15

A Summary of Techniques

This final chapter brings together many of the techniques used in the making of model period ships. The majority of them have appeared either in the same, or similar, form in earlier parts of this book where they have been recommended in the making of specific models. I have chosen to summarise them in this reference section for use in a more general sense.

Again, I would stress that these are methods that I use and find successful. They are not purported to be the only, or the best, way of doing things. Indeed, some situations call for a variation on the main theme, which is why you may find subtle differences between what is written in this chapter and what has been read in earlier sections of this book. I have no doubt that many readers will have their own preferred methods which will be different to mine. Nonetheless, for newcomers to the hobby, I put my preferences forward for consideration in the knowledge that they work and should make reasonable starting points for the less experienced modelmaker to build on.

Deck planking

There are several methods by which decking can be laid or simulated and the system to adopt is really dependent upon the physical size of the model, your own patience and to how much trouble you wish to go to in order to achieve the result you want.

In the simplest form, the deck can be lined out by drawing the plank widths and butts directly onto the base material, which should have been previously well sealed and lightly rubbed down. Black drawing ink in a proper drawing pen is the best medium, this type of pen ensuring a consistency of line thickness. The secret of this procedure is in the sealing. If, at any point, the ink penetrates through to the wood it will spread into the grain and blotch.

Another apparently simple method recommended by some kit manufacturers, is to score the lines with a scriber and run a soft pencil into the grooves so produced. A word of warning about this method. If the grain of the deck material runs away from the straight

edge along which the scriber is guided, it will almost certainly take the scriber with it. The results of this can be quite disappointing.

If you really want a quick job, it is possible to buy deck planking in sheet form — cut it out and stick it on. However, this can sometimes look a bit artifical and it is usually obvious as to what has been done. Unless you are building a fully framed model where decking will be laid in proper dockyard fashion, without doubt, the best results are attained by laying individual planks using 0.5 mm or 0.6 mm thick strip of suitable width stuck down to a false ply deck. (Fig. 15.1).

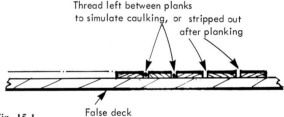

Fig. 15.1.

Caulking can be simulated in one of several ways, but the most flexible method I have found is to lay thread against the edge of each assembled plank before positioning its neighbour. According to the scale of the model (and your own visual preference), this can either be left in place or stripped out after all the planks have been set. (Fig. 15.1) On relatively small scales, the soft shadow in the gap left after stripping out the thread can often give a more natural look to the deck. Alternatively, rather than using black thread, dark grey can be quite effective on the smaller model. If it is decided to leave the thread in place, then take care to ensure that its thickness is somewhat less than that of the plank and also that it is well adhered to the deck. Failure in these areas will not permit final sanding of the planking without furring up any thread left protruding above the deck surface.

As to the laying of the planks, a contact adhesive is probably as good as any. The white PVAs are alright, but tend to distort and warp the very thin material being used. This can cause problems with the correct laying of the thread caulking and during the subsequent sanding operation. Commence by laying the margin planks around the outside of the deck followed by one long plank down the centre of the deck (or one each side of the centre line). This provides a datum for the remainder of the planking. It is worthwhile making a simple cutting jig to ensure that all planks are of identical length and, incidentally, a razor saw will usually give a better result here than the modelling knife. (Fig.15.2.)

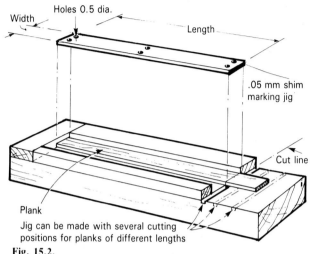

Fig. 15.2.

A brass shim template, the same size as a plank with fine holes through it at the position of the plank fixings, is a simple way of identically marking the planks with a sharp soft pencil. Lay the planks from the centre outwards, remembering to stagger their positions in order to keep the butting of the ends in line at every fourth row. As you come closer to the margin plank, recognise that the planks have to be tapered and let into the margin plank. (Fig. 15.3.) Note that the tapered planks never come to a sharp end and should never be less than half

the full width at this point. Once the end of a plank needs to be trimmed, such that the length of taper is more than twice the width, it should be joggled in to the margin plank.

Having laid all the planks it only remains to sand the whole area smooth. Bearing in mind the amount of handling the model is still to have, it is a good thing at this point to give it a couple of thin coats of matt or satin varnish to protect the surface from the inevitable finger marks.

Hull planking

The planking of a model ship is a feature that discourages many would-be modellers from embarking upon this fascinating branch of modelmaking. Yes, it can be long-winded, and sometimes tedious, but the satisfaction of a job well done is very much worth the effort. Patience is an essential quality with which, hopefully, all modelmakers are endowed and planking a model ship should not unduly stress that capacity. An excellent result does not always stand out in the overall picture, but everyone and his grandma will recognise a lousy planking job.

These notes are aimed at the type of construction used in many kits where frames or bulkheads are mounted onto a false keel and filler blocks glued in position at stem and stern. The first essential is to prepare the edges of the frames so that they follow the lines of the hull and permit the planks to lay across the full edge thickness of the frame. (Figs. 15.4a, 15.4b.)

A flexible strip of 3 mm ply faced with coarse glasspaper or garnetpaper is ideal for the convex surfaces,

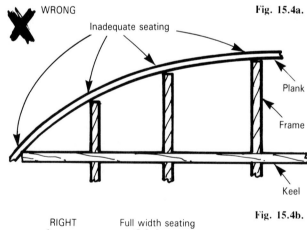

Fig. 15.4a.

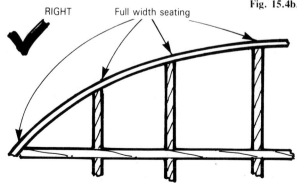

Fig. 15.4b.

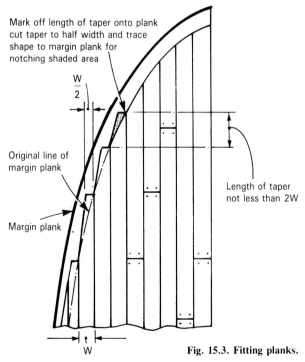

Fig. 15.3. Fitting planks.

while a piece of 16 to 20 mm diameter dowel rod is ideal for working in the concave areas around the stern. To minimise breakout, always aim the strip or dowel against the frame edge from which most material has to be removed and use one of the planking strips to constantly monitor progress until such time as it makes contact across the entire thickness of all frames concerned. (Fig. 15.4c.)

Fig. 15.4c.

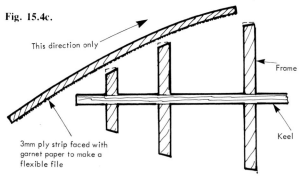

This direction only

Frame

Keel

3mm ply strip faced with garnet paper to make a flexible file

As to the planks, remember that apart from perhaps a couple each side, few planks retain full width over their entire length. One or both ends have to be tapered to suit the contours of the hull and one edge of the plank has to be bevelled in order to attain a snug fit alongside its neighbour.

A word about tools. A small razor plane is ideal for both tapering and bevelling and a small low-voltage electric mini-drill for drilling holes to take the fixing pins. Make sure you start each project with a new blade in the plane.

Examine each plank carefully and discard any that have knots or a complex grain pattern. These can be useful for stealers or other details later in the construction, but will either be very difficult to shape prior to fixing or will break when bending. Also watch which way the grain runs, and where possible taper so that the plane does not 'lift' the grain. (Fig. 15.5.)

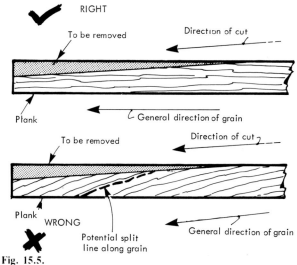

RIGHT

To be removed

Direction of cut

Plank

General direction of grain

To be removed

Direction of cut

Plank WRONG

Potential split line along grain

General direction of grain

Fig. 15.5.

In the case of walnut particularly and, to a lesser extent, mahogany, planing the 'wrong way' can split a plank of the section normally encountered. At this stage, you have to consider whether or not the planks will need

'steaming' to get them round the curves of the hull. There are no hard and fast rules here and many models can be planked without the application of heat, particularly if you are using lime or mahogany. The Amati plank nipper is a boon when using most types of timber but walnut is a different kettle of fish, being very short-grained, and you may well have to consider steaming. For this, I favour an electric kettle with a 1 metre length of 32 mm diameter plastic waste pipe placed over the spout. Keep the water at or near boiling point for as long as it takes to make several strips placed in the pipe sufficiently pliable to pull round a forming fixture. (Fig. 15.6.)

Fig. 15.6.

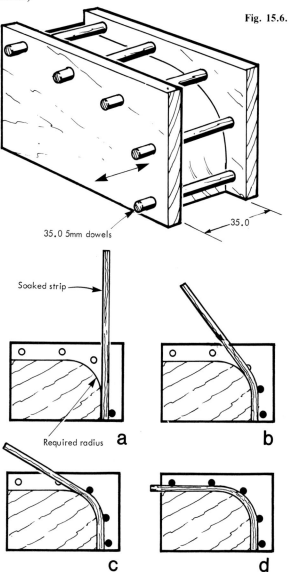

35.0 5mm dowels

35.0

Soaked strip

Required radius **a**

b

c

d

Having prepared the frame edges, selected the timber and gathered together all necessary tools, we can now start planking. It is generally required to leave a convenient area for the later fixing of the bulwarks and, to provide this facility, the first, untapered, plank is usually positioned some 6 to 10 mm below the line of the deck. Pin and glue this in position using PVA adhesive, not forgetting to drill the pin holes through the plank. A drill 0.3 mm−0.4 mm diameter is alright, but ensure that the hole is applied square to the frame *not* square to the plank surface. Also try to keep the line of holes straight down each frame. This can be done with greater ease if the centre of the hole is marked and indented with the sharp point of a hard pencil; done properly, the drill will not run off, but centre itself on the marked position.

When the top plank has been laid each side, it is then necessary to lay the second untapered plank. This needs to be positioned with a little care at, or around, the waterline. To avoid awkward gaps later on, its final position should be an exact multiple of the plank width measured down from the underside of the first plank. (Fig. 15.7.) Fix the plank thus on the two or three widest frames amidships and bend the plank to follow its natural course towards the bow and stern. A 'dry' run is advisable to ensure that at the bow the distance down from the underside of the top plank has not decreased to less than half that at the midships position. If it has, move the lower plank accordingly. The basis for calculating the taper on the rest of the planking has now been established.

Referring again to Fig. 15.7, it will be apparent that the distance along the edge of the frames from deck to keel is different at each frame. In order to determine the width of planks at each frame (and hence the taper) it is necessary to measure and record the distance L at each frame. It is anticipated that L will be almost identical on the two or three midships frames and decrease frame by frame towards the bows. This may also be the case on the frames towards the stern, but in many cases L can increase, thus indicating the later use of 'stealers'. In theory you might therefore expect that tapering the planks would be unnecessary. In fact, tapering is done for convenience of fitting and fixing and has to be judged according to the contours involved. To get back to the tapering. Take dimension L at the centre frames and divide this distance by the basic plank width. This will tell you how many planks it will take to cover that section. Now divide that figure into all the other values of L and the result will be the width of plank at which that particular value of L was measured. Transferring this data to the planks will define the degree of tapering required.

A reminder of the need to watch the run of the grain is pertinent at this point — try to arrange for the taper to run across the rising grain so that the razor plane does not 'pick-up' and perhaps split the wood. Remember also to bevel one edge of the plank in order that it sits snugly against the edge of the previously fixed strip. You will find that for nearly all circumstances you taper the 'keelside' of the plank and bevel the upper 'deck-side'. Make sure that not only are the planks well glued to the frames but also to each other, edge to edge.

When all the full length planks have been fitted it will then be necessary to fit the stealers into any gaps left, mainly at the stern. Stealers never finish at a sharp point,

Fig. 15.7.

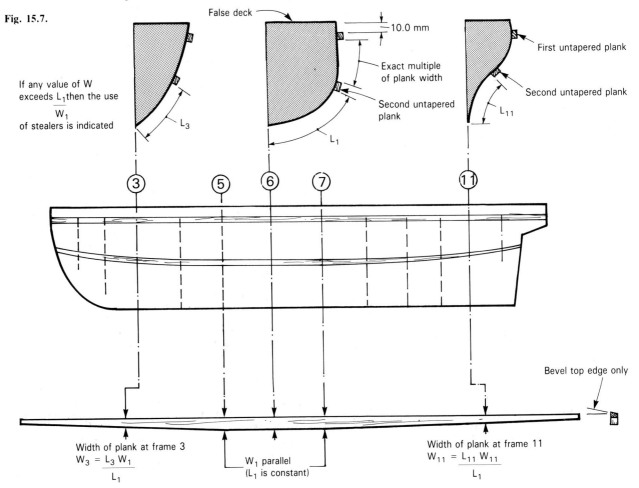

so one adjacent plank should be trimmed to allow the stealer to be no less than half a plank width at its narrow end (Fig. 15.8), so that it can be conventiently drilled and pinned.

Fig. 15.8.

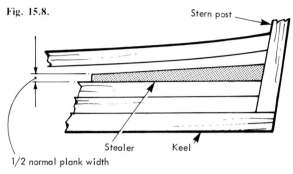

Stern post

Stealer   Keel

1/2 normal plank width

It now only remains to finish off. First, I chose to remove all the pins used to fix the planks. You will understand why if you have ever torn the pads of your fingers while sanding across the partially removed head of a brass pin! When the sanding process is complete you can replace the pins of your choice, or, at smaller scales, fill the holes with a dark coloured filler and sand smooth. This gives a very subtle impression of nail heads without being overbearing and obtrusive.

Masts and spars

Even in the top quality kits, masts and spars are rarely supplied tapered and turned and, in the vast majority of cases, all that is given is straight dowelling of suitable diameter. However, it should be noted that some masts are of square or rectangular section at deck level and also at the top, where trestletrees and crow's nests are later assembled. Thus, dowel rod may not always be as convenient a material as would at first appear.

Starting with a dowel rod or length of square sectioned timber, it is essential to ensure that the grain be long and straight with no knots or other obvious blemishes. Select a length that is at least 25 mm longer than the finished

requirement. This little bit of extra length is useful for holding during turning and tapering and, of course, can be cut off later.

Having chosen your material, you are now faced with the tapering operation. Whether you are working from scratch or building from a kit, the plans should enable you to define the length, position and diameter of the tapered sections. Such data should be marked on to the material. The first step is to carefully file four flats each opposed at 90°, roughly tangential to the finished diameter over the length of taper required (see Fig. 15.9). Secondly, file four further flats in the same manner to produce an octagonal section. Obviously, one can continue by filing the eight corners off to produce a shape nearer to the circular section required, but except where diameters of, say, 20 mm or larger are involved, an octagonal section will reduce quite readily by sanding during the next stage of working.

The first piece of equipment to come to mind for reducing the mast to circular section is a lathe. However, I have not found this to be the ideal tool for the task in hand and prefer to use an electric drill held in a horizontal stand. The spare 25 mm length of mast is held in the drill chuck and using various grades of abrasive paper, the mast is finished by hand. A few words of caution. Don't use the continuous run button on the drill, use the trigger only. Hold the abrasive paper between thumb and forefinger to provide both pressure and steadying action (see Fig. 15.10). Make sure that the paper is folded correctly relative to the direction of rotation in order to avoid 'snatch' and don't squeeze too hard — it can get somewhat hot. Try to anticipate when, for any reason, you need to stop and then release the trigger before removing the working hand. This helps to retain good axial alignment between the mast and drill centre lines.

Some care will be needed if the small end of the taper runs into the underside of a larger square section, both from the point of view of producing the shape required

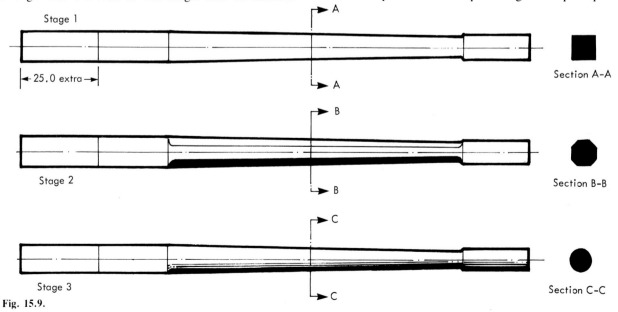

Stage 1

25.0 extra

Section A-A

Stage 2

Section B-B

Stage 3

Section C-C

Fig. 15.9.

181

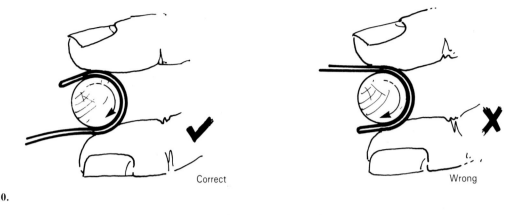

Correct   Wrong

Fig. 15.10.

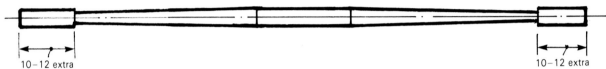

10–12 extra   10–12 extra

Fig. 15.11.

and preventing pulling the mast out of the drill chuck. Small outside callipers will be needed to check diameters at various places along the taper of such a mast, but if the tapered portion runs out to the end, a most useful tool for measuring diameters is the draughtsman's circle template. They can be bought at most reasonable stationers and have the added advantage of being useful in the marking out process as well — so quite a good investment.

The procedure so far described is for masts, bowsprits, booms, etc., where the tapers run in one direction only. Spars, having to be tapered towards each end can be done in a very similar manner with one or two essential differences. First, you need about 10 mm–12 mm spare lengths at each end and secondly, considerably more care is required due to the smaller diameters involved (see Fig. 15.11). In view of this, it is often a good move to use a new scalpel and gently scrape longitudinally to attain the section required, using the electric drill only for knocking off the last corners. Final sanding should be done longitudinally by hand.

Fig. 15.12.

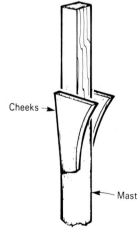

Cheeks →

← Mast

Having got your masts and spars tapered and turned, there are several things to be done before the various pieces can be assembled together. On masts, flats should be filed on those areas where the hounds, or supporting

cheeks for trestletrees fit (see Fig. 15.12). There are also several holes that are more easily drilled at this stage rather than after assembly. Holes for fitting eyebolts and sheave holes for the passing of some of the upper rigging come immediately to mind, but careful and continual study of the plans is most worthwhile to ensure that all such features are taken care of.

Remember too, that spider bands together with trusses and futtock bands (see Fig. 15.13) should also be fitted to the lower masts before assembling cheeks, trestletrees and crosstrees. Woldings are also best wound on at this time.

Fig. 15.13.

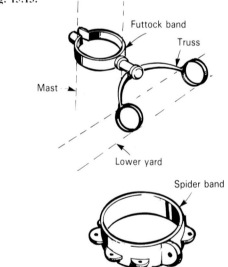

Futtock band

Truss

Mast →

Lower yard

Spider band

Flats should be filed on to spars for the seating of the battens. These should be glued into place and left to thoroughly set before proceeding with the fitting of stirrups and jack-stays (see Figs. 15.14 to 15.16). Whilst there is some time to go before you start rigging, again it is worth consulting the plans and look ahead to see what will be needed in the way of blocks for clews and buntlines etc. You should also consider fitting the brace block pendants at this stage.

Fig. 15.14. Fitting battens.

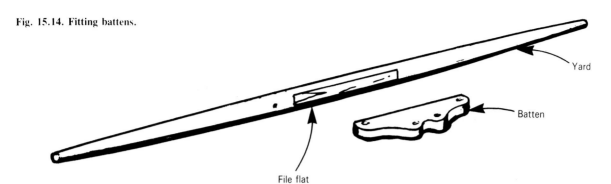

Fig. 15.15. Jackstays footrope and pendant.

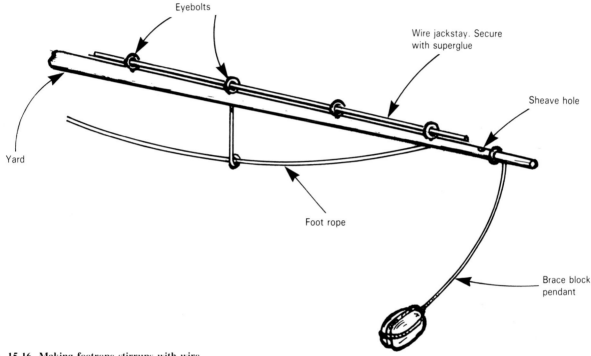

Fig. 15.16. Making footrope stirrups with wire.

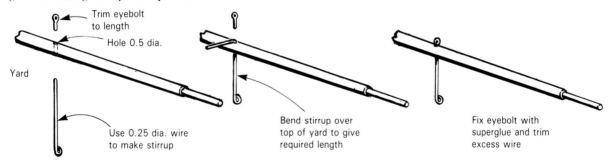

Now that as much work as possible has been done on the individual masts and spars, all pieces can be assembled together. It should be pointed out that depending on the scale of your model, it may be more expedient to assemble the lower masts to the hull and rig the shrouds and stays before assembling the upper masts. The larger the scale, the more likely is this to be the case and the convenience gained is entirely dependent on the actual model being built and your own preference of working procedures. There are no hard and fast rules.

Building the tops calls for considerable accuracy. The physical sizes of the parts involved is on the small size but nonetheless the trestletrees should be notched to receive the crosstrees to give the best job and added strength (see Fig. 15.17). Cut and notch the trestles in pairs to ensure squareness of the crosstrees, carefully measuring the actual size of the mast to get the spacing correct. The decking of the top is best made as a sub-assembly and fitted separately on most medium scale models, but again judge each case on its merits. Keep looking at the plans to make sure that all the various rigging points are recognised and catered for where possible before final assembly.

183

Fig. 15.17. Assembling tops.

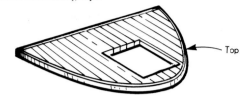

Top

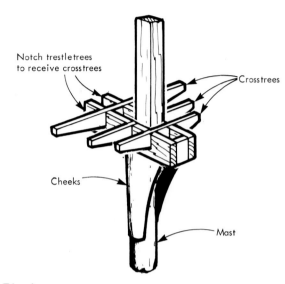

Notch trestletrees
to receive crosstrees

Crosstrees

Cheeks

Mast

Rigging

Before starting to rig a model ship, it is well worth doing a bit of reading on the subject in order to familiarise yourself with the basic fundamentals. Once you understand what each part of the rigging does, it becomes more clear why particular lines are belayed where they are and certainly, what at first appears to be a total maze of rope, takes on a much more comprehensible picture.

The better books on the subject do tend to be a little on the expensive side so a visit to the local library will usually help. Two works are particularly recommended, *Plank On Frame Models* by Harold Underhill and *The Masting and Rigging of English Ships of War* by John Lees (Conway Maritime Press). When you have managed to acquire the desired basics, the first things to look at are the rigging materials, cordage, blocks etc. Since the aim of this text is to hopefully be of assistance to the less experienced, I am going to assume that you have been supplied with these items in a kit or you have bought them from one of the well known fittings lists. Either way, you are not going to lay your own rope or make your own blocks. Having said that, it is wrong to suppose that such provided, or bought, items are immediately ready for use.

Taking the cordage first, a range of 6 sizes from 0.25 mm diameter through to 1.5 mm diameter should suffice. In general, the smaller sizes would be a light brown or tan colour (for running rigging) and the larger diameters, dark brown or black (for standing rigging). Both light and dark colours for the 0.75 mm diameter

are usually found necessary. Unfortunately, far too many kits supply all thread in sparkling white and this, or course, has to be washed and dyed. In fact, this is a chore that should be done at the start of the project so that the drying out process can have plenty of time. Rewind the thread to be treated into hanks about 250 mm long and dye according to the instructions given with whatever dye you purchase. Hang the hanks up to dry and hook on some weights to the suspended hanks. This should take all the give, and the natural tendency to twist, out of the thread.

As far as blocks are concerned (see Fig. 15.18), the main thing is to clear out the holes and generally clean off any 'whiskers' left from the manufacturing process. A low-voltage electric drill is absolutely ideal for these operations. It may seem a little long-winded — and even pointless — to redrill holes already provided, but there are few things more frustrating than a length of thread that gets stuck halfway through a block. You can lay odds that such a block will have been rigged in the one place you can't get the drill into!

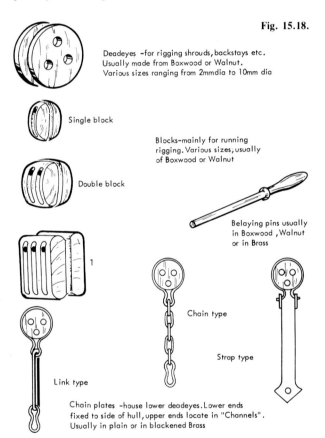

Fig. 15.18.

Deadeyes –for rigging shrouds, backstays etc.
Usually made from Boxwood or Walnut.
Various sizes ranging from 2mm dia to 10mm dia

Single block

Double block

Blocks–mainly for running rigging. Various sizes; usually of Boxwood or Walnut

Belaying pins usually in Boxwood, Walnut or in Brass

Chain type

Strap type

Link type

Chain plates –house lower deadeyes. Lower ends fixed to side of hull, upper ends locate in "Channels". Usually in plain or in blackened Brass

The other essential material that should not be overlooked is adhesive. The most efficient one that I have so far found is the original cyanoacrylate. The smallest touch to a moistened knot or serving allows it to be trimmed really close to a point where the end of the residual thread is completely unseen. An equally effective medium is acrylic varnish, although it obviously takes longer to harden off. White PVA is useful for laying down the surface of the thread. Pulling a cut length of thread between thumb and forefinger liberally coated with PVA not only stabilises the cordage and stiffens it up, but also smooths off all the little surface fibres which stick up and later act as 'hooks' for any dust to settle on.

As far as tools are concerned, I have found that three or four pairs of different ended tweezers are essential. A slim-handled scalpel or good modelling knife (kept specifically for rigging) is most useful, but for trimming ends close, without doubt the most efficient tool is a pair of good nail clippers, either the square ended gentleman's pocket style, or, the smaller side cutters used by a pedicurist. I generally prefer the clippers to the scalpel, one slip with the sharp edge when in amongst the rigging can cause havoc. Supplement these implements with a few different sizes of crochet hook for general 'fishing' and you should be well set to start the rigging process.

Looking at the completely rigged ship, it may at first seem a difficult decision as to where one starts the rigging. Obviously, different types of vessels present a different content and complexity, particularly in running rigging. However, there is a logical breakdown and allocation of sub-divisions of working, which help the modelmaker avoid creating problems for himself, particularly those of inaccessibility. The first two divisions are fairly obvious. The standing rigging is that part of the set-up that is permanently fixed and holds the masts

and bowsprit in their correct relationship to the hull and to each other. Secondly, the running rigging, which is the working part of the rigging and used for raising and lowering yards etc. on the masts, adjusting their position on the mast relative to the centre line of the ship and for raising and setting the sails.

Each of these two divisions should be taken separately. Take the standing rigging first, and further subdivide into areas of working. Starting with rigging basically on the ship's centre line and closest to deck level, work upwards toward the upper masts. Now move from the centre line outwards, again considering the lower rigging first. Putting the system into practice, the bowsprit will get first attention and specifically the gammoning. This lashes the bowsprit to the forward part of the ship. The rope passes over the bowsprit and down through a slot in the prow then back up the opposite side continuously for a number of times, and finally finishing with several frapping turns to tighten everything up. The gammoning is usually applied such that the fore part of the winding at the bowsprit passes to the aft side of the slot in the prow to provide a twisted appearance. The forestays from the bowsprit to the foremast followed by the stays from the underside of the bowsprit to the stem sometimes via the dolphin striker, are next to be rigged. The accompanying sketch shows a typical sequence of applying this initial rigging (see Fig. 15.19).

At this stage, before continuing with the shrouds and

Fig. 15.19.

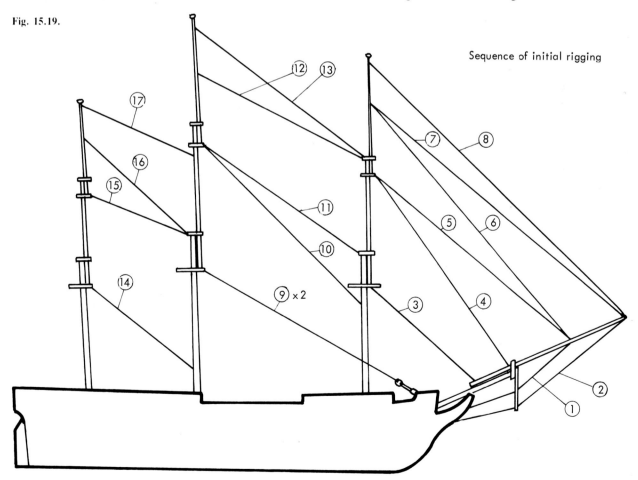

Sequence of initial rigging

backstays it might be as well to say a few words about knots and generally tying off the various parts of the rigging. 'Knots' in the true sense are virtually non-existent in the fixing of standing rigging and for the most part, the end of the stay (or whatever) is passed around or through the feature concerned and is then lashed to its incoming self. Most modelmakers will have, or will develop, their own way of best accomplishing this. I offer mine as a basis for starting — you can vary it to suit yourself (see Fig. 15.20). Some years ago I purchased some very small electrical 'crocodile' clips and today, would not consider starting rigging without them. Buy the very smallest size possible and whilst, in theory, one is sufficient, three or four is a more practical figure to consider. The cost is insignificant in the overall scheme of things, but you will find that they are worth their weight in gold.

As to their use for rigging, Fig. 15.20 illustrates my preferred procedure. For all lashings I use 0.25 mm diameter black thread. Obviously, for relatively small scale models say 1:100 or smaller, this would be inappropriate, but then the rigging techniques would, in any case, be different. Whatever feature of rigging I am involved in, every length of thread cut is automatically given the PVA treatment, even the 0.25 mm

diameter lashing. As explained earlier, this not only provides anti-dust adhesion properties, but in the case of lashings, permits a simple hitch, once pulled tight, to remain tight without slippage whilst the next part of the procedure is carried out.

A far more difficult aspect to cover is that of tension. How tight to apply each part of the rigging? I would be less than honest if I said that there are rules to follow which would guarantee correct results. How do you explain a sense of 'feel' or gut feeling that a particular tension is about right? I guess only experience will tell, nonetheless, the whole object of this book is to try and help the less experienced, so I will do my best to lay down a few basic rules.

The first essential is 'do not over-tension'. This not only tends to pull masts out of line, but is a totally irreversible situation. There are always means of tightening things up — albeit cheating — but it is almost impossible to slacken a line, once set up. My own tensioning device involves the use of a crocodile clip. I attach one clip to the line midway between its fixing points and tension up until the line is pulled straight. Alright, I know the weight of the clip and length of line is significant, but at least I have a consistent basis upon which, with experience, I can apply variations.

Fig. 15.20. Tying stays.

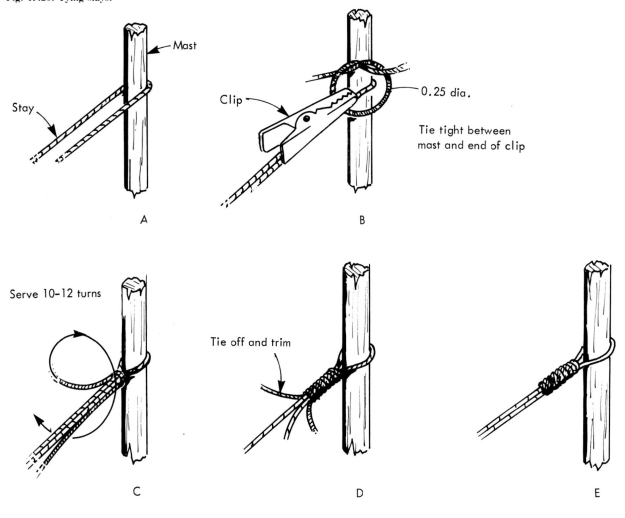

The setting up of the shrouds and backstays is carried out in a precise sequence. The shrouds are set up in pairs alternating from starboard to port, the first shroud starting at the foremost starboard deadeye, going up around the mast head and returning to the second starboard deadeye. A similar pair are set up next for the port side, followed by the shrouds for the third and fourth starboard deadeyes and so on, until all deadeyes have been provided for. It is best to secure each shroud pair at the mast head as they are first assembled. A simple method is to pinch the two ropes together close to the mast with a small crocodile clip and seize them with thread between the mast and the end of the clip. The clip is then removed and the seizing completed over the doubled rope (see Fig. 15.21).

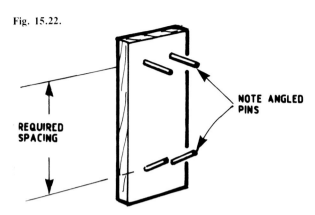

Fig. 15.22.

NOTE ANGLED PINS

REQUIRED SPACING

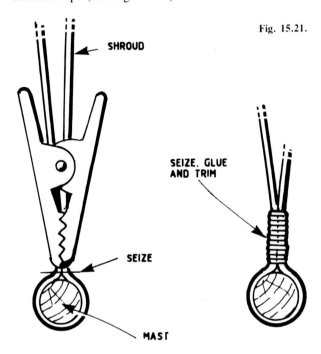

Fig. 15.21.

SHROUD

SEIZE, GLUE AND TRIM

SEIZE

MAST

The fitting of deadeyes to the lower end of the shrouds needs a little care to ensure that when the lanyards are subsequently tightened up, the separating distance between upper and lower deadeye is roughly the same across the whole assembly. The lower deadeyes have, of course, by this time been correctly assembled with chainplates etc., during the construction of the hull. To get the deadeye separation correct, I make a very simple jig from a small length of scrap hull planking and four short pins (see Fig. 15.22). One pair of pins of the jig locates in holes in the lower deadeye and the upper deadeye assembled to the other pins. Holding the jig and loose upper deadeye in position with forefinger and thumb of one hand, the relevant shroud is passed between the finger and thumb, round the deadeye and doubled back up to be gripped with a small crocodile clip, and the doubled shroud then seized close to the deadeye. Before applying a touch of superglue to the seizing, make sure that the holes in the upper deadeye are in correct alignment. Having trimmed all loose ends we can now consider reeving the lanyards.

Cut an adequate length of suitable size thread and give it the usual PVA treatment by putting a drop of glue on the fingers and pulling the thread through a few times to stiffen it up. In addition, to assist in the threading through the holes in the deadeyes, smear one end of the thread with a touch of superglue to provide a built-in bodkin. A set sequence for rigging lanyards should be followed as shown in Fig. 15.23. At this stage I find it preferable to only just take up the slack, leaving the final tightening until both port and starboard shrouds have been rigged on a particular mast. This helps to make sure that the mast is not pulled out of line and that the upper deadeyes can take up a reasonably straight line. The free end of each lanyard can now be tied off to the shrouds above the upper deadeyes. The PVA treatment will have prevented the lanyards slipping back through the deadeyes so that tension in the shrouds will not be reliant on the final tying off.

We now come to the dreaded ratlines. A great number of modelmakers (including myself) have spent hours trying to evolve an easy, but effective, way of getting around this chore. In spite of several inspired bouts of enthusiasm I, like the others, have learnt the hard way that the best way is the obvious way — tie them all on.

Fig. 15.23.

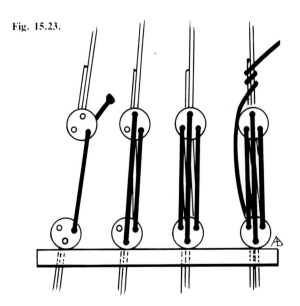

**SEQUENCE FOR RIGGING LANYARDS.
NOTE RELATIVE POSITIONS OF DEADEYES.**

187

Prior planning can relieve some of the monotony. For instance, make up the yards at various intervals to avoid a continuous spell of knot tying. I normally use clove hitches on models with scales larger than 1:50 and simple granny knots on smaller scales and, in this instance, do not use the PVA treatment.

Being right-handed I find it easier to start on the left-hand end of the group of shrouds to be rattled down and using fine-nosed tweezers to thread and guide the free end, work my way across from left to right. Keep all knots inboard of the shrouds for best effect and do not pull everything up too tight — the shrouds should still be straight when you have finished (see Fig. 15.24). The series of photographs in the chapter on the *Royal William* illustrate the technique described.

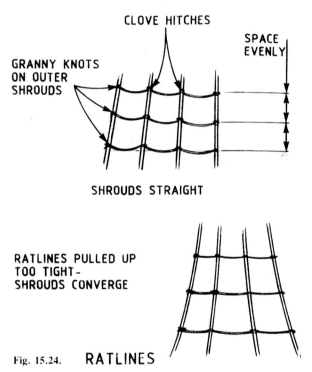

Fig. 15.24. RATLINES

On smaller scale models, the finer thread does seem to have a mind of its own when it comes to laying straight and it is almost impossible to attain the slight downward sag of the ratline between each shroud without some additional coercion. A method I have found effective is to use a small piece of polythene, or other plastic, impervious to the action of superglue, as a 'stroker' and, having dabbed all the knots, smear any offending ratline with superglue and stroke it to shape. It takes a little practice but it does work. A lot of the problem can be avoided by trying not to tie the knots against the natural twist of the thread — not always easy to accomplish, but it does help to reduce the problem.

One key thing to bear in mind is that ratlines do have to be applied and it really is not helpful to put the problem off until a later stage in the rigging process, when any additional rigging will inevitably get in the way of fingers and tweezers. The running rigging on a ship is that which moves yards on the masts, either to

haul them up and let them down, or to alter their angle relative to the centre line of the vessel. Running rigging also raises and lowers the sails and trims them to the most efficient shape to suit prevailing weather conditions and the required 'way' of the ship. It is important, fairly early in the model building process, to decide whether or not to fit sails. There are many arguments for, and against, making up sails and this is not really the forum for such a discussion. Suffice to say that your choice will affect both the content and placement of the running rigging and the position of the yards on the masts (see Fig. 15.25). When in port for any length of time, sails would be unbent (taken down), repaired as necessary and stowed. Some of the rigging, such as leechlines and buntlines, would also be removed. Other lines would be pulled out and conveniently hooked up. This meant that the amount of rope in the coils hanging at the belaying points would be far less. Without sails, yards would normally be lowered on to the tops and not hauled up in their operating position (again see Fig. 15.25).

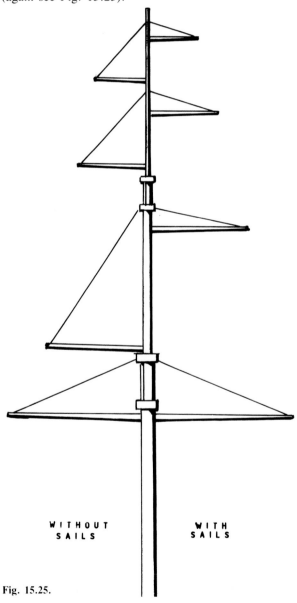

WITHOUT SAILS   WITH SAILS

Fig. 15.25.

Before starting to rig, it is a good idea to have a check around the masts and spars to make sure that all possible blocks are in place; it becomes increasingly awkward to tie on blocks as the rigging process develops. Also ensure that the holes in them have been cleaned out. Where to start? In general it is easier to start with those lines that are tied off nearest the centre line of the vessel and gradually work outwards. Combine this with working on the lower spars first and it will be easier to see the best run for each line; obviously no line should interfere with the working of another. Having adopted the basic rule, centre and lowest first, it has to be said that there will inevitably be exceptions depending on the rig in hand, but it is a good basis for working and the exceptions can usually be conveniently and sensibly sorted out.

When it comes to belaying and tying off, most drawings provided in kits indicate the correct belaying points, sometimes even to the extent of a separate belaying diagram. If this information is not given, you have a bit of a problem. Two courses are open to you — further research on the particular vessel concerned or research to find the details of a similarly rigged ship. One thing that always followed a set pattern was the rigging of the halliards. On the foremast the topsail halliard is rigged to port, on the main mast to starboard and on the mizen again to port. On each mast the topgallant and skysails alternate port to starboard so that the loads would be more evenly distributed to both sides of the ship.

When tying off, a turn and a half around the belaying pin or bitt, with the spare end of the line held taut for the application of a spot of superglue, is all that is needed (see Fig. 15.26). Snip the spare off close to the pin rail and all that remains is to hang a coil of thread onto the pin to complete the job. If tying off to a bitt, take the spare end to the deck and lay on a flat coil to simulate a continuous length of rope. Making up coils of rope needs a little care or they can look somewhat artificial. This is where, if you have chosen to fit sails, you get an advantage in that generally there is less spare rope to coil up. Flat coils to lay on the deck are not too much of a problem, just don't make them too even.

Fig. 15.26.

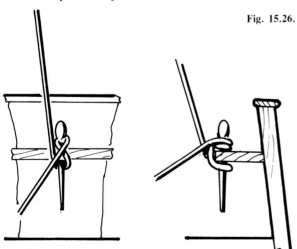

Coils for hanging on belaying pins are a somewhat different story. The task is to coil them so that they appear to hang naturally from the pin and to do this, I use a simple jig (see Fig. 15.27). Mine is made such as to be able to make a dozen coils at once, but obviously you can extend the principle to any convenient number you like. Again, do not apply the thread too evenly and use an extra dose of the PVA treatment so that the finished coils, when cut from the jig, retain their shape.

Fig. 15.27.

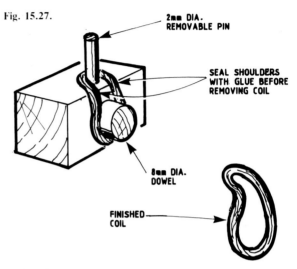

Adhesives

The proper use of the correct adhesive in model boat building can generate quite a bit of additional cost to that already expended on the kit, or other basic materials if building from scratch. The technical advancement made in the world of adhesives during the past few years is quite staggering and has reached a point today where there are very few materials that cannot be stuck together or to each other. Having said that, selecting the right adhesive for the job in hand is important, both from a technical and a cost standpoint. For example, it would be most expensive to plank a hull using superglue.

Probably the most important aspect of joining materials together is preparation. This applies to any adhesive and, in general, the more high-tech the 'glue', the higher the degree of cleanliness and surface preparation needed. The instructions found with the adhesive pack will usually tell you what is required to attain a good joint and list the materials for which that particular adhesive is not suitable. Most poor, or failed, joints occur due to disregard of the instructions given.

Obviously, it is highly desirable to produce a good mechanical joint prior to sticking the subject parts together. The mating surfaces of a butt joint should be flat and mitred corners should come together without major gaps. Many adhesives have gap-filling properties, but proper fitting makes for a far superior joint, both in strength and appearance.

Cleanliness is most important, the major contaminants being oils, greases, paint, varnish and finger marks. Oils and greases are more easily removed from metal and plastic parts, but almost impossible from wood. Paint and varnish should be carefully scraped away from the area to be stuck to reveal the base material. Clean hands are essential when working with wood, the natural oils produced by the finger tips are sufficient to contaminate a joint and even leave finger marks that are difficult to remove. Some woods produce their own oils. Teak is such a material and this can often make it difficult to stick.

As to the adhesives themselves, there are four that I keep to hand that are particularly useful in model boat building. I am not saying that after purchasing your basic materials you should go and buy all four, but I guess that after a few models you will accumulate them and like me, will keep stocked up.

White PVA. You will probably use more of this than any other and it is well worth buying the largest size you can afford, it certainly comes much cheaper that way. Whilst it takes quite a few hours to thoroughly 'cure' or harden off, it does have a fairly quick 'grab' time. With reasonable planning you don't find yourself waiting about for the glue to dry before proceeding with the next stage.

One word of warning though. If you are planking a hull and intend to finish leaving the natural wood, make sure you remove all excess glue from the surface and wipe off with a damp cloth. Failure to do this will leave you with lightly stained patches where the adhesive has bleached the surface to a depth that involves more than a little sanding to get out. For best results, the parts

should either be jointed together or mechanically held in place by pins or clamps whilst the adhesive 'grabs'.

Clear glue. Useful for sticking various plastics, wood, metal, card etc. Normally it is supplied in a tube and can be difficult to apply in the sparing way necessary so as not to make a messy joint. Some make 'string' very easily and this can be an additional hazard. It has a very useful place in the overall scheme of things, but needs a little care in application.

Contact adhesive. Ideal for second skinning on a double planked model or the application of thin strips for decking. Once the thickness of material being used gets below 0.75 mm (0.30 in) the use of PVA, because of its liquidity, tends to warp the strips as it dries, hence contact adhesive comes into its own. The secret is undoubtedly to make sure both surfaces to be joined are thinly, but fully, covered and that sufficient time is allowed for the adhesive to become touch dry before bringing the parts together.

Cyanoacrylate. Will bond virtually all materials except polythenes, teflons and silicone-based rubbers. It is very clean and easy to use and its major advantage is its speed of cure. If it has a disadvantage it is its inability to cope with larger gaps, so joint preparation is again most important. On the domestic market, it comes in two main forms, liquid and gel. The liquid is extremely useful for rigging — no blobs, no big knots and extremely close-trimmed ends. The value of the gel for fixing long strips ie. rubbing strakes, around the curves of hulls, cannot be overstated.

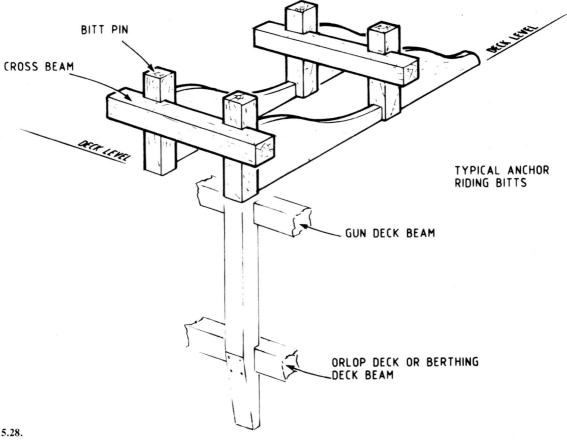

Fig. 15.28.

You should, of course, not forget that all cyanoacrylate adhesives bond skin very easily and very quickly. This is a hazard which is very real, but one which should not be exaggerated. Contamination around the eyes would be serious, but fairly warm water will permit fingers and thumbs to be peeled apart without damage. Some manufacturers supply a solvent which is even better.

There are a number of other adhesives of course, notably the two-part epoxy resins, Araldite for instance. These undoubtedly fulfil a very valuable function when building working model boats and in areas around glow plug and diesel engines, where its resistance to oils and solvents comes into its own. For the static model, however, it is not often one comes across a situation that cannot be equally satisfied by one of my main choice of four previously mentioned.

Deck fittings

Significant among the fittings are those concerned with the handling of the anchor cable; the riding bitts, the capstan and/or the windlass.

The riding bitts were massive timber constructions used to secure the cables while the ship was riding at anchor. Such was the force acting on the bitts, that the vertical members extended to the beams of the deck below (see Fig. 15.28). The sizes of timber and proportions of these assemblies were governed in the man-of-war by the number of guns carried. To give some idea of the sizes involved, for a 74-gun ship the timbers were in the order of 500 mm square. It is important for the modelmaker to be aware of the use of fittings in order that he can not only reproduce them at the correct size and scale, but put them in the correct position for this purpose.

The windlass was a mechanical device used particularly on smaller vessels for hauling up the anchor cable. In basic form, it consisted of a wooden barrel, usually octagonal in section and horizontally supported at each end by bearings housed in the bitts and associated cheeks. Earlier versions were turned by handspikes inserted into holes in the barrel (see Fig. 15.29). These were later discarded and the equipment turned by cranked handles at the extreme outside ends of the barrel

spindle. For heavier use, the mechanical advantage was enhanced by offsetting the crankspindle from the barrel centreline and transmitting the manual power via a pinion on the crank and a wheel on the barrel. The barrels were ridged with eight whelps or cleats. These were also tapered, so that not only did the cable move along the barrel as it was turned on, thus tending to reduce slip, but the effective diameter of the barrel was increased. A ratchet device was fitted at the centre of the barrel to prevent the loss of manual control when the cable was under strain (see Figs 15.30 and 15.31).

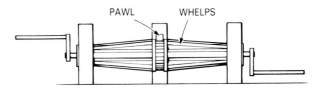

EARLY WINDLASS

WINDLASS WITH CRANKED HANDLES

Fig. 15.30.

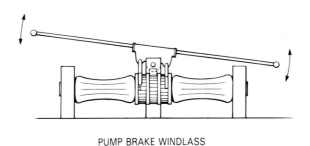

PUMP BRAKE WINDLASS

Fig. 15.31.

One could almost describe the capstan as a vertical version of the windlass (see Figs 15.32 and 15.33). By the end of the 17th century the double capstan was not uncommon. This allowed two capstans, one on a deck immediately above the other, to share the same spindle. The advantage was that twice as much effort could be employed to more readily raise the anchor, the crew on the upper deck not having to be encumbered by any cable. A later innovation produced the double-tier capstan which had a device that allowed the upper

Fig. 15.29.

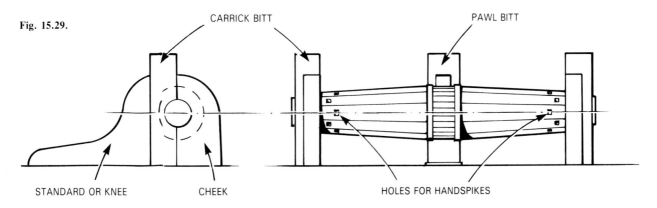

CARRICK BITT

PAWL BITT

STANDARD OR KNEE   CHEEK

HOLES FOR HANDSPIKES

capstan to be disengaged from the lower, thus allowing the two capstans to be used for different tasks at the same time (see Fig. 15.34).

Fig. 15.32.

EARLY CAPSTAN

Fig. 15.34.

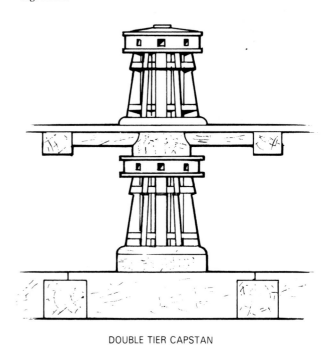

DOUBLE TIER CAPSTAN

Fig. 15.33.

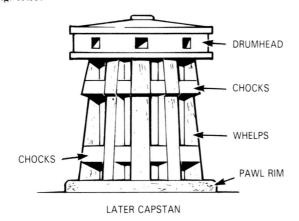

DRUMHEAD

CHOCKS

WHELPS

CHOCKS

PAWL RIM

LATER CAPSTAN

Fig. 15.35.

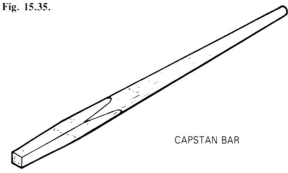

CAPSTAN BAR

The modelmaker should bear several points in mind. Obviously you always need to recognise scale, and one particularly good tip is to remember that the height of the capstan bars above deck level should be about chest high on a scale man. A capstan is usually best fabricated rather than adapted from a solid turning. This allows the holes for the capstan bars to be correctly formed in square section. Finally, don't forget to make, and conveniently stow, the actual capstan bars near to the capstan. They were normally of round section at the handling end and had a tapered square section at the heavy end to make a snug fit into the capstan head (see Fig. 15.35).

Pumps were an essential part of every ship's equipment, to remove water from the bilges, to fight fires caused by enemy action or to supply water for washing the decks. The main chain pump was usually installed on the lower gun deck and is not always seen on a ship model. However, on a large man-of-war this was a sizeable piece of gear employing some seven or eight men to operate it. The parts visible above deck level are the cisterns and the cranks (see Fig. 15.36), although, of course, the pipes through which an endless chain pulled the buckets extended right down to the bottom of the ship. The pump well was at the deepest part of the vessel, usually just aft of the main mast. The singular term 'pump', is something of a misnomer, because it was usually a combination of two or four pumps on larger vessels.

In addition to the main chain pump, larger vessels would also have one or more Elm Tree pumps for the more domestic purposes, although on the smaller men-of-war it would also serve as a bilge pump. Its name derived from the fact that the main pump case was made from elm because of its natural ability to withstand long periods of exposure to salt water (see Fig. 15.37). Again, from the model standpoint, you normally only see the working head above deck level, although these

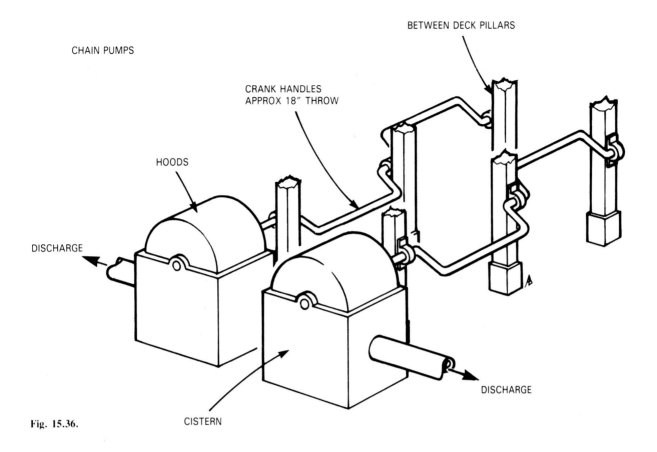

CHAIN PUMPS

BETWEEN DECK PILLARS

CRANK HANDLES
APPROX 18" THROW

HOODS

DISCHARGE

DISCHARGE

Fig. 15.36.

CISTERN

ELM TREE PUMP

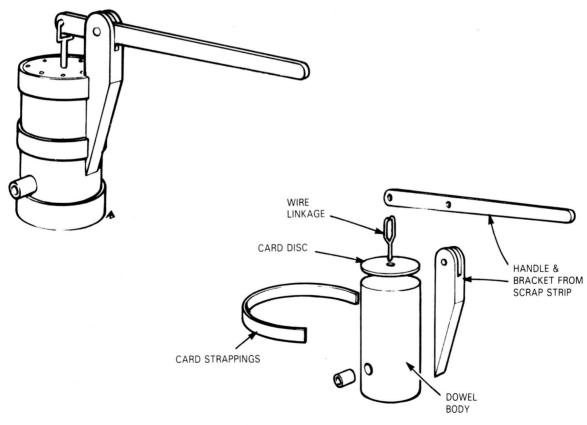

WIRE
LINKAGE

CARD DISC

HANDLE &
BRACKET FROM
SCRAP STRIP

CARD STRAPPINGS

DOWEL
BODY

Fig. 15.37.

MODEL CONSTRUCTION

pumps either draw their supply directly through the bottom of the ship adjacent to the keel, or from a cistern that could be flooded via pipes and valves that led from the cistern to the outside of the hull below the waterline; simple, but not very effective. Plunger pumps improved the situation somewhat, in that being mounted in pairs and operated by a rocker arm, the downstroke on one was the upstroke of the other and thus, every stroke brought up water (see Fig. 15.38).

Fig. 15.38.

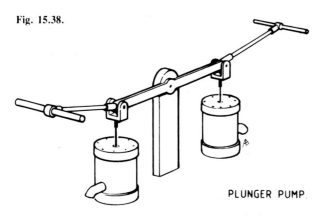

PLUNGER PUMP.

Diaphragm pumps of later introduction were much more efficient, a much shorter stroke delivering a greater volume of water (see Fig. 15.39). On some larger ships these would be mounted in pairs with their plungers connected to a crank shaft driven by two men each side. The motion was smoothed out by the action of flywheels at each end of the shaft (see Fig. 15.40).

Fig. 15.39.

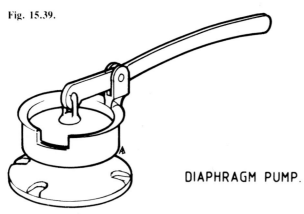

DIAPHRAGM PUMP.

The rudder

An area where many kits fall down is in the construction and hanging of the rudder. There are several features which, with very little effort, can be recognised and yet add considerably to that 'authentic' look.

Firstly, the rudder on most men-of-war was fabricated from several pieces. For reasons of strength and durability this involved different timbers and so the modelmaker need not worry about contrasting grain or shade. The edge of the rudder adjacent to the stern post, and indeed the stern post itself, was usually enhanced by a strip of elm for durability. This bearding was of triangular section to permit adequate movement of the rudder. Similarly, the bottom edge of the rudder was usually fitted with an elm sole but of rectangular section (see Fig. 15.41).

Fig. 15.41.

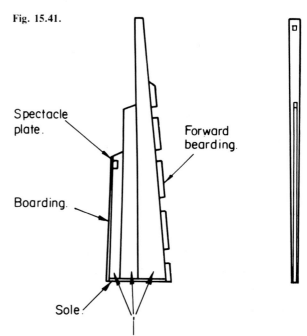

Spectacle plate.

Forward bearding.

Boarding.

Sole.

Rudder fabricated from 3 separate pieces prior to edging with sole and boarding

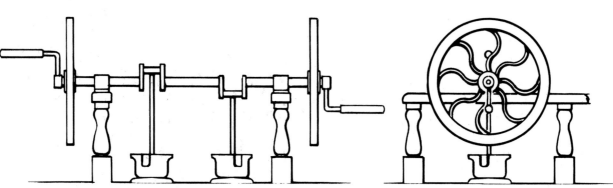

Fig. 15.40.   FLYWHEEL PUMP.

Hanging the rudder to the stern post, if given some thought, can often be made to look better than the 'kit' formula. Let us take the hinges first and make sure that they are fitted the right way round. The pintle (pin) fits on the rudder above the gudgeon, which fits on the stern post. The eye of the gudgeon stands proud of the stern post but the pintle is housed in a gap cut into the bearding on the front edge of the rudder. The length of the gap should be such as to allow the gudgeon to pass under the pintle before the rudder is lowered to make the hinge. A recess on the starboard side of the gap nearest to the waterline permitted the fitting of a wood-lock, which, after hanging the rudder, prevented the pintle lifting out of the gudgeons (see Fig. 15.42). Since several pintle/gudgeon units are involved, this calls for care in marking out, but well worth the effort when you see the result. There certainly won't be that incorrect gap between rudder and post seen on so many models built from kits.

A further enhancement to consider is the fitting of a spectacle plate to the rear edge of the rudder. This is essentially a metal 'U' bracket holding a ring each side to which an auxiliary steering system could be attached if the wheel or tiller sustained damage in action. But be careful not to overgild the lily, the spectacle plate was not normally fitted until the latter part of the 18th century (see Fig. 15.43).

The vast majority of kits supply pintles and gudgeons in the shape of pre-formed brass strips ready drilled for pinning to the rudder or hull. Both pieces of the hinge are identical and a separate pin to make up the hinge assembly is required — sometimes provided, sometimes

Fig. 15.43.

SPECTACLE PLATE

not. In the less sophisticated kits the modeller is left to make everything from brass strips and heavy gauge wire. While I appreciate that not everyone has workshop facilities available to make pintles and gudgeons in a more authentic way, using what is supplied can be made to look neater, assembled more easily, and will avoid too much deviation from the real thing (see Fig. 15.44).

Model stands

One very important aspect of model boat building, so often, in fact too often, neglected by kit manufacturers, is the provision of a stand. A stand serves two significant purposes. It supports the finished model for display purposes and, thus, needs to look neat and tidy without detracting from the appearance of the model itself. Secondly it has to have sufficient substance and strength to provide adequate support during the construction of the hull. Sometimes it is almost impossible to satisfy these two requirements and one has to consider a design that will hold the hull with sufficient stability to permit lateral working, cross drilling etc., but capable of being modified to provide a stand of display proportions.

In many instances, of course, where plank on frame

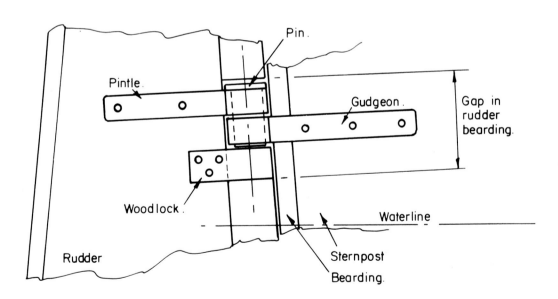

Note :- Woodlock fitted one position only.
i.e. on starboard side of gap
immediately above waterline.

Fig. 15.42.

Fig. 15.44.

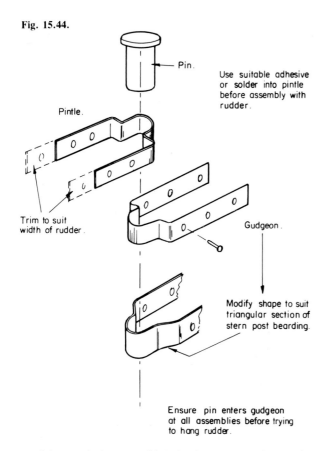

Pin.

Use suitable adhesive or solder into pintle before assembly with rudder.

Pintle.

Trim to suit width of rudder.

Gudgeon.

Modify shape to suit triangular section of stern post bearding.

Ensure pin enters gudgeon at all assemblies before trying to hang rudder.

Fig. 15.45.

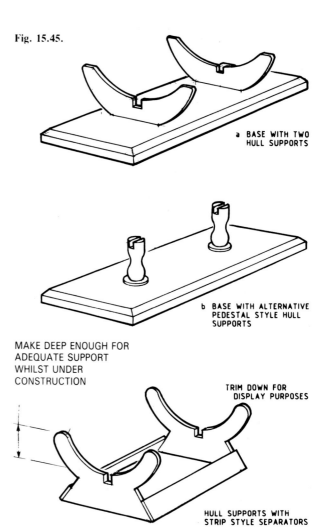

a BASE WITH TWO HULL SUPPORTS

b BASE WITH ALTERNATIVE PEDESTAL STYLE HULL SUPPORTS

MAKE DEEP ENOUGH FOR ADEQUATE SUPPORT WHILST UNDER CONSTRUCTION

TRIM DOWN FOR DISPLAY PURPOSES

HULL SUPPORTS WITH STRIP STYLE SEPARATORS

models are being considered, the construction techniques are such that the model is built on, or within, a framework that makes the requirement for a stand at this stage redundant. However, there does, inevitably, come a time when such constructional framework is discarded and the practical support problem rears its head.

Discounting all the fancy shapes and decorative work, with which you can embellish a stand, design usually falls into one of two basic categories — a base with two hull supports or, two hull supports tied together with longitudinal separators of one sort or another (see Fig. 15.45). The inner shape of the hull supports is the key to stability and, early on in the construction process, it is wise to consider where, within the length of the hull, the model will be supported. Having made this decision, the inner shape can be traced and transferred from the lines plan to the stand material. If you are building a kit in which a lines plan is not provided, use the shape of the frames or bulkheads nearest your chosen support points as the basis of your stand. Don't forget to add on the thickness of any planking, so that your final profile is the outside sectional shape of the hull.

The hull supports should incorporate a centre notch for locating the keel. This is important as it enables the model to be located, as well as supported, in the stand. It is often advisable to extend the supports fairly high up the sides of the hull for maximum stability whilst fitting out and rigging is in progress. Once all work is finished the shape can be altered to provide a more aesthetically pleasing profile for display purposes. The supports can be screwed to a base plate or separated by the use of

dowel rods or strips, remembering to make provision for a suitable nameplate.

A nice touch involves lining the inner shape of the supports with a thick felt or baize strip. This not only makes a seating that will not mark the hull of the model, but also takes up any minor inaccuracies sustained when transferring the shape from the plans (see Fig. 15.46).

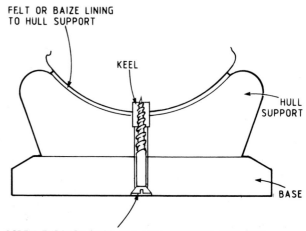

FELT OR BAIZE LINING TO HULL SUPPORT

KEEL

HULL SUPPORT

BASE

SCREW THROUGH BASE AND HULL SUPPORT INTO KEEL. ALTERNATIVELY, BUILD CAPTIVE NUTS INTO MODEL CONSTRUCTION AND USE BOLTS AND WASHERS.

Fig. 15.46.   FIXING MODEL TO STAND

I find it useful, for handling purposes, to fix the model to the stand, although I always leave access to the screw heads in case I need to remove it at a later time.

Kit enhancement

I suppose most modelmakers make their first model sailing ship from a kit. There are exceptions, of course, but for those with limited facilities, the kit provides the means to enable the newcomer to model ships to produce something reasonable and presentable. However, if you aim to build a model that has that something extra in terms of quality, accuracy and overall presentation, there are many things that can be done to improve the kit-based model.

When it comes to accuracy, you would expect that having paid, in some cases, up to a couple of hundred pounds for the kit, the manufacturer would have done all the necessary research to provide drawings and documentation that were right. Unfortunately, this is not always the case and indeed, it is quite surprising the degree of error that can sometimes be found with a kit for an extremely well-known and documented vessel. So, the message is to do some research of your own, not only to confirm what you are given in the kit, but also to stimulate a more personal contact with the subject. This has a knock-on effect in that you attain a higher interest about aspects of the ship other than its construction and, I believe, you therefore make a better model. I would hasten to add that any research that you do should be done before the commencement of building so that the results of your findings can be built into the model, rather than be the subject of later modification.

The quality of the model can be enhanced in several ways. I have already spoken of accuracy in terms of whether the vessel has the correct shape and proportions, but another area that is well worth looking at, is in the fittings supplied in the kit. For the most part, these are drawn from a proprietary range of parts and may fall into the classification of being 'near enough', rather than being 'just right'. Look particularly at anchor styles, pumps, binnacles, ships' wheels and rigging blocks. With regard to the latter, the usual problem is that the blocks supplied are too big for the rigging at the top end and some will need replacing with a smaller size. The other bits and pieces can usually be modified or adapted to present a more truthful representation of the equipment in question.

Now we come to the point where your research pays off. What can you add to the model that is not shown, or provided for, in the kit? Are there details that can be applied more authentically for the sake of spending just a little more time? There are certainly many little details that can be quite simply added that can transform the model from what might be seen as obviously kit-built, to something just a little bit special. Probably one of the most significant failures in the ship kit concerns the masting. In too many instances the drawn detail is in-

correct and the material supplied of limited value.

Does your research show you that the masts really do have a circular section throughout their length, or, should the heel of the topmasts have an octagonal section? (See Fig. 15.47.) Again, yards on English warships were certainly not of circular section throughout their length after about the middle of the 18th century, when centre sections became eight or sixteen squared. Indeed, if the yard was made in two pieces, the central area would have been battened and bound with iron hoops (see Fig. 15.48). Bearing these features in mind, the provision of nice round dowel rods in the kit is not quite the asset it would first appear to be. In fact, there is much to be said for straight-grained, square-sectioned material. After all, there is little of the original outside surface of a dowel rod left after making even a completely round-sectioned mast. So with all the tapering

Fig. 15.47.

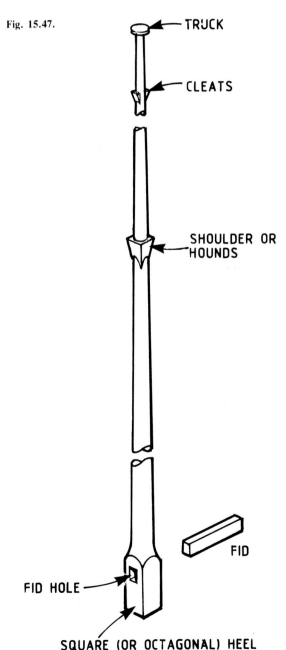

TRUCK

CLEATS

SHOULDER OR HOUNDS

FID

FID HOLE

SQUARE (OR OCTAGONAL) HEEL

Fig. 15.48.   THE TWO-PIECE YARD

involved, it could be said that it is easier to do the job right starting from a square section.

Check, too, how the stays are to be attached to the masts. So many times one sees the stay simply lashed around the mast with no means of preventing the stay slipping down the mast. The mast should either have a built in swelling, or the provision of one or two cleats. It certainly wasn't a case of the biggest man in the dockyard putting his thumb more heavily on the knot! There was also quite a bit of complexity in the construction of the tops. Now I am not suggesting that, at 1:48 or 1:50 scale, all this detail can be reproduced. But there are a number of items which could be added to advantage. The fid in the heel of the topmasts for instance or, bolsters in the structure of the trestletrees (see Fig. 15.49). Another simple touch is to recognize that, in some instances, the main caps were bound with an iron band, more than adequately simulated with a strip of card, suitably coloured (see Fig. 15.50).

Fig. 15.49.

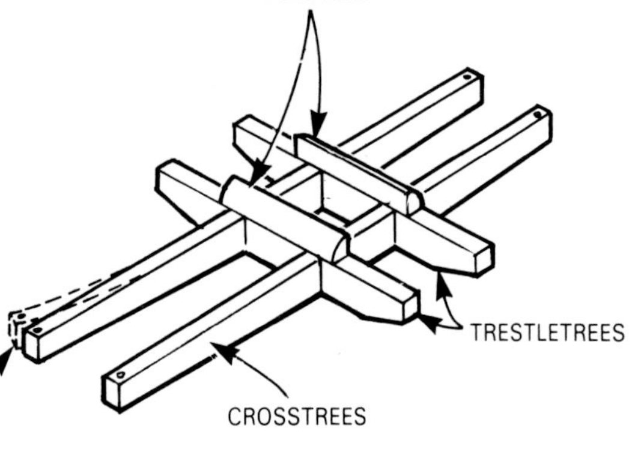

BOLSTERS

TRESTLETREES

CROSSTREES

CHECK WHETHER CROSSTREES
CURVED BACK, OR WERE STRAIGHT

Fig. 15.50.

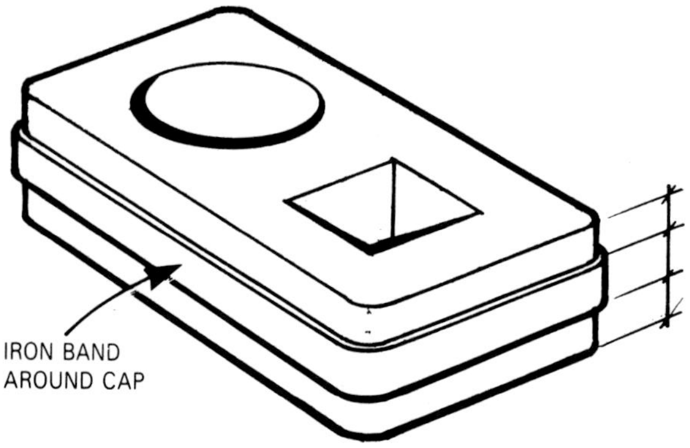

IRON BAND
AROUND CAP

In the early part of the 19th century jackstays were added to the yards of English warships. They were, of course, not the only type of vessel to have them and it is worth checking to see if your particular vessel

featured them or not. If the kit in question does allow for them, there is an excellent chance that they will be too big. For those who have not yet come across them, jackstays were rails running along the near top of yards to which the footrope stirrups and, sometimes, the bunt clewline blocks were attached. The stanchions through which the rails ran were fixed into the yard such that the rail was but two or three inches above the surface of the yard. Thus, it will be realised that the 'eyebolts' provided in the kit and normally advised for simulating the stanchions, are far too big. The rail should really be no larger in diameter than 0.031 in (0.75 mm) and the stanchions are better represented by twisting a length of soft wire around the rail at the salient points, trimming the twisted ends fairly short and inserting them into holes drilled into the yard.

The stirrups are secured to the jackstay and drape over the rear of the yard, the lower end having an eye through which the footrope passes. This eye would normally be between 30 in and 36 in below the yard, say 11/16 in at 1:48 scale. Stirrups and footropes should be made from a suitable size of rigging thread, but because it is not possible to scale down the volume/weight ratio, neither will hang in a natural fashion. Fine soft wire, suitably coloured, will fulfil the requirement much better and the modeller should have no trouble achieving that graceful hanging sweep of the footropes between the stirrups.

The buntline and clewline blocks are normally seized to the jackstay, but do make sure that you use the smallest of blocks and having done so, remember to run a drill through them before assembly to make their subsequent rigging that much easier.

There are many occasions when you see a more than respectably built model spoilt by lack of attention to the installation of the guns. There really should be a little bit more finesse than just a blob of glue under each wheel of the gun carriage to hold the assembly to the deck. Obviously the scale of the model can be a limiting factor as to the amount of detail that can be applied and, at smaller scales, the art is perhaps knowing what to leave out, rather than what to put in. Consideration of the overall picture can help to make your decision (see Fig. 15.51).

The gun carriage had to be in the in-board position to permit access to the muzzle for swabbing and loading. The bore had to be swabbed out in case any residual powder, from the previous discharge, prematurely ignited the new charge. Charge and shot were then rammed home and the gun run out to the firing position. This was effected by block and tackle on either side of the gun carriage running to the inside walls or bulwarks of the vessel. The tackle could be transferred to another, more widely spaced, pair of eyebolts to assist in the

Fig. 15.51. The gun and carriage.

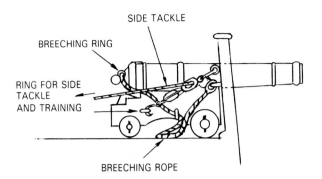

Fig. 15.52. The carronade.

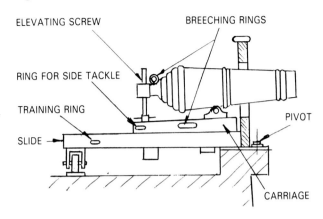

lateral training of the gun. After firing, the recoil was controlled by the breeching rope which ran through a ring at the rear of the barrel and was tied off at rings on the inside wall of the gun position.

Even at a scale of 1:96 the majority of the tackle described previously is quite achievable, even if only in representative form. At 1:48 scale there really is no reason why a full set of blocks and tackle cannot be rigged. The breeching rope is of quite substantial thickness, whereas the gear for running out and training the gun is of manhandling size. The carronade, with its shorter, but larger bored barrel, sported a similar set of

tackle although the barrel, instead of being mounted on a wheeled carriage, was fixed to a sliding carriage that traversed, under recoil, in a slide. The slide was pivoted at the muzzle end for training the gun and was supported on the deck, under the inboard end, by a small pair of wheels (see Fig. 15.52).

The breeching rope, together with the block and tackle on either side of the unit, were used in exactly the same manner as described for the gun on the wheeled carriage.

199

Conclusion

One of the problems when writing a book such as this, is deciding when to finish. The making of model ships is an ongoing thing and one learns new facts and develops new techniques during the making of nearly every successive model. I suppose that this is one of the attractive features of the hobby — there is always a challenge and, certainly, always a great sense of achievement when the job is done. However, total satisfaction is rarely, if ever, attained; there is always something that comes to light that you know you could have done better had you realised there was yet another way of doing it. Thus, there never can be a finite end to such a book as this because, the very next model could be the source of another chapter.

And so it goes on and on. How many more models are there to build, where is all the time to be found? One thing is certain, while there are models to build and while time can be found, then they will be built. I sincerely hope that this book may help in the continuance of this most satisfying of hobbies.

Index

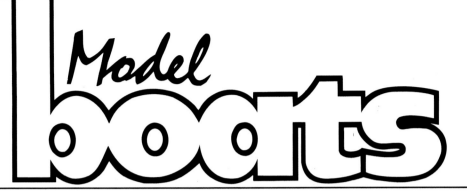